Fay Taylour

Dedication

Tapadh leat a Mhàiri Anna,
mo bhean, mo ghaoil,
a chagair mo chridhe.

Fay Taylour

'The World's Wonder Girl' – A Life at Speed

Stephen M. Cullen

PEN & SWORD **HISTORY**

AN IMPRINT OF PEN & SWORD BOOKS LTD
YORKSHIRE – PHILADELPHIA

First published in Great Britain in 2023 by
PEN & SWORD HISTORY
an imprint of Pen & Sword Books Ltd
Yorkshire – Philadelphia

ISBN 978-1-39909-938-4

Typeset by Concept, Huddersfield, West Yorkshire, HD4 5JL.
Printed and bound in England by CPI Group (UK) Ltd, Croydon, CR0 4YY.

Pen & Sword Books Ltd incorporates the imprints of Aviation, Atlas, Family
History, Fiction, Maritime, Military, Discovery, Politics, History, Archaeology,
Select, Wharncliffe Local History, Wharncliffe True Crime, Military Classics,
Wharncliffe Transport, Leo Cooper, The Praetorian Press, Remember When,
White Owl, Seaforth Publishing and Frontline Books.

For a complete list of Pen & Sword titles please contact
PEN & SWORD BOOKS LTD
47 Church Street, Barnsley, South Yorkshire, S70 2AS, England
E-mail: enquiries@pen-and-sword.co.uk
Website: www.pen-and-sword.co.uk
or
PEN & SWORD BOOKS
1950 Lawrence Rd, Havertown, PA 19083, USA
E-mail: uspen-and-sword@casematepublishers.com
Website: www.penandswordbooks.com

Contents

List of Plates

(All photographs © The Fay Taylour Archive)

The Taylour family before the First World War

Last year at Alexandra College, Dublin

With the family car in England

Broadside Queen

Lionel Wills during the International Six Days Trial, 1928

On tour, Perth, Australia, 1929

The Douglas

Victor in the 'Skerries Race', 1934

Brooklands, 1934

Engines, cars, and the racetrack

Early years of midget car racing in England

Fay Taylour on the water

Pre-race publicity

Dublin, 1946

'Tufty'

Leaving for the USA

A Jaguar for Clark Gable

On the US midget car circuit

An Irish woman driving an English car

Midget car racing, Portland, Oregon, 1951

Trouble ahead

Racing in Sweden

Brands Hatch, 1953

Midget car racing in Australia, 1953

Broadsiding, in a midget car

Publicity shot, Australia, 1953

Mercedes-Benz advertising car, Melbourne, 1953

The 50-year-old speed queen

Back in the USA, 1955

Retired from racing, 1959

Acknowledgements

My thanks go to the holders of the Fay Taylour Archive who very generously gave me access to Taylour's surviving papers, and patiently waited for me to produce this biography. I am also greatly indebted to Mairi Ann Cullen, whose painstaking skill turned that archive into a useable resource, cataloguing Taylour's unpublished writings, letters, and other papers so that her impatient husband could write this book.

Prologue

In August 1929, 168 motorcyclists took part in a six days' time trial over the Bavarian Alps, a gruelling test of their skills and machines. In chaotic scenes in Munich the entire field began at once, rather than three riders each minute. Escorted by large numbers of police and a huge crowd, the mob of motorcyclists was eventually stopped outside the city and the trial was restarted. It proved to be a dangerous ordeal, as the Press Association's special correspondent attached to the British team reported:

> Crossing the Bavarian Alps nearly every competitor was unseated. The road over Mount Ettallerberg – approximately 3,250 feet – presented an amazing spectacle, guides and spectators, of whom there were thousands lining the whole route, toiled up the steep ascent escorting the small army of riders, whose task of pushing their machines to the peak of the pass was an unenviable one. Many, in fact, collapsed exhausted before they reached the top. The pass itself is a disused rocky narrow passage – it could hardly be called a road – very steep and full of loose rocks and small stones. It was an ordeal for the ordinary pedestrian, let alone the man with a heavy 10 h.p. combination, to push to the top. At frequent intervals the passage was completely blocked, the riders who collapsed under the terrific strain having no means of retiring out of the way of the oncoming competitors.[1]

This was merely the first day of the 600-mile-long trial course, in which each competitor began with a score of 100 from which marks were deducted for various penalties, such as putting one's feet to the ground. At stake were the International Trophy and the International Vase, both held by Britain, which had entered one team of three riders for the Trophy and two teams of three for the Vase. In addition, there were eighty-four other British riders competing as individuals, including six of the total of seven women in the event, the seventh being a German woman. At the end of the event, the British Trophy team was the only team to finish, and a British team also took the Vase, with Ireland third behind France. In fact, British and Irish competitors dominated the whole event, taking the majority of gold, silver and bronze individual medals. *The Irish Times* reported:

> among the women riders, Miss Marjorie Cottle, Mrs Louis M'Lean, Miss Fay Taylour, Miss B. Lermitte, Miss C. Herbert, and Miss M. Mewton all won silver medals [awarded to competitors who lost less than 15 points]. In the conditions theirs was a truly magnificent performance.[2]

1

Although Fay Taylour was variously described as British or Irish, she was, in fact, Irish, and the Irish press maintained a long-time interest in her racing fortunes, with, for example, *The Irish Times* carrying a feature article on her as late as 1953.[3] In part, this was a result of her famous victory in the Leinster Trophy Motor Race at Skerries in August 1934. But Taylour also had a flair for self-promotion and traded on being Dublin's Alexandra College 'girl' who had forsaken respectable bourgeois life for motorsport. Characteristically, although Taylour had been one of the tiny number of women competitors in the Bavarian Alps trial, she had gone one better than the others, and attracted additional attention by setting 'a new fashion [of] making her toilette match the colour of her machine'.[4] This combination of fearlessness, undoubted racing skill, and the ability to compel attention, marked Fay Taylour's long life in motor racing.

Chapter One

Early Years and the Beginnings of a Racing Life

Fay Taylour, christened Helen Frances Taylour,[1] was born on 5 April 1904 at 9 Oxmantown Mall, Birr, King's County (now County Offaly), Leinster, Ireland. She would be the middle of three sisters, Hilda the oldest and Enid the youngest. Fay Taylour's family were a long-established part of the Anglo-Irish Ascendancy. Her father, Herbert, had been a junior officer in the British Army before joining the Royal Irish Constabulary (RIC). He enlisted as an officer cadet in August 1893, being promoted to District Inspector (DI) 3rd Class in March 1894, DI 2nd Class in May 1898, and DI 1st class in December 1906. He eventually reached the rank of County Inspector in April 1920.[2] The RIC was a unique force in the United Kingdom, and different in composition and tasking from police forces in England and Wales or Scotland. From its founding in 1836, the Irish Constabulary had a semi-military character that reflected its dual role of law enforcement and an armed counter to possible Irish republican militancy. It was a largely barracked force, although most 'barracks' were little more than houses and even, at one time, portable huts. The 'barracks were strategically centred in the most likely trouble spots', the authorities regarding the RIC as 'a highly efficient force [which] supplied Dublin Castle with most of its intelligence information'.[3] Almost all the 10,000 or so RIC rank and file were Irish and Catholic, mostly the sons of farmers. As an officer, Herbert Taylour was typical of his rank:

> Of the 250 officers in the Force in 1900, 60 were English, and the remainder were Irish; 50 had come from the ranks [...] Of the Irish [officer] cadets who entered the Force many were graduates of Trinity College, Dublin, the younger sons of the landlord classes, sons of clergymen and army officers; the majority, the sons of police officers. They were the pick of 10,000 men.[4]

Being an RIC officer came with good social standing, especially among the Anglo-Irish Protestant elite. An RIC officer enjoyed a 'social standing [...] superior to that of most people in the town and he generally mixed with the local magnates and land proprietors from which class he often came and from among whose daughters he often chose his wife'.[5]

Fay Taylour's mother was Helen Webb, who had been born in Dresden while her parents were visiting Germany. Helen was of Scots and English descent and spent her early years in Gibraltar where her father, Randolph Webb, was

3

stationed. He had served in the Crimean War, the Indian Mutiny and in Abyssinia,[6] and rose to become surgeon general of the Royal Army Medical Corps. He subsequently moved to Dublin following his appointment to a post at Dublin Castle, the centre of the British administration in Ireland. He had three other children after Helen. These were Mabel, Hilda, and George.[7] Fay Taylour later remembered her mother Helen, or 'Nellie', as an often sickly woman:

> 'As delicate as Dresden china' was an apt and two-way description of her. She was born in Dresden when her parents were vacationing there, and her dainty waist resembled the fragile Dresden china statuettes that Dordy [her husband] so loved to buy. And, alas, she was so delicate that my main memory of her is a darkened room and the smell of eau-de-cologne. She had a weak heart and suffered bad headaches, but in between she played tennis with us, entertained and went to parties.[8]

Fay Taylour's two aunts were, however, quite different. Neither woman married but lived in their father's Dublin house, *Lis-na-Crum*. Aunt Hilda became an active suffragette and was imprisoned in Holloway Gaol, where Fay was taken as a child to see her. Taylour later described her suffragette aunt as 'a man-hater'.[9] Aunt Mabel became a teacher at the famous Dublin girls' school, Alexandra College, which Fay was to attend herself as a boarder. During term-time weekends, Taylour would stay with her two aunts. Taylour's Uncle George was a mathematician and philosopher, a professor and fellow at Trinity College, Dublin. His wife, Dr Isabella 'Ella' Webb, was a notable and quite remarkable medical doctor. In 1904, Isabella Ovenden (her maiden name) was the 'the first female student to achieve first place in the final medical examinations of the Royal [University of Ireland]. She won a travelling scholarship to Vienna and was awarded a doctorate in medicine in 1906.'[10] Her career was outstanding in many respects. She was a pioneer in the treatment of tuberculosis, opened free clinics for women and babies, worked as both a practitioner and a lecturer, and volunteered at two Dublin 'Babies Clubs'. During the Easter Rising in Dublin in 1916:

> As Lady District Superintendent in the St John Ambulance Brigade at the time of the 1916 Easter Rising, she took command of and quickly transformed the St John headquarters at Merrion Square, Dublin into a temporary emergency hospital. Thereafter she worked in the hospital and cycled repeatedly through the firing lines to attend there and at other St John locations. In recognition of her Easter Week efforts, she was made a Member of the Most Excellent Order of the British Empire (MBE) in 1918.[11]

Webb subsequently became the first woman anaesthetist in Ireland, at the Adelaide Hospital in Dublin. She then turned her attention to the treatment of rickets, working at St Ultan's hospital as well as establishing the Children's Sunshine Homes. She worked, volunteered, wrote, taught, and campaigned almost up to her death in 1946.

In addition to her mother's siblings and sister-in-law, Taylour also had two aunts on her father's side, Evelyn and Helen. Neither of these women married, but they were notable in the Taylour sisters' childhoods. Fay Taylour remembered that 'we spent holidays with them, and Aunt Evelyn, like the Dublin aunts, chiselled away at me so that the finished product [...] must surely bear their mark'.[12] This remark is an interesting insight by Fay Taylour into her own character and development. As an adult, she was to make her way in motorsports in which women were absent or only rarely involved. She faced numerous obstacles in her motorcycle racing career, and in car racing and midget car racing. Yet she persevered, refusing to take 'no' for an answer. As a girl she was part of a family in which strong-willed and very capable women were prominent. Among her five aunts there was an extraordinary medical doctor, a teacher at the renowned Alexandra College, an active suffragette, along with two more unmarried women who 'loved us as if we were their children'.[13] These women not only had an impact on Fay, but also on her younger sister, Enid, who followed in her Aunt Ella's footsteps and studied medicine at University College, London and became a doctor. She was highly regarded in her profession, with an early testimony to her work in 'strenuous house surgeoncy' noting that 'she is enthusiastic, very capable and brings an intelligence and scientific spirit to her work which is far above the average'.[14] Enid married another doctor in 1934, had two children and was in the Far East with her husband when war with Japan broke out. She and the children were evacuated to Ceylon, then Northern Rhodesia where she set up a clinic, while her husband was captured and interned by the Japanese. After the war, Enid worked with her husband across Africa on behalf of the United Nations and the World Health Organization. Like her aunt, Enid died in her mid-sixties, working almost up until her death. The oldest sister, Hilda, married a British Army officer and had children but after her divorce lived on alimony for the rest of her life. The young Taylours, then, grew up in a family environment dominated by able, independent-minded, and determined women. In fact, the only male influence in Fay Taylour's early years was her RIC officer father, Herbert.

Fay Taylour remembered her father, whom the sisters called 'Dordy', as 'handsome, gay and autocratic, and all-round sportsman. He loved sailing, hunting, fishing and shooting; and he played tennis and golf, winning trophies in all these sports. He was also a good dancer, and played billiards and Bridge with the best. He was a strict disciplinarian'.[15] An official estimation of Herbert Taylour was that he 'is a capable painstaking officer and has experience in handling large numbers of men. He is a man of a most kindly amiable disposition [...] a man with a high sense of honour and loyalty and his private character is irreproachable'.[16] Altogether, Herbert Taylour sounds very much like the personification of the Victorian officer and gentleman, with country interests, and a strong sense of duty. There was more than a bit of hero-worship in Taylour's description of her father. In part, that was due to the contrast between the outdoors, military man that her father was, and the feminine nature of her mother, the 'Dresden china doll' with her illnesses and hypochondria, and love of parties, entertaining and tennis. Taylour herself admitted that as a child, 'I was obviously pulled in opposite directions, my mother's very feminine characteristics opposing the he-man traits of my father'.[17] But Fay Taylour was undoubtedly close to her father, and he was a hands-on parent. He went riding with his daughter, and taught her to shoot, and, when he bought a car, he taught her to drive, despite his own limitations with the new form of transport:

> Driving the Buick was another big delight, but sitting beside Dordy driving was quite another matter. From the moment he got the car and took us for the first drive I was instinctively aware not only that my father was a bad driver but of the factors pertaining to danger, such as entering a turn on a wet road too fast for the high centre of gravity. I was as nervous as an adult could be, but it was Dordy who should have been nervous. Sitting in the driver's seat without really knowing how to handle the levers and pedals, because he didn't know himself, I would round a corner to find the road strewn with sheep or cattle. I can only remember hitting the garage wall after I made the difficult entrance which involved extra throttle to climb over a plank spanning the door.[18]

Although Fay Taylour saw herself as the 'tomboy' of the three sisters, adding driving to riding and shooting was just part of being the daughter of an RIC officer in rural Ireland.

Fay Taylour had a strong relationship with her father, which proved able to withstand some strong shocks in later years. In particular, her detention in 1940 by the UK government as a threat to national security put great strain on their connection. Herbert Taylour was understandably upset by his daughter's arrest and detention, and in August 1940 she told the Advisory Committee examining her detention in Holloway Gaol:

> My people [family] are very distressed. My father is what is termed a real old die hard. When Ireland became a Free State he came to live here. He wrote me a frightful letter when I went to Holloway; he said he could not believe that a daughter of my mother could turn out as I had done. He did relent and sent me flowers the other day.[19]

It was to Herbert Taylour's credit that he did not cut himself off from Fay, given that many people regarded all those detained and interned as traitors, or enemies of the UK. Her father even visited her once in gaol in May 1941, wrote to her and occasionally sent parcels to her while she was detained. She was aware of the distress her internment and her views caused to her father, and was herself upset by the difficulties this caused in her relationship with him:

> Our relations are friendly [...] he wrote to me for my birthday the other day. I am terribly sorry for him. It is grim enough for me to have had my freedom taken from me, but for him, who has been such a good loyalist, to have to be punished like that, it is rather difficult for him.[20]

In later years, Fay Taylour would also become a proponent of Irish Republicanism and the armed struggle in Northern Ireland, but by then, her father, the 'good loyalist', 'real old die hard', and 'a strong Conservative',[21] was dead.

Fay Taylour remembered her early childhood as something of a rural idyll. She and her younger sister, Enid, were taught by a succession of governesses, some bad, some good, but much of Fay's time was spent outside. She roamed around freely, played with her pets, rode, and occasionally made friends with local children both within and without her parents' social circle. One friend in particular, she remembered. He was a local boy she had seen while out in the trap with the governess, Miss Orr. He had gone past them downhill in 'a wooden box on wheels'.[22] On saying that she would love to be able to try the 'box on wheels', she was told by Miss Orr that 'it was only a game for boys'.[23] If the intention was to prevent Fay from trying the 'soap box' cart, then Miss Orr said exactly the wrong thing. Matters were complicated further when Fay discovered from Bennie the bread delivery man that the boy was only a local tradesman's son and, furthermore, a Roman Catholic. Undeterred, Fay arranged through Bennie to meet the boy and his cart. The meeting was a success with the two driving the cart down a back lane, which was 'exciting. It was narrow, and I spent most of the afternoon in the muddy ditch each side because the steering was very sudden'.[24]

Herbert Taylour was posted to different towns several times, and the family moved with him. The outbreak of the First World War saw Herbert volunteer to return to the Army, but that was refused given his age and rank in the RIC. The sisters' favourite governess, Miss Orr, left to become a wartime nurse, and Fay's older sister, Hilda, was at Alexandra College in Dublin. Fay briefly attended a local boys' school, the Royal School, Cavan, but in August 1917, aged thirteen, she went to Dublin to begin her time at Alexandra College. The school was founded in 1866 by Anne Jellicoe, a Quaker who believed that girls were entitled to the same educational opportunities as boys. Under Jellicoe, the school became a significant pioneer of girls' education in Ireland and the rest of the United Kingdom. Jellicoe campaigned to enable women to take university degrees, something that was achieved in Ireland with the Royal University of Ireland Act 1879. As a result, the first women in the United Kingdom to receive university degrees were six former pupils of Alexandra College, who studied at Dublin's Royal University and Trinity College, Dublin. At first, Taylour was at the preparatory department, known as Alexandra School. This was run by three spinsters, the Misses Fletcher. Hilda was at the college, although, according to Fay, Hilda was uninterested in schoolwork and saw her future in terms of making a good marriage. Fay was not academic either, but she was keen on hockey, tennis, and gym. She also enjoyed being 'a mischief', as she later wrote, 'everything except the lesson books was diverting'.[25] She quickly became part of a group of girls, some of whom remained friends for life.

From the Misses Fletcher's school, Fay moved, in 1919, to Alexandra College, at that time sited at Earlsfort Terrace, Dublin. By then, the First World War was over, but the war for Irish independence had begun, following the failed Easter

Rising in 1916 which had, nevertheless, reignited the idea of armed struggle against the British state. Although most fighting took place in County Cork and County Tipperary, Dublin was the focus of a particularly vicious urban conflict between the Irish Republican Army (IRA) and the various forces of the British Crown. For Taylour and her school friends, however, events outside the world of Alexandra College were merely a backdrop to their teenage school-focussed lives:

> I was hardly aware that the first world war was ending. Rifles were cracking all over Dublin from sporadic, and later continual outbursts by the Sinn Feiners. The big flu epidemic in November 1918 came home, however, as several girls caught it, and our favourite Miss Fletcher died.[26]

For Fay Taylour's father and his men in the RIC, the guerrilla war was anything but a background to their lives.

Herbert Taylour was stationed in County Galway during the period, where fourteen RIC men were killed,[27] mostly assassinated in the street or killed in ambushes. Herbert would have been a prime target for assassination himself, and when Hilda married her British officer fiancé, David, in Dublin in June 1921, care had to be taken. The reception was held at Fay's Aunt Ella's house in Hatch Street, and 'everyone breathed a sigh of relief when Dordy arrived and then tried to keep him away from the windows'.[28] Only seven months earlier, on 'Bloody Sunday', the IRA had killed British officers in their homes in Dublin, along with other members of the security forces. This had sparked a massacre of Gaelic football spectators at Croke Park by British forces. The city was still very tense, and as Taylour remembered, 'as Dordy had ordered de Valera's arrest in County Clare earlier it was no wonder everyone was jittery'.[29]

Fay started her last year at Alexandra College in September 1921 as a 'House-craft' student: 'instead of the ordinary classes I would now learn to cook, sew, and manage a house'.[30] By the time the Christmas holidays arrived, and Fay returned home, it was clear that major constitutional changes were in the making and that the future in Ireland for Herbert Taylour, now stationed at Dublin Castle, and his family, was in doubt. During that Christmas holiday, both Enid and Fay contracted measles and were looked after by a nurse, their mother being in bed already. One night, while still poorly, Fay was woken by noises outside the house. Looking out from her upstairs window, she saw men climbing over the 'high yard gate'. She secured the house front door with the 'door log' which 'fitted into deep slots in the wall, transversing the door'.[31] Outside, the men took away Taylour's car, but, although they broke into the basement, they made no attempt to come upstairs. After they had gone, Fay found that the gardener, Gallagher, was also missing, and that the bicycles and all the motor equipment had been taken along with the car. Gallagher turned up the next day, having been held by the IRA men until they had made their getaway. Fay asked him why they had not attempted to come upstairs, to which Gallagher replied, 'I told them yez was sore afflicted with the scarlet fever and it was mighty catchin'. They believed him because they 'had first awakened the Swans half a mile down the road thinking it was Claymore, our house, and their man had said we were all sick.'[32]

The Irish War of Independence was drawing to a close, as was Fay Taylour's school career. The Anglo-Irish Treaty was signed on 6 December 1921, being subsequently ratified by all the parties involved, which in the case of the newly emerging Irish Free State led to the Irish Civil War. The RIC was disbanded, and Herbert Taylour and his wife left Ireland, moving to England. Fay remained at Alexandra College for her final term and her examinations. She finished her time there by winning the tennis finals, being part of the school rowing eight, and winning second place in the Housecraft examinations, which came with a cash prize of £50 (worth around £6,000 in 2022). It proved to be an important windfall in relation to Taylour's future career. A few days later, Fay Taylour left Ireland for England. She would return many times to Ireland, as a place for motorsports and as a refuge, and, as she grew older, she saw herself as being entirely Irish.

Fay had finished school, was eighteen, and initially excited by the prospect of a new life in England, which she imagined as an extension of her life in Ireland, although with even more social life. As she later remembered, she imagined that England would be a new adventure, 'where I would now be grown up and meet young men, and go to dances and parties, and have a marvellous time like Hilda'.[33] At first, the Taylours lived with relatives or in hotels while they were house-hunting. In October 1922, the family moved into Burghfield Bridge Lodge, Berkshire, in a small hamlet on the River Kennet, part of the parish of Burghfield, a few miles from Reading. Enid was continuing her education, and had moved to Cheltenham Ladies' College, while Hilda lived fifteen miles away, her husband having left the army to take up farming. Fay's mother was increasingly incapacitated with the illness that would kill her, and Fay was responsible for running the house with a live-in maid and a daily 'help'. The First World War, however, had an impact on the labour market for domestic servants, and it was one of the few areas that saw a marked decline in the size of the labour force.[34] As a result, Fay Taylour spent a good deal of time trying to hire and keep a maid, something that seemed, at times, next to impossible. The result for Fay was that a good deal of housework fell to her and the 'help'. There was a worse problem in that moving into a new house in rural Berkshire was not the same as moving into a new house in rural Ireland prior to 1922. In Ireland, her RIC officer father had always been a key part of local 'society', both by virtue of his position, and his religious affiliation. In England, he was merely a retired officer in a country that was predominantly Anglican. As a result, the Taylours were not immediately invited to local functions or parties, and Fay was not automatically included in the social round of local middle-class youth. For Fay, 'I was finding that the new life was not so wonderful after all'.[35] Emerging from Alexandra College at eighteen, but now in England, she found that all her Irish friends were too far away, and none of her expectations of life as a young woman were likely to be met.

To break out of the isolation she felt, Fay joined a women's hockey club in nearby Reading. At first, that move did not seem to help: 'most of the women were older, and were married, and their husbands whisked them away after the game. It was very formal, not a bit like Ireland, and they all called each other by their surnames'.[36] However, after being hit in the eye during a game, she found that the social ice was broken, and that 'suddenly I had new friends, and invitations to play in different hockey matches'.[37] That was an advance, but she still wanted to meet young men so that she could go to parties which were based on invitations addressed to 'Miss Taylour and partner'. When she did go dancing, Fay had to dance with another young woman called Mimi. Sadly, she realised that part of the problem was the impact of the First World War on the numbers of young men still alive. Among Fay Taylour's papers there is a small, undated newspaper cutting (probably from 1919) that is headed 'France's War Losses' and provides the total known numbers of casualties for the main combatant nations. For Britain the figures given are 706,726 dead, and 2,037,325 wounded, in addition to those still classified as 'missing'.[38] Many of those wounded were, in fact, mutilated, and would never lead a normal life. Many young women found that they were 'surplus women'.[39] As Taylour ruefully realised, 'too many young men had been killed, and the rest had left the country towns for big cities'.[40] So Fay, as a young woman, was isolated and lonely in what was, in some respects, a strange country.

However, Fay thought that things had changed when, having taken the family car to a garage to have its bumper repaired after it was damaged while she was playing hockey in Reading, she met a young mechanic, whom she called 'Fred'. He was friendly and pleasant:

> His hair was the gorgeous colour of café-au-lait with a few strands aiming at his forehead. He reminded me of the fair boy at the Royal School though his chin was less square, but he was quite a bit older, twenty-nine as I learnt later. He was wearing white overalls covered with grease marks, yet he looked fresh and clean.[41]

The car took a couple of days to repair, and Taylour went twice to the garage, where Fred gave her tea and they talked. Finally, the car was ready, and Taylour had no further excuse to visit the garage. Fred solved the problem by asking her if she wanted a ride on his motorcycle. She had never ridden one before but wanted to. This began a platonic but, for her, intense teenage love affair, accompanied by learning to ride a motorcycle. Fred was a mechanic, and so she kept him secret from her family, using as cover imagined sewing classes at the Women's Institute on Monday and Thursday evenings. This was a universal teenage experience for Fay:

> We met at the lonely cross-road, at first pretending that the lesson was the object. We sat on his raincoat, or straddled the gate [...] I was content to sit beside him. To be with him was all I wanted, and he never attempted to make love, about which I knew nothing. He called me Paddy because I came from Ireland and was different, he said, from English girls.[42]

But towards the end of March 1923, not long before Fay's nineteenth birthday, Fred ended the relationship. He had promised to marry the daughter of the family he lodged with. According to Fred, this girl had been in love with him for three years, but his seeing Fay had brought matters to a head, and he asked the girl to marry him. For Fay, this was an upsetting end to the relationship, 'what I'd wanted I didn't know, except happiness. Loving someone was happiness. I'd been lonely, terribly lonely, before meeting Fred. Now I was lonely again, and unhappy'.[43]

Life went on, however, and was enlivened when Fay's friend from school, Norah, came to stay. They went to parties, played tennis, and Fay continued to play hockey. She heard about other young women whom she had known at Alexandra College being married, and the women at her hockey club were enjoying their married lives: one friend left to follow her British Army husband to his posting in India. But Fay seemed to have no luck when it came to meeting single young men. By the time her twenty-first birthday came, she was worried that she had been 'left on the shelf' as far as boyfriends and potential husbands were concerned. Her mother, suffering from cancer of the liver, became progressively weaker, and her father had to commute part of his RIC pension in order to pay for a live-in nurse.[44] Her mother died in November 1925.

The following year, 1926, saw Fay Taylour take the first steps towards becoming a motorsport star. Riding into Reading on her bicycle with her Post Office savings book, she returned on her first motorcycle, a small Levis machine. As she said, 'the housecraft prize won at college had come in useful though I doubt it was presented for such a purchase'.[45] However, she was soon dissatisfied with the little Levis, which was probably that company's 211cc model, and changed it three days later for Levis's bigger 246cc-engined lightweight motorcycle. This, too, failed the Taylour test: 'I'd ridden it on the Common and found I wanted more speed'.[46] Fay's father appears to have taken a benign view of his daughter's new interest, although he was surprised when he realised that she had bought a new motorcycle so quickly after the first. He probably did not realise that for Fay this was the beginning of a life-long passion.

As the second Levis machine had also proved to be underpowered, Taylour advertised for a good second motorcycle, 'and that brought dozens of tow-headed motorcyclists to the house with every kind of used motorbike, from the racing Norton to the gentler B.S.A.'[47] She greatly enjoyed test riding all of them, but decided that none of them was in good enough condition. Instead, she replied to an advertisement in the 'For Sale' column of a motorcycle magazine and bought 'a "350" A.J.S. [...] from a one-legged airman at Hendon air base'.[48] This was much more to her liking. The bike featured AJS's overhead valve engine, with which the company had taken the first four places in the 1921 Junior TT race and first and second place the following year. These successes 'marked the early beginning of the legendary "big-port" AJS, a giant killer'.[49] Taylour assessed the AJS compared to the Levis, writing that the 'docile Levis was a side-valve two-stroke while the A.J.S. was an overhead-valve four stroke, which was faster and peppier'.[50]

Now that she had a 'peppier' motorcycle, Taylour wanted to race. Her first race was probably a 'Ladies Race' organised by a London motorcycle club. However, she discovered that the 'contest was a trial, not a race, and I'd entered it looking for excitement only to find that the main feature was a SLOW hill climb'.[51] Worse, not fully understanding the mechanics of her AJS, she burnt the clutch out. She then enrolled in a motorcycle school in Chelsea to learn more about engines and motorcycles. Not only did she find the instruction valuable, but she also discovered that the club provided a new friendship circle, as all the other members were young men who were 'interested to talk to me'.[52] With her new knowledge and a sense of belonging that she found among the enthusiasts, she spent much of her time with motorcycles. That Easter, she and a group of the 'boys' went on a motorcycle tour of Devon. Among the young male motorcyclists, she was treated 'in open comradely style' by the others whose 'sweethearts were the motorcycles'.[53]

The next step in Taylour's motorcycle life came when she went into a Reading motorcycle repair shop in early 1927 to see about adjustments to her AJS. The owner was Charles Harmon, a motorcycle racer. He suggested that she enter the Southern Scott Scramble, held near Camberley, Surrey. The 'Camberley Scramble', as it was known, was held each year: 'entrants included professional factory and T.T. riders, and three factory-sponsored women riders who vied each year for a special trophy called the Venus Cup'.[54] The course was across the undulating heath and scrubland of the area, including some very steep ascents and descents, all on sandy surfaces. Harmon took Taylour to see the course and start to practise on some of the lesser hills. These included one nicknamed 'Kilimanjaro'. In the weeks prior to the competition, Taylour 'returned again and again to the course, determined to conquer every hill and tricky stretch so that I might wrest that Venus Trophy from the famous Marjorie Cottle who won it each year'.[55] Cottle was a few years older than Taylour and was already a well-known name in motorcycling. She competed in a variety of forms of trials and racing but is 'perhaps best remembered today for Raleigh's famous 1924 publicity stunt, in which she rode a 2¾hp solo model around the coast of mainland Britain – a journey of over 3,000 miles'.[56] The race was run on 5 March 1927, over two circuits of a 25-mile course, one held in the morning, the second after lunch. Taylour's AJS shed its chain at one point, but she repaired it and carried on. The gruelling event reminded Taylour of horse-riding across country: 'I felt like a point-to-point rider across his horse for I was part of the nifty A.J.S. as we took stoney hills, heathland, mud and sand in our stride'.[57] At the end of the race, the riders gathered in a local pub to await the results. For Taylour, it was triumph.

> I'd not only won the Venus Trophy but also the 350-Class Cup which was vied for by all the competitors riding the same sized engine as mine, and also

a team prize. The Reading Motorcycle Club had honoured me with inclusion in their No.2 team, which finished first.[58]

This was the beginning of Fay Taylour's motorsport career.

After her victories Taylour wrote to the AJS company in Coventry, and was taken on as part of their works team. She subsequently switched to Rudge Whitworth Ltd in the summer of 1927. In the fourteen months between competing in the 1927 Southern Scott Scramble and her victories in the May 1928 Southern Scott Scramble, Fay Taylour had a string of other successes. She won:

> Gold Medals in the National Alan and Travers Trophy Trials and Silver in the Colmore, Cotswold and Victory Trophy Trials [...] She took a Bronze Medal place in the Bemrose Trial, the Wood Green M.C. Ladies' Trial and won a Gold Medal in the Auto Cycle Union's Six Days Trial, run over a 750-mile route.[59]

It was a startling, successful opening to her motorcycle career, which she was to build on over the next two years, becoming known worldwide.

Chapter Two

Speedway Queen, 1928–30

Towards the end of 1927 Taylour's father moved from Burghfield Bridge Lodge in Berkshire to a new home, 'Derryquin', which he had built in Lymington, Hampshire, and shortly afterwards he remarried. This marked another change in Fay Taylour's life, and she later described her father's move, saying 'our English home was broken up'.[1] Herbert's new wife was a young woman only a few years older than Fay. Prior to the marriage, Fay described her stepmother-to-be as being 'sisterly'.[2] In all her various autobiographical writing, Taylour never named her father's second wife, always referring to her as her stepmother, or, occasionally, as 'Mac'. Although Taylour and her sisters appear to have been welcomed or at least tolerated as visitors to Derryquin, it was made clear, according to Fay, that it was not a family home. Burghfield Lodge had been Fay Taylour's home, where she had a central role in housekeeping, but after her father's second marriage that was no longer the case. The change in domestic circumstances dovetailed with Taylour beginning a new phase of racing that would take her around the world. From then on, with the exception of her years in detention, Taylour would have a peripatetic life following the racetrack. As she described it: 'my father married again in 1928, and, after seeing him off to France honeymooning, I went on to the dirt tracks'.[3]

The 'dirt tracks' Taylour referred to were the home of the latest motorsport – speedway – which was to become one of the outstanding spectator events of the day. The novelist and future MP A.P. Herbert, on first experiencing speedway, wrote:

> Heavens, the noise! It is like 10 million mechanical drills performing in unison. It swells and falls as the riders take the corners; it echoes about the cavernous concrete halls, drowning the feeble acclamations of the crowd; it dies slowly as the riders stop, and the end of the race seems like the end of a battle. It is titanic and terrible and monstrous; and yet in that enormous place, made by those monsters, it seems appropriate and right.[4]

There is some debate around the origins of speedway, with the term itself being used in the USA as early as 1902, while early variants of motorcycle track racing were found in both the USA and Australia.[5] However, Australia has probably the best claim to inventing the sport, with a meeting held at 'the Hunter River Valley under floodlights at West Maitland Agricultural Showground [New South Wales] on the 15 December, 1923'.[6] Its first appearance in Britain is generally regarded as being the meeting at High Beech in Epping Forest in February 1928, when at least 15,000, and perhaps as many as 30,000, spectators attended.[7] Although the popularity of speedway in Britain would be characterised by 'almost inexplicable crazes and falls',[8] it attracted huge crowds and was a cheap, immensely popular sport among working-class spectators. In 1946, for example, six million people attended speedway events in Britain. Only a year after the introduction of the sport, there were two speedway leagues, with thirteen clubs in the north of England, and twelve in the south.[9] By the end of 1928, there were speedway meetings at thirty-four tracks, rising to over sixty within a year. However, the first explosion of speedway quickly fell back to ten tracks by 1932, and seven by 1935, followed by some recovery prior to the war. Nonetheless, it remained a popular sport. For example, 93,000 people attended the 1938 World Championship Final at Wembley.[10] From the outset, speedway was a dangerous, exciting, dramatic, professionalised sport that threw up famous names, such as James Lloyd 'Sprouts' Elder, an American rider who was one of the most well-known competitors during the late 1920s and early 1930s. Elder's take on the sport was that 'for excitement, it licks a bull-fight. Once you get the speedway habit you look upon bull-fighting as a kind of dairy farming'.[11]

Speedway was a professional sport, and one that depended very much on promoters and prize money. It was governed by the Auto-Cycle Union, which forbade women from competing in the speedway leagues.[12] However, women were permitted to compete in non-league races, and Fay Taylour was 'one of around half a dozen women [who] took part in speedway races against each other and against men'.[13] Other women speedway riders in Britain included Eva Askquith, Marjorie Cottle, Edyth Foley, Jessie Hole and Louise Ball. Eva Askquith was to become as well known in Britain as Fay Taylour, and a rivalry was to develop between the two women, but it was Taylour's successes against the top male riders in Britain, Australia and New Zealand that marked her out for speedway fame.

Taylour first saw speedway racing at Stamford Bridge, Fulham. Following her successes at the Southern Scott Scramble in March 1927, she had been taken on by the AJS company in Coventry as part of their works team. She soon switched to Rudge Whitworth Ltd where she had the same role as a trials rider. The 'Reliability Trials' were important for the motorcycle companies as success in those challenging races against the clock over rugged terrain was essential to sales of their motorcycles. Any model that showed its strength, endurance and reliability in trials was guaranteed greater sales. Taylour spent a very successful year and a half as a works team rider, gaining victories in a whole string of events. But, true to form, she soon wanted to move on to greater challenges, particularly involving speed. She had, of course, heard of the new sport of dirt-track racing when it was first introduced to England in the summer of 1928:

I'd seen hair-raising pictures, and read stories of how Australian promoters were building these special loose-surfaced tracks in several English cities, particularly London, and had a batch of their fastest racing boys, including

Sig Schlam, to demonstrate and keep the crowds thrilled till the English riders had learnt the art of 'broadsiding'. Broadsiding was the word used to describe the method of taking the turns, and the conservative 'London Illustrated' likened it to the Chariot Races of old. The rather inelegant word 'dirt', which came from Australia where unsurfaced by-ways are called dirt roads, was becoming the most romantic in the dictionary for tens of thousands including the aspiring competitors.[14]

Taylour saw herself as an aspiring competitor in this new sport and tried to interest the competitions manager at Rudge Whitworth in the dirt track. The answer, however, was that the firm was not interested as it did not see how, unlike the reliability trials, dirt-track racing could be used to boost sales of the firm's machines. That did not stop Taylour wanting to see and learn more about speedway. One afternoon she left the Rudge Whitworth showrooms early and took the train to London for a mid-week speedway meeting at Stamford Bridge, Fulham. She intended to return by the night train.

Stamford Bridge was packed and the first race had started by the time Taylour took her seat halfway up the stands over the starting line:

> I had a perfect view of the whole track. It was oval, two straights joined by two sweeping curves, approximately a quarter of a mile to the lap, and of course with the loose or 'dirt' surface. The queer sweet smell of racing fuel was everywhere, and there was an atmosphere of compressed excitement though nothing very daring was happening on the track. I watched the riders with curiosity, the loose surface was giving them trouble on the bends, one or two went into a skid and came off and the others looked wobble-y. A girl behind me was saying: 'they haven't learnt to broadside yet', and I gathered they were all new to the game.[15]

Broadsiding was an essential technique for speedway but, as the girl spectator realised, at this early stage in the sport in England it was only Australians and Americans who had mastered the skill. Taylour and the crowd were soon treated to a demonstration by a master, the American 'Sprouts' Elder, who had already made a dirt-track name for himself in the US, South America and in Australia. In 1928, he dominated speedway in England and Scotland. Elder 'became one of the real big money riders [...] he seldom rode unless he received at least £100, plus his other winnings at each track'.[16] Later he would be instrumental in establishing speedway across the US. Elder's performance that night at Stamford Bridge was all that Fay Taylour needed to convince her where her motorcycle racing future lay:

> Elder came out of the pits now crouched over a small machine which had no footrest on the left side, which was the inside since the track was driven anti-clockwise, and I noticed as he stopped on the starting line to be introduced that there was a shallow hook on the right side of his small petrol tank which fitted over his knee. His motor was dead but two overall-ed men called

'pushers-off' leapt from the infield and gave him a shove, and the special little dirt track bike, called a Harley Peashooter, sprang to life.

Like a huge gorilla, Elder's tall figure leant forward over his racer, his right knee tucked under the hook and his left leg trailing full length behind him. So that was why he had a steel cap over the toes of his left boot! For three or four laps he circled the track with never a wobble, and I thought: that's it. Then suddenly, as he entered the straight on the far side, he opened his throttle with a roar AND KEPT IT OPEN. It must have jammed I thought as he approached the bend at an impossible speed, but I stared fascinated although I didn't really want to see him going through the fence. The next moment he was on the bend and his bike was lying inwards at such an angle that he'd obviously skidded and was crashing – but that would be better than hitting the fence head on.

But he neither hit the fence nor the ground. He came out of that turn with the bike upright, roared straight under my stand and slammed full throttle into the next bend in another enormous slide as if it were perfectly safe. So that was 'broadsiding'![17]

This demonstration was followed by a match race between Elder and Art Pechar, another American who was a favourite of the Stamford Bridge crowd. Against Elder, however, Pechar crashed spectacularly and was taken from the field in an ambulance. Taylour was captivated by all of this: the special dirt-track bikes, the loose track, the atmosphere of the crowd, the new technique, and the skill and speed of riders like 'Sprouts' Elder and Art Pechar. From then on, Taylour was determined to take part in speedway. It was, as she would frequently tell reporters in the future, 'the love that lasted', in contrast to her many relationships with men.[18]

Taylour did not return that night to her job at Rudge Whitworth in Coventry. The next morning she went to see if the Stamford Bridge speedway promoter would let her practise on the dirt track. Perhaps predictably, he 'just laughed'. Taylour then went to another promoter, but he said that a woman could not possibly have the physical strength or nerve to race on the speedway track. Writing many years later about these early rejections, Taylour made the revealing comment, 'But every "no" made me all the more eager'. [19] That statement could stand for much in Taylour's personal and political life, not just her sporting life. Still determined to try speedway, Taylour visited all the promoters except at Crystal Palace. She decided that she would have to 'gate-crash' a practice session and thought it best to leave one promoter unaware that she was looking to try the dirt track. She then went to a sports clothing shop, Lewis's Leathers. While she was trying on helmets the shop's owner, Sammy Lewis, recognised her, and when another customer came in, he introduced Taylour to him. The man turned out to be a speedway rider, Lionel Wills, whom Taylour had seen racing at Crystal Palace the previous evening. Wills pointed at the crash helmet Taylour was holding and, 'asked if I was going to have a shot at dirt track racing'. Taylour's answer, of course, was yes, and instead of dismissing her as a woman, Wills replied, 'it's great fun, but I'm absolutely terrified every time I go into a turn'.[20]

Meeting Wills was a key moment for Taylour's sporting and personal life. The 'tall distinguished-looking young man'[21] was a year older than Taylour, a Cambridge graduate, the heir to a shipping agents' company, George Wills & Co.,[22] and an aficionado of speedway. His job regularly took him to Australia, and it was there that he had first seen speedway, writing enthusiastic accounts of it for the sporting press in Britain. Taylour claimed that it was Wills who was responsible, along with his Australian friend, Johnnie Hoskins, for introducing the sport to England. She wrote, 'on a recent business trip to Australia [he] had discovered dirt track racing and persuaded Australian promoters to introduce the sport to England'.[23] Norman Jacobs, the historian of 'The Glaziers', the speedway team whose home was Crystal Palace, confirmed this, and gave an account of how Wills's sports journalism from Australia in 1926, then his meeting with Fred Mockford and Cecil Smith, who ran path racing at Crystal Palace, convinced them of the viability of a speedway track. They then contacted Johnnie Hoskins, a renowned speedway promoter in Sydney, and he cabled advice leading to the building of the Crystal Palace speedway track:

> Mockford and Smith took his advice, converting the old football pitch into a 440-yard-long dirt track, 33 feet wide on the straights and 55 feet wide on the bends. The track was banked 1 in 20 at both ends, with a riding surface consisting of several inches of finely graded cinders. The safety fence was made of sprung wire netting and was 4 feet high on the outside of the track, behind which there was some 6 feet of no man's land and then a 4-foot iron railing fence. There was seating accommodation for 8,000 people and stepped standing accommodation for a further 65,000. The cost of the conversion was £5,000.[24]

It was here that Wills took Taylour to smuggle her onto the track incognito, her sex hidden under padded leathers, crash helmet and goggles. She had taken her AJS motorcycle along with her on the back seat of Wills's old 1907 Rolls-Royce Silver Ghost Tourer. Wills saw the pit marshal, Frank, and he agreed that Taylour could try the track. Taylour rode out when the track was fairly clear of others who were practising, entered a bend and, 'off I came!'[25] As Wills explained, her AJS did not have enough power. Her Rudge might have been better, but what was really needed was a 'Dirt Track Special'. Wills was still waiting for his 'Special' to be delivered. Despite the AJS, Taylour kept on practising until Fred Mockford appeared and told the staff to flag in 'that lad' so the track could be raked for the next day's racing. That lad, of course, was Taylour, and when Wills laughed and told him it was 'a girl', Mockford flew into a rage. Taylour then came into the pits, but Mockford did not let Wills introduce her, saying to her, 'you have a nerve, haven't you?'[26] Wills suggested that Mockford book Taylour, but the promoter replied, 'I'd sooner book the devil himself'. Wills then told him a white lie, saying 'but all the other promoters are booking her'.[27] At this point Taylour left, saying she had to wash, but in reality she could not face another 'no'. She was surprised when she emerged from the washroom to hear Mockford say to her, 'How would you like to ride at our meeting a week from tomorrow? You can practise during the week.'[28] Taylour was 'in' and it was largely due to the good-humoured persuasion of Wills.

Lionel Wills became an important figure in Fay Taylour's life. Not only was he instrumental in helping her gain a foothold in speedway, but he also became important to her personally. At this point in Taylour's life, she was still very unsure how to deal with men on a personal basis. She was attracted to men, and was apt to fall for them in a romantic fashion, but she was still a virgin, remaining so for several more years. Matters were more complicated in that she realised that she would not be able to link her life with any one man. She was also affected by the advice of a friend, a married woman married to a British officer in the Indian Army, who had once told her, 'never let a man you're fond of know that you care'.[29] Taylour took this to heart, and despite her developing feelings for Wills, she kept an emotional distance. There was a pronounced element of naivety and inexperience surrounding Taylour's relationship with Wills, but there was also the troubling realisation that she did not feel sexually attracted to him. All in all, it was a confusing and difficult time for her. She later wrote, 'although we were often alone together our relationship was that of brother and sister'.[30] Eventually, Wills asked Taylour to marry him, but her response was 'no'. Wills was subsequently married twice, but Taylour and Wills kept in touch for most of the rest of his life. For the rest of her life, despite many male partners, both short and long-term, Taylour kept referring to her early relationship with Wills. In that sense, Wills became a sort of cipher for what might have been. She built her adult life around her determination to race, to be independent, to 'laugh at security' in all its forms, including personal. Yet she often, especially when in financial or sporting difficulties, thought of Wills and his offer of marriage. She knew that it could not have lasted, but the thought that she might have married him was a strange sort of comfort and regret in difficult times.

For the moment, however, what mattered above all else was the break that Mockford had given her when he invited her to race. First, she had to learn how to broadside. Taylour was still using the factory Rudge that she had thanks to her job in Coventry, a job she held on to in order to have a motorcycle to race. She stripped the left footrest, lamps, mudguards and other parts from the Rudge in an effort to lighten it and make it speedway ready, but it was still too heavy a machine. Each day saw her at the Crystal Palace speedway track, riding, falling, and riding again, all to develop the skills needed, especially broadsiding. This was a controlled skid at speed that enabled the bike and rider to slide around the bends, with the front wheel upright, the rear wheel slanting, and the rider's inside leg trailing back in line with the rear wheel. The skill and strength needed to successfully 'broadside' was one of the reasons given for why women would not be able to compete in the event. Fay Taylour was to disprove this, developing her broadsiding technique to a level that enabled her to beat the best male competitors. She was undoubtedly highly skilled, but she also possessed upper body strength and large, strong hands. Indeed, someone who knew Taylour at the end of her life remarked that for such a small woman, she possessed very large 'men's hands that looked as if they had been transplanted onto her arms'.[31] Speedway racing required a combination of the right machine, skill, strength, and undoubted courage:

> The afternoon before race day I was actually broadsiding! But it was a touch and go business, and the Rudge Whitworth bike was really far too heavy, even for the men who were riding especially lightened frames. 'Dirt Track Specials' were being built by factories. But the engine of the Rudge was the right size. It had the power to put me in a slide. I had neither the power nor the experience to hold it for more than a few yards. I'd been heeling the bike over at the start of the bends, giving full throttle at the same time, but no sooner had I started to slide than I was in trouble. I was in deep water without knowing how to swim. Then came the sensible idea of waiting to start the slide till just before coming out of the turn so that I could enter the straight before losing control. And gradually I was able to put the bike into the slide earlier and earlier till I was making quite a professional broadside from about half way round, at the same time rolling into the curve as steadily as possible without siding. Instead of flying into the bend fast and falling off I was able to come out of it on full throttle and down the straight at speed. Falling off was a tiring business![32]

Race day arrived, and Taylour was ready. It was 9 June 1928 at Crystal Palace, it was her first speedway race, and she would be the first woman in England to race on the dirt track. She appeared in a special race against the two Australian stars Sig Schlam and Ron Johnson. The event was designed to maximise the entertainment value of introducing a woman on the dirt track while providing the two 'aces' with an opportunity to show their broadsiding and speed. Taylour was given a handicap start, because she felt that the two men were so skilled that in the event that if she came off her bike, they would be able to avoid her:

> I did fall off in spite of all my planning. With a super effort I'd taken the heavy bike round smoothly for three and a half laps of the 4-lap race. Then, on the last bend, I lost control and went head over heels. I saw the Pathé Gazette Newsreel later. The two boys were behind, and I doubt they could have caught me, but their handicap was too stiff so it was fairer for it to end that way.[33]

Despite, or perhaps because of her fall, which left her bruised but able to walk away, the event was a success. *Motor Cycling* magazine commented: 'The prospect of watching a lady rider, Miss Fay Taylour, matched in a handicap race against a star such as Ron Johnson was chiefly responsible for the excellent crowd at Crystal Palace Speedway last Saturday'.[34] Throughout her career, Taylour was well aware of the value to her, and promoters, of being a woman competitor in largely male preserves. The novelty of Taylour's racing skill was particularly valuable to speedway promoters who were engaged in a business that depended for its survival on continuing to draw crowds beyond those that were initially attracted by the new sporting import.

The next Saturday, Taylour raced again at Crystal Palace, but only against Ron Johnson. Again, she came off her bike 'after getting into a fast front wheel wobble'. Falling heavily, 'I was bruised and winded, but in the spirit of those days when all the amateurs were falling off you walked away without assistance, unless it was a stretcher exit, and declared if you had any breath left that you were unhurt'.[35] The spectators were appreciative and Mockford hired her for a further meeting, but this time a demonstration, not a race. Lionel Wills, who would also be on the Crystal Palace track that evening, had taken delivery of his new 'Dirt Track Special', and offered to loan it to Taylour for her ride, which, as she said, 'was an incredibly sporting gesture since the odds to date were in favour of my falling off, and bikes also get bruised!'[36] She had a few practice laps on Wills's bike and was determined to hand it back to him without any damage after her appearance. The need to stay on the bike was further enhanced by the news that officials from the Auto Cycle Union (ACU) would be at the meeting, and Mockford warned her that if she came off again then the ACU intended to ban her from the dirt track. But having a motorcycle purpose built for speedway made all the difference, and she successfully completed her third appearance at Crystal Palace.

Taylour next raced at Hove, near Brighton, on her own 'Dirt Track Special', which was delivered just in time, enabling her to beat the local champion, Bob Barker. She was now firmly on the speedway circuit. Races followed at High Beech in Essex, Salford near Manchester, Liverpool, and Birmingham before the end of the 1928 season in England. At the new Albion Greyhound Arena, Salford, she won a match race and the handicap event. In Liverpool she was second in the Golden Gauntlet Race. In three months, she had established herself as a notable speedway rider:

> After Salford Taylour was seen as a dashing and clever rider, who seemed to refute the assertion that considerable physical strength was a prerequisite if a machine, travelling at speed round the corners, was to be safely controlled. She also challenged, by her very presence, the notion that the dirt-track was essentially a place for men only. Fay was given the credit of being the superior in skill in each of the Salford races in which she took part. Her cornering was daring and performed at speed, and she appeared to have the ability to cope at critical moments, such as when finding her path blocked on a bend.[37]

Taylour's fame spread. She was being referred to in the daily and specialist press as 'Queen of the Dirt Track', and the 'Broadside Queen'. That press attention may well have encouraged a handful of other women to switch to speedway, with women like Eva Askquith and Jessie Hole soon becoming as well-known as Taylour.[38]

The final piece in the puzzle of successful dirt-track racing for Taylour had been her acquisition of her own 'Dirt Track Special', a 494cc Douglas, the most successful speedway bike of the time. One of the engineers involved in its design was Freddie Dixon, one of the great motor engineers and motorsports champions of the interwar period.[39] Dixon retired from motorcycle racing in 1928 after returning to the Douglas company as both a rider and engineer. He had been employed by Douglas as part of its attempt to develop the flat twin engine and prove its worth at the Isle of Man TT road races. But there were fundamental difficulties with the engine that neither Douglas nor Dixon could overcome. Dixon finished 18th out of 21 in the Junior TT and had to retire from the Senior following a crash. These disappointing results marked the end of his racing career on two wheels, but he continued to work on the development of motorcycles until 1930 before turning his attention to racing motorcars.[40] For speedway riders 'a Dixon tuned engine for the dirt track bikes was available for an extra £10. This gave an extra 7bhp and was a worthwhile investment'.[41] It was on a Dixon Douglas that Taylour won some of her most famous dirt-track races. But Taylour's links with Freddie Dixon were more extensive than merely riding one of 'his' machines to victory on the dirt track. These links would develop decades later when she became much more interested in politics and political activism; activism that led her to being detained in 1940 under the Defence Regulations 18B for her pro-German and anti-war stance.

In December 1940, some six months into her detention in Holloway Gaol, Taylour managed to smuggle out an uncensored letter to Dixon. The letter briefly laid out Taylour's explanation for why she had been detained – 'my only crime is that I disapproved of the war'[42] – and asked Dixon if he could send her a small food parcel containing, among other things, five carrots as a sign that her unofficial mailbox (possibly smuggled out via another detainee visited by her husband) was working. Clearly, Taylour thought that Dixon was a reliable person to establish contact with on the outside, which raises the question of Dixon's own political views. She had, before detention, given him literature from Oswald Mosley's British Union (BU, *aka* BUF). An MI5 report, by agent M/3, dated April 1940, noted that at a race meeting, Taylour 'gave a quantity of B.U.F. literature to Freddy [*sic*] DIXON with which he was very impressed'.[43] Dixon also appears to have offered her a job driving for him if she was released (he had lost his licence), but, in fact, it was Dixon who revealed Fay's letter to the authorities. He took the letter to his local police station in Reigate, and, speaking to Inspector Edward Ayres, he said that it was 'from a lady-friend' and 'he was somewhat disturbed by the contents of the letter'.[44] At first, Dixon refused to give Taylour's name, or show the letter, but in the end did both. Interestingly, he told Inspector Ayres:

Although he himself did not altogether agree with our [the UK's] present position [i.e. the war] brought about by promises, he felt that as the country had made such promises it was our duty to abide by them and therefore the war was inevitable. He regarded the letter with suspicion and refused to allow himself to be used as a medium possibly for some act of doubt to the detriment of the National interest.[45]

In the late summer of 1928, however, all this was far in the future. Buoyed up by her new-found success in speedway, Taylour agreed with a suggestion by Johnnie Hoskins that she travel to Australia and race there, in the home of speedway, for Australia's 1928–29 summer season. But before she did, she accepted Lionel Wills's invitation to join him in the International Six Days Trial.

This reliability trial started in Munich, before the riders crossed through the Austrian, Italian and Swiss Alps, 'with a hotel stop every night at such romantic places as Oberammergau and Chamonix, touching also Savie France and finishing up in Geneva'.[46] Wills and Taylour rode together each day as they had drawn consecutive competitors' numbers and stayed at the same hotel each night. In her unpublished biography, *I Laughed at Security*, Taylour makes much of the romantic element of this trip. Nothing sexual happened between Taylour and Wills, although her account reads as if they were each waiting for the other to take the initiative. For Taylour, it became part of her mythology of her relationship with Wills. After the event was over, they went to Paris where they spent two nights before flying back to England. At the airport, Wills engaged a freelance photographer to take a photograph of the two 'stepping on to the plane complete with weekend suitcases and happy smile'.[47] Wills subsequently showed the photograph to his mother and family and thought that their shocked reaction was 'hysterically' funny. It had the effect of making Taylour *persona non grata* with Wills's family. Later, as Taylour reflected, 'I couldn't share his amusement though I loved his rebellious trait of not caring a hoot what anyone thought'.[48] In fact, Wills did 'care a hoot' about his mother's opinion, as he subsequently retired from racing following a crash which his mother decided was the last straw. His future was with the family shipping company. There was also another aspect to the Six Days Trial experience. A large part of the backdrop to Taylour and Wills's intense European interlude was in Bavaria. Later, her professed 'love' of Germany would be one of the contributing factors to her detention without trial, and it is clear that her personal experiences of Germany in the 1920s and 1930s were strongly positive. Within a year of Taylour and Wills's fortnight on the Continent, Wills was to marry someone else, while Taylour returned for the International Six Days Trial in 1929. But before she did so, a highly successful speedway tour of Australia and New Zealand made her international reputation.

Chapter Three

Australia and New Zealand:
Tour 1, with a Wembley Interlude

Taylour left Liverpool for Australia in November 1928, sailing on the White Star liner SS *Euripides*. Family, friends and speedway racers waved her off as she boarded the boat train in London. Lionel Wills gave her a rag dog mascot and a parcel of records to play on her portable blue leather-cased gramophone. As the train drew out, Taylour realised that she would miss Wills. She opened the parcel of records and found that he had included 'two extra ones [. . .] not exactly Lionel's taste in popular music, but the words carried a message: YOU BELONG TO ME and YOU'RE THE CREAM IN MY COFFEE. I hummed them to myself, repeating the last line of one verse, "I'll be lost without you". So he too would miss me!'.[1] Taylour's lone trip to Australia was something of a gamble. All she had to break into speedway in Australia was the knowledge that Johnnie Hoskins had written to the Perth speedway track management, and that she had a clippings collection of 'wonderful write-ups in the English papers'.[2] She had deliberately not contacted any of the Australian promoters prior to leaving England as she had not wanted to receive negative replies. She would, instead, rely on her ability to 'satisfy the promoters and their spectators with my ability to slide the bends'.[3] She would also rely on the force of her personality.

In early January 1929 Taylour and her two motorcycles, the speedway Douglas and the Rudge as a back-up machine, disembarked at Albany, 260 miles from Perth. She was met by some speedway contacts and put on the night train to the Western Australia capital. She had relatives in Australia on both sides of her family. In time, she met some of them, but the first thing was speedway. She received the sort of reception at Perth station that she came to love, 'a regal reception awaited me at Perth where speedway officials, riders, fans and press reporters had gathered at the station'.[4] Taylour enjoyed the attention and the social life that surrounded her racing, but she also knew that if she were to sell herself as a racer, that sort of attention was vital. She never had a manager, and filled the advertising and promotion gap herself. Taylour developed a good relationship with journalists wherever she went, seeking out opportunities to promote her racing in newspapers and on the radio. She was also quick to see the value of advertising that linked her name to motorcycles, engines, tyres, oils, and anything else that would earn a fee and push her name.

The first mention of Taylour in the Australian press came in a long piece in *The Daily News*, of Perth, Western Australia, headed 'Girl Speedster/Only One of

Her Sex/MISS TAYLOUR HERE'. The article showed Taylour's skill at presenting herself to the Australian public. She was described as being 'of medium height and in her neat-fitting costume presented a trim, athletic figure, leaving no doubt as to her ability to handle a machine at speed'.[5] The welcoming party in Perth had included the leading Australian riders, Sig Schlam and Charlie Datson. She told the press that she had come to Australia because of the impact of riders like Schlam and Datson in England, where they had created 'a very favourable impression', and because Australia was the home of the sport. In her numerous interviews in the Australian press, Taylour frequently praised Australian sporting life, with its appreciative crowds. She also compared Australia to England in terms of attitudes to women in motorcycle sport. In return, the Australian press routinely wrote of her in very positive terms.

Taylour's first race in Australia was at the Claremont ground in Perth, on Saturday 5 January 1929, where she beat a local ace, Frank Brown. *The Daily News* described the action, and the crowd's response to Taylour:

> Appreciative of good riding, the crowd had simmered its appreciation of Miss Taylour's practice run when she playfully showered many of the bystanders with cinders in the most approved Speedway fashion. The simmering broke into a roar as the two speeding riders [Taylour and Frank Brown] raced over the line on the start of their match race. Miss Taylour at once took the lead and was never headed. Her riding was pretty to watch and fast into the bargain. Brown did well, but his 2¾ machine had not the pace of the other's 3½ h.p. mount. The winner received a splendid ovation – a win by a woman rider over a mere man being particularly popular with the feminine element. Miss Taylour's time was only a few seconds outside the record for the course. She covered the distance in 1.20 2–5.[6]

Taylour's ability and fame undoubtedly inspired other women to race. On arriving in Australia, she had noted that 'although many women in England used the motorcycle as a means of transport, not a great many rode it in competition'.[7] But her successes had the direct effect of doing just that – inspiring more to race. For example, Mrs Medwell, the chairwoman and general secretary of the Women's Motor Cycle Club in Southern Australia, explained a year later that the example of Taylour had been behind the founding of the club. The club captain, Miss Joan Carter, commented: 'the girls have been further fired with determination to become capable riders by the example of Miss Fay Taylour, the woman speedway rider who was in Adelaide this season'.[8] Both in the UK and Australia it was the case that 'speedway attracted many women and children as spectators to the tracks',[9] and they now had an internationally successful woman ace.

Taylour's victory over Frank Brown at the Claremont Speedway, Perth, on 5 January, was a fitting prelude for her next battle against the dominant speedway rider of the day – Australia's 'Super' Sig Schlam. Taylour had hoped to acclimatise to the bigger Australian tracks before competition riding but was thrown into racing immediately. Following her victory over Frank Brown there was much expectation and speculation in Perth regarding her match against Sig Schlam. Newspapers carried full-page advertisements for the Schlam versus Taylour match at the Claremont Speedway, and Taylour later described a banner 'in huge letters' on the way to the track which read, 'FAY TAYLOUR will RACE SCHLAM'.[17] Schlam held the lap record for the Claremont track, which had stood for over a year; he had an unrivalled victory record, and, unlike most Australian riders at the time, he also rode a speedway Douglas. It looked very much as if Fay Taylour's task was an impossible one. To make matters worse, she became embroiled in an argument about appearance fees and prize money with E.L. Baker, the director of Speedways Ltd, which was responsible for the Claremont races. Taylour's demand for a £50 race fee on top of appearance money was deemed excessive, despite the fact that she was a major crowd-puller who brought bigger than average gate numbers.[18] The dispute was settled, presumably because her appearance against Schlam could guarantee a bigger than normal crowd, and they raced on 26 January 1929.

The build-up to the race was nerve-wracking for Taylour. By the time she was in the pits waiting, she later recalled that 'the fire in my tummy was too fierce and everything else was vague. Even the mechanics' voices seemed far away'.[19] Friends had come to wish her luck, and Sig Schlam spoke to her:

> I was literally dazed with nerves, and it didn't make it any better when Sig came up and said quietly: 'I have to beat you this time'. He seemed to be saying he was sorry, and of course he was referring to our last meeting on the track at the Crystal Palace in London. It was clear now that if I hadn't fallen he was then going to let me finish first. This time it was out of the question, and I wouldn't want it. But I didn't want a run-a-way race either. Why hadn't they matched me against a rider of my own standing?[20]

Taylour stayed with her bike and the mechanics in the pits as the other races were run. She concentrated on the race ahead, realising that if she was to prevent a 'run-a-way race' by Schlam then she would have to have her motorcycle's throttle wide open, and it would 'take a lot of throttle I'd never used before'. Her thoughts continued, 'that dash into the first bend after the flying start ... it would have to be full throttle, and if I were on the inside, which would make the bend more acute, I'd probably overslide'.[21] The mechanics told her that they had fitted a larger sprocket to her Douglas, 'it'll give you just that extra speed'. Yet, as she knew, she had yet to get as much speed as she could out of the machine. It was a long wait, but eventually she was on the starting line with one of the staff telling her that the track was heavy, and speeds slower. 'I still felt nervous, but there was no way out now and the nerves were giving way to more urgent and factual thoughts'.[22]

Sig Schlam pulled up on the outside of her. It was a racing start, so both riders rolled around the track together, then opened up at the ten-yard point to cross the starting line. The race was on:

> I didn't shut off for that dreaded plunge into the first bend, nor did I overslide. Sig was beside me, but his whereabouts could make no difference

because I was going as fast as the bike could take me. To stay on and to remember to pump [oil at each lap] was all that seemed to matter at the moment, and I pumped as I raced down the back stretch. Then into the second bend full flight, and on to the home straight to complete the first lap.

I was so engrossed that I didn't notice at first that Sig was no longer beside me. He was just behind, unable to overtake but waiting for me to lose ground through the slightest fault if not a fall. But I was still alone and still on the saddle as I completed an equally fast second lap and took the white flag for the third and final round.[23]

Halfway around the first bend on that last lap Taylour hit a bump in the track with her back wheel, de-throttled momentarily and regained 'bite' on the track before accelerating again. On the final turn, Schlam was right against Taylour's back wheel:

Heeling the bike inwards to start the slide, I felt the rear wheel slip out at rudder angle and then grip as the loose surface piled up sufficiently to provide the necessary bite. Perfect! Then, as my left leg streamlined to the rear, my knee nearly touching the ground and the steel toecap on my boot lightly trailing on the track, I settled into the long power-slide that would take me on to the finishing straight, the back wheel sending up a fan-shaped wash as I slid. The trickiest moment was over![24]

Fay straightened up from that final power-slide and shot down the final straight on full throttle. She had beaten Sig Schlam on his home ground. Spectators poured over the fences, although there were still races left, and Taylour had to be rescued from autograph-hunters by the police.

Fay Taylour's race against Schlam was a triumph. She led the Western Australia star for the whole three laps of the race, equalled the track record, and achieved the fastest time of the night. The speedway newspaper, *Hoskins Weekly*, reported, 'in the international match, Taylour versus Schlam, Miss Fay Taylour beat Sig Schlam in convincing style. She registered 1.17, the fastest for the night's racing, and equalled the track record in spite of heavy going. Her riding can only be described as brilliant'.[25]

The victory was reported in *The West Australian* under the simple but dramatic headline 'Miss Taylour Beats Schlam':

The warm evening and the meeting of the international rider, Miss Fay Taylor [*sic*] and S. Schlam, drew a large crowd to the Claremont Speedway on Saturday night. Schlam had insufficient speed in the match races and was well beaten by the woman rider [...] In his race with Miss Fay Taylour he gave her the inside position and she drew away at the start and was never headed. Miss Taylor was cheered heartily and her time (1.17) and the fact that it was Schlam she defeated speaks eloquently of her ability as a match rider.[26]

The tone of this report is interesting, in that it typifies most reporting of Taylour's riding. The press treated her as a competitor, in just the same fashion as they reported male riders. There were occasional mentions of clothes and make-up, but these came in feature articles or social pieces; when it came to race reporting Fay Taylour was treated as a major international player, albeit one who had a particular following among women fans of the sport. Not only had Taylour ensured herself a permanent place in the early history of speedway, and on its home ground, but she had also demonstrated, in dramatic fashion, that a woman could compete on equal terms with the best men in the speedway arena.

After the race, Taylour took the night train to Melbourne, washing and changing on the train, elated by her victory over Schlam. It had been just the boost that she needed, and, coming at the beginning of her tour, gave her the confidence that she could win against all that Australian speedway had: 'I was looking forward to Melbourne now without the fears that assailed me in Perth'.[27] She also now had full confidence in her 'Speedway Special' Douglas, her 'Duggie'. It would give her the edge over other riders not equipped with Duggies and, having beaten Schlam on his Douglas, she knew that she had mastered the motor-cycle too. Later she also realised how much more she had to put into dirt-track racing in terms of physical strength compared to men: 'a man might be using fifty percent of his strength where I would need a hundred, but I'd never have made that admission then if indeed I ever stopped to work it out'.[28] The train made a stop at Adelaide, and she was met there by officials from the Adelaide speedway. They had previously rejected her suggestion that she race there, but following her performance in Perth they now wanted her to race on their track. They were too late, as Taylour had bookings at Melbourne and Brisbane, and tracks in New Zealand were negotiating with her by cable.

Taylour claimed another match win at Melbourne but lost to Vic Huxley at Brisbane. She later described that race. 'I was pitted against the great Vic Huxley who rode his home track like a tornado. It was a peculiar track, with an extra bend and only one straight, and in spite of a practice run in daylight I felt completely lost under floodlight'.[29] After the race she danced at Lennon's Hotel with Charles Kingsford Smith, Australia and Brisbane's great air pioneer, who had, along with Charles Ulm, made the first trans-Pacific flight in May 1928. This was the type of encounter that Taylour loved and that came to be part of her life when travelling from racetrack to racetrack, staying at the best hotels.

At the beginning of March 1929, Taylour went to New Zealand for a month. Before the ship docked in Wellington, the harbour pilot gave her a copy of a morning newspaper with the front-page headline, 'Good Morning Miss Fay Taylour'.[30] A reception awaited Taylour at her hotel, including an American director for General Motors in New Zealand who presented her with a white Chevrolet for her use while in the country. Her first races in New Zealand were in Wellington. By the end of the evening, the track was showing signs of wear. In her last race of the meet Taylour crashed, hitting a hole in the track, then 'the fence, crushing my third right finger between the fence and the handlebar.

I refused aid at the track but at midnight a doctor was summoned to the hotel to sew up the gash'.[31] Either that night, or subsequently at the hotel, her left racing boot went missing. This was the steel reinforced boot that enabled broadsiding and drew sparks from the surface of the track. A few days later, Taylour was out shopping with a former pupil of Alexandra College, a young woman called Olive, when 'suddenly Olive shrieked "look"'! And there, all alone in a shop window, stood my boot in its mud-spattered and un-beauteous glory. A notice boldly said FAY TAYLOUR'S BOOT as if I were some national hero who had died with his boots on'.[32] The theft and exhibition for sale of Taylour's racing boot was also reminiscent of the display of a religious relic, but in a secular, sporting fashion. Taylour's stay in Wellington also saw her perform in a short silent film, *Shifting Cinders*, made by a local producer, in which Taylour played the part of a speedway rider's girlfriend who saved the day for the hero by riding as him in an important race after he had been injured. In Hollywood many years later, Taylour would come close to having a movie made based on her racing career, but, apart from newsreel film, this lost silent film proved to be her only appearance on the silver screen.

From Wellington, Taylour drove in the white Chevrolet to Auckland for two race meetings. At the first she beat Bill Herbert, and when she arrived at the following week's meeting, Herbert met her outside the stadium. He told her that she had two match races that night, not just the one she was booked for, and he said she 'must win'. Herbert told Taylour that there was a belief among the other male riders that he had let her win the previous week, and that her victory had been a set-up. As a result, two of the best riders, Alf Mattson and Jack Garmston, were scheduled to race against Taylour. Inside the stadium, Herbert's mother also put in an appearance, saying to Taylour, 'See you beat them [...] they're too cocky'.[33] The pits were full of expectant mechanics, riders and officials, while the crowd was lively. The two races were run in succession, and Taylour won each of them. 'After I'd shaken hands with opponents they both clapped Bill on the back and apologized for ever having doubted him, and Bill's mother confided to me later that they weren't so cocky after all'.[34]

After Wellington, Taylour raced at Christchurch and then at Dunedin, before leaving by ferry for Wellington, from where she would return to Australia. She had given some thought to going instead to the USA from New Zealand, but she also knew that there would be letters from Lionel Wills waiting for her in Australia and she wanted them more than an unplanned trip to America. It would be another two decades before she would visit and race in the USA, and then on four wheels not two. On the voyage to Melbourne, the captain of the ferry invited Taylour to his cabin to meet the American aviator and Antarctic explorer Richard E. Byrd. At the time, Byrd was involved in the first of five explorations of the Antarctic, utilising three aircraft and two ships. Taylour described him as being 'neither bearded nor salty but young and handsome',[35] and he was just the sort of person she loved to meet, enabled by her own growing fame as a motorsports star.

Taylour only had a few weeks back in Australia, with her first race being at Melbourne. She collected the letters from Wills:

> His letters which had accumulated at Melbourne were full of speedway chat interspersed with sardonic references to his family's taunts every time a letter from me arrived. I wrote to his office but he would take the letters home and flaunt them with triumphant glee. His last to me ended: come back soon, and come back in one piece.[36]

It is difficult to entirely understand Wills's behaviour in relation to his family's disapproval of Taylour, especially as he was soon to submit to his mother's pressure, give up racing and take over a role in the family firm. Similarly, Taylour recognised, both then and later, that despite her feelings for Wills, there was something missing and, despite what she would occasionally tell herself, she was never going to marry him.

Taylour was unwell prior to her race in Melbourne, with bad headaches, something that affected her throughout her life, usually at times of stress. She took three aspirins and slept for most of the day of the race. At the track, she met up with some of her Australian cousins who informed her that 'everyone is falling off'.[37] The track was heavy and uneven, and Taylour did fall off in the first lap of a match race which was restarted as her opponent also fell. The Melbourne *Sporting Globe* subsequently reported:

> Brilliant Fay Taylour – Smashes Record and Defeats Reg West. Fancy anyone rising from a sick bed, breaking two records, equalling another, winning an international match race against one of the most renowned riders in the Commonwealth, then finishing up the night's racing by winning the A Grade Handicap in hollow style... such was the phenomenal performance put up by Miss Fay Taylour at the Exhibition Speedway on Saturday night.[38]

Fay's tour of Australia and New Zealand had been a resounding success, and she was probably at the peak of her motorcycle speedway career during this period. She sailed back to England having earned over £1,500 in prize and appearance money, the equivalent of around £106,000 in 2022.

Taylour arrived at Tilbury from Melbourne on 31 May 1929,[39] three months after the start of the British speedway season. She was welcomed at Tilbury by 'a whole bunch of speedway boys',[40] plus Lionel Wills, Johnnie Hoskins and two newspaper reporters. One of the reporters may well have been representing *The West Australian*, as an interview with her appeared in that newspaper on 3 June. In it, Taylour noted that her experiences in Australia 'had established her belief that efficient women riders were as popular as men [and] the British prejudice against women riders did not exist in Australia'.[41] Unknown to Taylour, there was more truth in this belief than even she realised. The 1929 season was to be her last season dirt-track racing in the UK. The 'speedway boys' and Hoskins took Taylour off to London in a truck decorated with her name and that of the Wembley Stadium speedway track, which Hoskins was now promoting. He told Taylour on the way to London that he had already entered her for the Cinders Trophy. The trophy was staged once a month and the aim was to beat the existing lap record from a flying start. Riders entered as representatives of their countries, and Taylour was to represent Ireland. As Taylour realised, although Hoskins told her that 'you'll do splendidly',[42] she knew that for the promoter, her taking part was good publicity however she performed.

Taylour had lunch with Wills in London and talked about speedway. Wills told her that he had fallen several times already during the few months of the 1929 season. Writing about their conversation later, Taylour reflected on the different motivations of speedway riders, including Wills and herself:

> No ambition drove Lionel unless the challenge to overcome something difficult can be called ambition. Prize money was a lure to the boys. They needed it, but not Lionel. Lionel raced and got fun out of braving its terrors solely to prove to himself that he could do it. I raced less gloriously to prove to others that I could do it! And in the proving was the satisfaction of having created something my own way and of being applauded.[43]

Taylour's reflection that she raced to prove to others that she could, that she could succeed in this difficult and dangerous game, and that she enjoyed the well-merited applause and attention, showed how straightforward and powerful the motivation was that drew her to the racetrack. She also had the necessary character to succeed. She was single-minded, totally determined, and absolute in her rejection of anything, or anyone, who forbade her to take part, to compete and win. Taylour also developed a keen, informed understanding of what was needed for a successful dirt-track racer:

> Racing is an art, and a fight. The art of drawing curves to an advantageous pattern, knowing where to dab in or erase throttle, where to use brakes on a powerslide, how to play a gearbox, and above all how to match your equipment to the surface, for whether the course is fast, slow, loose or slick you are going as fast as possible under given conditions. And because you are on that limit line shooting to win, it is also a fight, a fight for mastery. Over that line is no demilitarised zone, if you cross it the others keep shooting.[44]

The next challenge for Taylour was the Cinders Trophy. She knew that the Wembley track would feel 'cramped and strange after the bigger Australia tracks'.[45] Her first appearance at Wembley only allowed her to get an initial impression of the track before her Douglas broke down, having just been unpacked after the long voyage from Australia. It had to be overhauled and fully serviced before her attempt on the Cinders Trophy two days later, on 6 June. She had a few warm-up laps. Her Douglas was running perfectly: in fact, its engine was delivering so much power that Taylour overslid on one of the bends. As she remembered, 'the track was tricky'.[46] Eventually, it was Taylour's start, and in a display of controlled and skilled riding she took the trophy. *The Motor Cycle* subsequently reported:

> On Thursday Fay was at Wembley again, and won the hearts of the crowd to a man – or woman. This time her engine was functioning well, and although her riding was excellent at the end of the last season it had nothing of the finish that it has now. After her experience of the large tracks in Australia I expected that she would find her style very much cramped on the rather acute bends at Wembley. However, near the end of the straight she would cut out for a few yards only, and then opening out flat would go full bore for the bend round the offside.
>
> Although fast and spectacular Fay never once went mad. At all times her riding was well controlled, and although the manner in which she took the bends showed she was fearless, it was obvious to a close observer that she was using her brains as well.
>
> In view of the fact that she was cheered to the echo it would have been quite understandable, and even permissible in a woman, if her success had gone to her head. But it didn't. Finally she had her shot at the lap record and lowered it to 20.8 seconds. The crowd went mad.[47]

Beating riders from five countries to win the Cinders Trophy was a major success for Taylour. As *The Motor Cycle's* correspondent had recognised, her season in Australia and New Zealand had enabled her to develop to new heights as a motorcycle speedway champion.

Fay Taylour was not the only woman speedway rider, nor the only woman to compete successfully against men on the dirt track. Her greatest woman speedway rival was Eva Askquith. A contemporary of Taylour's, Askquith was born in 1905 in Bedale, North Yorkshire, the daughter of a butcher. She first came to notice riding in the 1927 Scott Trial in Swaledale. From there she moved to speedway, riding at Leeds in October 1928 at the end of the season. When the 1929 season opened in March, Eva returned to Leeds, now riding a Douglas. By the summer she had beaten one of the leading male riders, Harold 'Tiger' Stevenson, at Lea Bridge.[48] She followed that victory by beating probably the most famous rider of the day, the American Sprouts Elder, in a heat at Southampton, although Elder won the match. Askquith was Taylour's main woman opponent, and Johnnie Hoskins was well aware of the crowd-drawing potential of a match between the two. For Taylour, 'it was important for me to defeat her since I held the internationally bestowed title of Woman Champion or Queen of the Speedways, and so the race assumed enormous significance'.[49] That 'internationally bestowed title' was, of course, entirely informal, but Taylour was correct in appreciating the rivalry of Askquith, whom she described as being 'a quiet unassuming girl whose riding skill was far superior to the small batch of women riders who raced among themselves'.[50] Hoskins arranged the meeting between the two for 4 and 27 June.

Taylour's later account of the matches between her and Askquith, in her unpublished autobiography, presents a detailed description of difficulties with the engine of her Douglas, and a fascinating account of the differing styles of racing adopted by the two women. However, the account also obscures the outcome of the two meetings at Wembley, seemingly combining the two events to give the impression that Taylour beat Askquith. Although Taylour was apt to understandable self-aggrandisement in her various autobiographical writings, this is the nearest that she came to omitting events to improve her racing record. Brian Belton, in his account of Taylour's motorcycle dirt-track career, gives the outcome of the two Taylour versus Askquith meetings at Wembley as Askquith beating Taylour 2–0 on 4 June, and Taylour beating Askquith 2–1 on 27 June.[51]

The 4 June meeting between the two women was a best-of-three meet, with four laps per heat, flying start. Taylour's account was that she won the first heat, then her Douglas developed engine trouble during the second heat and Askquith won. The mechanics worked on Taylour's bike, but it would not start for the third heat. It was pushed back to the pits and the mechanics returned to its engine. Other races were run while they worked, but Hoskins was desperate to run the third heat. He insisted that the third heat be started, telling Taylour that it had to be run, and Askquith that she should keep on racing even if Taylour's Douglas stopped. Askquith led from the start and Taylour's engine kept misfiring before stopping, then starting again, finally giving full power. Taylour then claimed she came from a long way behind to pip Askquith at the finish line. If Taylour's account was accurate, then she would have won the 4 June meeting 2–1. In her unpublished autobiography she then fails to mention the 27 June meeting. It seems, then, that Taylour combined her account of the two Wembley meetings into one. Given the importance of the Askquith races to Taylour, it is unlikely that this was a misremembered account. It is more likely that the defeat, in the first of the two Wembley matches with Askquith, was just too much for Taylour.

Despite the obfuscation of Taylour's later account of the Wembley meetings, the memoir does contain a fascinating description of the differing techniques adopted by the two women. Taylour had made a great success of the leg-trailing technique of broadsiding, whereas Askquith was a very early proponent of a different technique that eventually became standard:

> She [Askquith] was a 'white line rider', riding close to the white line on the inside of the bends. She sat more upright on the bike, and instead of trailing her inside leg in a straight line to the rear she held it upright with knee bent so that her heel rather than her toes touched the ground when necessary. She was way ahead in this respect because a couple of years later the leg-trailing style disappeared and all the boys became white line riders. Early fans regretted the change, lamenting that the spectacle of flying wide around the bends in a fast streamlined powerslide, which had lent so much thrill and grace to the proceeding, had been lost.[52]

What is fascinating about Taylour's account of her Wembley races against Askquith[53] is the degree to which it reveals Taylour's attitude to other women riders, especially those few who met men on equal terms. For Taylour, women on the speedway track were primarily rivals to be beaten. In this, she regarded female riders in the same way as she regarded her male opponents. Yet there was something more, as she was keen to 'beat' other women in relations with men too, something that became apparent from the mid-1930s onwards, when Taylour became sexually active. Taylour desired to be the centre of attention, on and off the track, and this did not go unnoticed. Another woman speedway rider, Jessie Hole, remembered, decades later, that Fay Taylour 'always used to be at all the parties – she was a favourite at all the tracks'. These parties were not just attended by the riders, but also 'the bigwigs, the owners of the stadiums, and people like that ... they were the people with the money'.[54] Jessie Hole's reminiscence had an element of jealousy about it, perhaps underpinned by a sense that Taylour was able to use her class background to gain access to the 'bigwigs', which may well have been the case.

As the 1929 season drew to a close in Britain, Eva Askquith travelled to Spain, racing at Barcelona, then in South Africa, Australia, and Denmark. Taylour, having already established herself as a speedway star in Australia during the 1928/29 season, returned there during October for the 1929/30 season.

Chapter Four

Australia and New Zealand: Tour 2, Success on the Track and in the Press

News of Fay Taylour's second season in Australia was greeted with much antici-
pation among speedway fans. Arriving in Fremantle, Western Australia, on
12 November 1929, the Perth newspapers carried reports of her return, including
photographs and accounts of her travel and racing since leaving Australia earlier
that year. Taylour told the Australian press and speedway public that England
was still attempting to catch up with the home of the sport:

> She said the English tracks were improving, and that the answer to the
> statements that the sport was waning in England would be the enthusiasm
> dominating dirt track events which were expected during the coming season,
> to be three times as numerous as during the previous best season. She had
> brought to Australia two of the latest models of English racing motor
> bicycles.[1]

There was also interest in Fay Taylour off the track, with her return to Perth
being marked by a dinner at the Savoy Hotel. Taylour was described in glowing
terms as 'a wonderful English sportswoman' who was 'the idol of Claremont
tracks', and 'an attractive young woman, whose instantaneous pleasing personality was lent effect by her becoming voile frock'.[2] Taylour was in her off-track
element at the Savoy Hotel dinner in her honour, and she greatly enjoyed dancing
with aviator Jim Mollison, who was later to set a record for the fastest flight from
Australia to England before marrying Amy Johnson. Mollison was famous not
only for his flying, but also for his drinking and womanising, against which
Taylour was warned. She subsequently 'agreed to fly as a passenger with him the
following Sunday in some advertising stunt, but declined an invitation to his
bachelor quarters after dinner'.[3] Instead, Taylour divided her free time between
the US Vice-Consul, Thomas Wasson, and a diamond dealer. The latter edged
the American out, much to his annoyance. Wasson was later US Consul General
in Jerusalem in 1948 when he was shot dead by an unknown assassin. Of the two,
Taylour preferred the ill-fated Wasson, but noted that, at that stage of her life:

> Perhaps he liked me more than I thought, and I was doing precisely what he
> did, not crediting myself with the ability to attract him. Was my early home

life which allowed me to grow up with the unruffled belief that I was not attractive, except in a friendly hail-fellow sort of way, not so advantageous after all?[4]

At the time, Taylour was still using her relationship with Lionel Wills to provide an alibi for her unwillingness to get involved with other men, despite knowing that he was actively involved with two actresses from London's West End.

Taylour spent the first fortnight of her 1929–30 tour racing at the Claremont track in Perth. Her first race was against Jimmy Datson, but she lost, barely avoiding a crash. After Perth, Taylour's next stop was at the Speedway Royale, Adelaide, where she was seen to be the major attraction, the Adelaide press enthusing: 'the opportunity to see such a skilful and intrepid woman rider should attract a record attendance to Speedway Royale'.[5] *The Advertiser* ran a speedway news column that put Taylour at the heart of the forthcoming races, and neatly captured the extent of her fame, and her tireless competitive spirit:

> The star attraction at tomorrow night's meeting at the Speedway Royale will be the appearance of Fay Taylour, world-renowned lady racing motor cyclist. Fay has appeared successfully at nearly every small dirt track throughout England, Australia, and New Zealand, and her appearance on the Adelaide speedway has long been awaited.[6]

Taylour lived up to these expectations, winning the A grade handicap at the Speedway Royale on 30 November, and thereby boosting the expectations of an even bigger crowd the following week when she was due to reappear at the track. It was, by now, Fay Taylour who headed the publicity for races, not because she was a woman rider, but because she was a winner and a dangerous opponent for other international speedway stars. As expected, her second appearance at the Speedway Royale also resulted in victory:

> Riding a 3½ Douglas racer, Miss Fay Taylour, the celebrated Irish lady rider was successful in winning the A Grade Handicap on Saturday night. She was never in danger of losing any of the events in this race, and her time in the semi-final, 1.33 4–5 seconds was the fastest recorded for the season. Miss Taylour has ridden several makes of machine, but she prefers the English Douglas for reliability. Charlie Gray, also on a Douglas, won the match race against Miss Taylour, and was second to her in the handicap.[7]

It was not only the speedway promoters who saw increased revenue thanks to Taylour, but also Douglas dealers. Gard Brothers of Gougher Street, Adelaide, had a prominent advertisement displayed next to this report: 'World's Wonder Lady and the World's Fastest Motor Cycle. FAY AND HER DOUGLAS!'.

After her victory at Adelaide, Taylour was met in the pits by her Fetherstonhaugh cousin, Stella, who had brought her brother, Cuthbert, to meet Taylour. Cuthbert was a wheat grower, horse breeder and polo player, and

Taylour now embarked on another unconsummated relationship. Cuthbert, like Lionel Wills, would become a long-running feature in Taylour's internal emotional life. As with Wills, she would keep in contact with him over the years, eventually seeing him again after the Second World War when she raced midget cars in Australia. By then she was a quite different woman in terms of her personal life, but Cuthbert was married. In 1929, however, Cuthbert was a bachelor, and he took Taylour back to his farm, 'Wyara', where they spent a few days along with his sister and two male friends of his. Taylour then returned to Adelaide for more racing at the Speedway Royale, before spending Christmas 1929 at Wyara. Their time together was taken up with horse riding and small parties. Then, in the New Year, Taylour went back to the tracks, with Cuthbert telling her, 'I'll telephone you every night after racing [...] to make sure you haven't crashed.'[8]

Crashes were a familiar experience for speedway riders; Taylour later estimated that she had fallen or crashed twenty-four times in her motorcycle speedway career. Many of the men she raced against were seriously injured or killed, including champions like Sig Schlam, who was killed at Perth in November 1930.[9] During her 1929–30 tour of Australia, Taylour injured her arm at Melbourne's Exhibition Speedway in December, and her face at the Speedway Royale at the end of the month. In a crash at the Wentworth Oval Speedway in April 1930, caused by her trying to avoid Sig Schlam, who had himself crashed, she badly injured a young spectator and broke her own thumb.[10] The Speedway Royale crash led to Taylour developing a legend about herself that she would often refer to in her interviews with journalists. Overtaking a rider who had started in front of her, Taylour lost control and crashed through the wooden safety fence. She was knocked unconscious and taken to hospital where she regained consciousness the next morning. Waking up in bed, she discovered that she had 'a gash on my forehead, another under my chin that had been stitched up, and I felt bruised all over'. But, worse, the wool hospital nightgown was 'irritating me more than the bruises'.[11] In future she always took 'soft satin pyjamas' with her to races in case she was ever hospitalised again. They became a lucky talisman, and she was never again hospitalised by racing. The satin pyjamas also became a feature of her publicity, eventually being replaced by a nightie when the pyjama top split 'when I tried to oblige a reporter by putting the top on'.

Following her hospital stay, Taylour spent more time with Cuthbert at Wyara until she was recovered enough to resume racing. The atmosphere was outdoors, horsey and sporting, and Cuthbert 'looked handsome in his working slacks and open shirt'.[12] In the evenings, they danced to records played on her blue leather HMV portable gramophone, their favourite record being Cole Porter's 1928 hit, 'Let's Do It, Let's Fall in Love'. Taylour met Cuthbert's mother, and in happy contrast to her total rejection by Lionel Wills's mother, she was accepted. Eventually, Cuthbert asked Taylour to marry him. She did not answer, and later wrote that she immediately thought of Lionel. Cuthbert recognised this, saying, 'There's another chap, isn't there? The one in England who races?'[13] This was true, but Taylour knew that she was not going to marry either man. Although

Taylour was still a virgin, she knew that she could not marry, in part because of 'those periodical attractions for other men which uninvitedly and inescapably turned up, the work of Nature which knows no marriage laws, the desire to go out with someone else which can only be quenched by going [...] a magnetic field so powerful yet so easily earthed!'[14] Taylour would later 'earth' that 'magnetic field' often, and she did not want to be married to have 'security'. Neither did she want to end her racing career, which marriage might threaten.

Having recovered from the crash, Taylour moved on to New Zealand. She had spent most of March 1929 there during her first tour of Australasia. Her crowd-drawing appearances in New Zealand during that first tour stood her in good stead for this return in January 1930. The New Zealand press anticipated her return with articles and photographs, lauding her as the 'dare-devil Irish girl', 'wonder girl of the cinder track', and 'the well-known British dirt-track rider'.[15] Taylour spent six weeks in New Zealand in January and February 1930, racing at the Western Springs Speedway, Auckland, Monica Park Speedway, Christchurch, and the Kilbirnie Stadium, Wellington. Wherever she went she was greeted as a sporting phenomenon, attracting large crowds and building an enthusiastic fan base. At the end of February 1930, Fay Taylour made her last appearance at the Western Springs Speedway:

> Idol of the Western Springs Speedway spectators, the little Irish daredevil cinder track rider, Miss Fay Taylour, came to Auckland, she rode, she conquered. With further wins and successes added to her already long list, she has gone south on her winning way. Fifteen thousand people cheered and admired her skill and daring on Saturday night, when again she triumphed over two Auckland riders. The great crowd revelled in a sustained succession of thrills. Truly Miss Taylour is a great rider. She knows no fear. For her the highest plane of riding was attained in the first contest, in which she was matched against Alf Mattson. Still, though the second match, against Ben Bray, was not as fast as the first, it was just as thrilling – it was merely the difference between the superlative and the good.[16]

Press reports focused on Taylour as a rider and a brilliant competitor. There was little in the way of gendered commentary in the sports reports: Taylour's sex was only raised and discussed in feature articles and pieces by herself. She had, in fact, transcended gender in the sports pages of the newspapers, which treated her simply as a sporting star.

Wherever Taylour raced abroad, she ensured, if possible, that she appeared on the radio airwaves. Later, some of these wireless broadcasts would cause difficulties for her. It is clear from British security files on Taylour that the authorities were concerned about her ready access to radio. They used the fact that she broadcast from Germany during a pre-war trip there to build a case against her in 1940. In fact, as she pointed out during her detention, she had 'spoken on the wireless [...] from practically every city in New Zealand and Australia, and I have spoken [...] at Malta, when I was there'.[10] Her wireless broadcasts appeared to have focused on her racing, the role of women motorsport competitors, and women's ability to race against men on equal terms. It was a message that she also put across in the print media, writing articles for the press throughout her career. For example, in a long feature article by her, which appeared in the Adelaide newspaper *The Register News-Pictorial* on 25 February 1930: 'Why not more women speedway riders?'. She drew on her own career, and Eva Askquith's, to argue that women who were determined to race could do so, and could beat men. She stressed that what was needed was an absolute focus on racing and winning:

> It is no game for the weakling nor for the woman who cannot take a licking. It is the game for the woman who is determined to get on or get out, who is prepared to meet the men riders on equal footing and ask neither quarter nor mercy because of her sex.[11]

Taylour argued strongly that there were women who could race successfully, and that they needed to come forward and challenge men:

> I feel convinced that there must be plenty of women motor cyclists in the country who, if given the chance to learn and practice, would make good on the track. Women have for too long left the world of speed and sport to men. We have our women air pilots, but what women do we see in the high speed events? There are women motorists, but there were none in the Ulster T.T. race. We have our women riders in the most important motor cycling road trials in the world, but what women do we see in the T.T. races in the Isle of Man?[12]

Taylour argued that speedway was 'probably' the first sporting arena in which women could meet and match men, and that success in speedway would open a

> great age for speedwomen – an age when they shall no more be regarded as inferior to men on the road and in the air, but one in which they will challenge on equal terms and with definite hope of success the men aces of car and motor cycle and aeroplane.[13]

Fay Taylour's optimistic view of the future for women in speed-based sports envisaged 'hundreds' of women coming forward to take part, all with the necessary determination to take on motor sports with the single-mindedness that would bring success. Nonetheless, she did not believe that in tackling this male sphere women had to abandon their sense of femininity. For Taylour, the feminism of competing in motorsports did not preclude interest in 'dancing' or 'smart clothes' – she was quite clear that women, like herself, could manage both sport and being feminine. She returned to these themes repeatedly in her press interviews and writings, clearly well aware of her status and importance for other women. Women commentators were also quick to highlight Taylour's successes, using them as inspiration.

In her two speedway tours of New Zealand, in 1929 and 1930, Fay became even more of a star attraction than she was in Australia. As well as being lauded for her skill and fearlessness by male sports writers, she was also held up as a model for aspiring young women. In a long article in the *Auckland Star* of 24 December 1932 – entitled 'Sport for Women' – the advance of women in 'Men's Domains' was highlighted. It argued that women were now firmly placed in men's spheres, an example being provided by Fay Taylour: 'to ride the hurtling wheel of the broadsiding track hardly seems the work of a gentle woman, but this, too, has had its heroines, one of whom passed through New Zealand some time ago in the person of Miss Fay Taylour'.[14] If Taylour was aware of her status as a role model for women in motorsport, then she was also assiduous in courting her fan base, and thereby building her career and money-earning potential. She was feted wherever she went in Australia and New Zealand, giving free access to the press, and broadcasting whenever she could. She was also careful to cut a distinctive figure on the racetrack, wearing racing leathers that drew attention to herself as a woman, but also as an Irishwoman. Racing in front of a crowd of 20,000 at Western Springs, Auckland, in February 1930, Taylour won two out of three races, and was 'given a series of ovations from the huge crowd'. She was the star of the evening, and 'although masked and helmeted and looking like all the other riders of the cinder track, she was easily distinguishable, for on the back of her scarlet jacket was the flag of Ireland'.[15] The same report gives a flavour of her ability to reach out to her fans. As well as the more traditional circuits of the track 'throwing' cinders at the crowd, which helped build appreciation, she mingled with the crowd:

> During the evening, Miss Taylour made a tour through the crowd, a pilgrimage marked by great enthusiasm, with hundreds of Auckland small boys following admiringly in her wake. In her three races, Miss Taylour showed a wonderful nerve in riding, and gave a finished exhibition of the new sport which has got such a hold in Auckland.[16]

Taylour was a pioneer, and a consummate rider, but also a highly effective publicist, able to project a powerful image of herself as a sportswoman, and a motorsport star of the first rank.

Fay's successes in New Zealand led to her postponing her departure by a week for a final appearance at Christchurch at the beginning of April 1930. She then left for Adelaide before returning to England. Her riding during this second tour of Australia and New Zealand appears to have moved to a new level, with one commentator noting that she 'rode with more daring and brilliance than she did [...] and her broadsiding was masterly. She did not make one mistake on the turns ...'.[17] It was another triumph for Taylour, who had twice taken her skills to the home of speedway, and twice shown that she was a world-class competitor in this difficult and dangerous sport. She finally left Adelaide on the Orient Line's SS *Orama* back to London, arriving there on 5 June 1930[18] in time, she thought, for the British speedway season.

Chapter Five

Banned from the Speedway Track, and on to Four Wheels

While Fay Taylour was still at sea, an event occurred in England that would have a major impact on her future as a motorsports competitor. At Wembley, on 15 May 1930, a procession of speedway riders took place before a race meeting. As women riders led by Jessie Hole began their circuit of the track, a male rider cut in front of them, throwing one of the women, Mrs Billie Smith, from her motorcycle. She required medical attention, and first aiders had to partially remove her leathers at the trackside. In the process her chest was exposed, supposedly leading to spectators seeing her breasts.[1] This incident was then used to justify a complete UK-wide ban on women riding in speedway.[2]

Fay Taylour's analysis of the ban, which she learnt about on her return to England, is interesting:

> I made another trip to Australia and New Zealand, a few more rides in England, and then promoters, finding their crowds dwindling and searching for ways to get extra publicity, decided to stage a women's race and then announce a ban on women riders. Apart from the northern girl, Eva Askquith, the few women riders whom some promoters had used occasionally were too slow to interest spectators, and it was a race between such riders that was now staged as a forerunner to the ban announcement. Conveniently one rider fell on the approach ramp before reaching the track and broke a collar bone. Next morning came the big announcement: women banned from speedway racing. It gave the promoters headlines. They'd put women on the tracks to get publicity, and now they were banning them for the same purpose. I was on my way back from Australia at the time, and when I arrived a friendly promoter said, 'I'm sorry, girlie, but it means you too'. His offer of a free ticket to watch the racing was galling.[3]

It is not entirely clear how the promoters would expect to make any sort of improvement in their financial fortunes from the ban on women riders. In fact, the experience of promoters in Australia and New Zealand suggests that, properly publicised, the presence of world-class women riders like Taylour could boost crowds and takings. Speedway, particularly in the UK, had problems maintaining adequate gates, with 'inadequate income from spectators [...] the basic reason for the collapse of speedway in so many localities',[4] and it is difficult to see how the ban on women would redress that problem. The countrywide ban was

41

confirmed by the sport's governing body, the Auto Cycle Union (ACU), but the records of the ACU give no clue as to the reasoning behind the ban. Fay Taylour may have been focusing her disquiet on the wrong group, as it could well have been the male riders, not the promoters, who were the source of the pressure that led to the ban on women riders. The male riders, whose 'attitudes to racing were highly commercialised',[5] were alive to anything that was perceived as a threat to their earnings. Certainly, in 1937 the British organisation of speedway riders, the Riders' Association, did attempt to prevent foreign riders competing in the UK for this reason. It may, then, have been pressure from male riders, concerned not only about being beaten by women, but also fearful that increasing numbers of women would lead to falling earnings, that led to the ban.

Taylour was 'permitted one last race, this time at Southampton against the northern girl, Eva Askquith'.[6] The race being near Lymington, Taylour invited her father and stepmother to watch her in what would be her last motorcycle speedway race in the UK. The combination of her rivalry with Askquith, the presence of her father in the crowd, and the knowledge that this would be her last race, gave the meeting an extra edge. Taylour had not raced at Southampton before but described the track as 'larger than Wembley and with well-shaped bends just asking to be eaten up in an all-out powerslide. As long as it wasn't full of hidden bumps! Eva had raced here, she'd know where the bumps were. It was a cinder track, and cinders could get rough... but they also give a better grip'.[7] On the way to the pits, Taylour was stopped by two excited girls who asked for her autograph, then she was at the pits with the mechanics ready to push her off for the warm-up laps. Taylour and Askquith chatted before the race, and discovered a shared interest in horse-riding, Askquith riding to hounds in North Yorkshire. The race was the best of three, but Taylour took the first two heats to win:

> A special match race was arranged between Miss Fay Taylour, the young rider who has been much in the lime light lately, and Miss Eva Askquith. It was Miss Taylour's first appearance at Southampton, but Miss Askquith has raced here before.
>
> Only two of the three heats were necessary as Miss Taylour won both quite easily. Although not unduly pressed she gave a good display of riding. Her time in both heats was 80 2/5 seconds, and in a special attempt to set up a ladies record for the track she returned the excellent time of 70 4/5 seconds.[8]

This was Taylour's last competitive motorcycle speedway race in Britain, but a year later, in 1931, she made one last attempt to get back on a home speedway track, turning up incognito at a practice session at Crystal Palace:

> She hid her red curly hair under her helmet and slipped out to practice with the novice riders. Her skill and style impressed promoter Fred Mockford who was convinced the 'new rider' was no novice. He called her into his office and told her to take off her crash helmet. Her red hair showed him it

was Fay Taylour on the come-back trail. Mockford tried to sign her for the Palace team, but the ACU refused to accept her contract.[9]

The ACU ban did not finish Fay Taylour's motorcycle speedway career entirely, as she spent most of the 1930 season in Europe, particularly in Germany. She raced at Hamburg and Munich, and 'she raced with her Douglas on the 14-mile dirt-track [at Oberhausen], defeating the local champion Herr Muller'.[10] Taylour was welcome in Germany, on and off the track. She had enough of a profile to be valuable to German businesses for advertising. For example, while she was in Hamburg, staying at the Berliner Hof hotel, the director of Gargoyle Motor Oil wrote to her hoping that, as before, she would both 'secure the usual laurels [on the track] and that you give preference again to our Gargoyle motor oil'.[11]

By the end of the 1930 season, Taylour was back in England. She now faced fundamental difficulties. Fay was single-minded in her determination to keep on racing, but the impact of the banning of women from speedway in the UK brought about a financial crisis for her. Her initial steps in motorcycle racing had been facilitated by her position as a works rider, first for Rudge and then for AJS. By moving to speedway she had taken a gamble, which paid off. Her successes in the UK, Australia and New Zealand enabled her to continue to race, but it is likely that her profit margins were small. She was able to take a 494cc Douglas and her Rudge with her on her first tour of Australasia, where she won £1,500 in appearance and prize money. This was a large sum for 1929 (around £105,000 in 2022) and enabled her to travel first class to and from the UK. However, keeping herself on the racetrack was an expensive business, as she pointed out during her second tour of New Zealand:

I am a professional, I suppose, since I make enough money to pay expenses. But there is not so much money in it as some people think, chiefly because the manufacturers are under agreement not to support speedway racing in any form. For instance, I paid full retail prices for my racing machines: I have to pay for tuning every week; big bills for spares, and huge prices for fuel, as I cannot use ordinary benzene in my racing engines. I had to pay a bill at Wellington the other day for fuel for £9 [approximately £670 in 2022]; and that was only for three meetings [...]. To pay for everything, including my return fare to England, I have to spend £45 a week![12]

The enforced end of Taylour's speedway career in the UK meant she would not be able to fund her racing. It is probable that she would have ended her motor-cycle speedway career in any case, but in her own time. Later, she explained:

I'd known that at my own decision I would give up riding two wheels sooner rather than later. The effort to hold up the two-wheeled charger on the tracks had been nothing compared with the effort to hold up my feminine status which was ever under interrogation, and which couldn't be held up. It was a he-man's sport, yes. Unladylike? Yes, too! And how carefully I had to wash the dust off my face and change from the racing leathers before being interviewed by the Press – if I could. At the very start I was interviewed by a woman reporter. She called herself Jane Doe, and she found me practicing with my face covered with cinder dust. She wrote that if SHE had a daughter who took up dirt track racing she would advertise: DAUGHTER FOR SALE GOING CHEAP.[13]

The woman journalist's jibe clearly struck home, and it does seem that Taylour faced other rumours about her being a 'manly woman', or a lesbian, which she was not. At this point, she was certainly still committed to the moral values that her upbringing had established for her, yet knew she was attracted to men. In that context, the questioning of her sexuality concerned her much more than it would in later years, when she laughed off similar accusations. The speedway ban was not just a financial blow; it was also a blow on a much more personal level. 'The decision to quit was made for me [and] I left the motorcycle world altogether. It had played such an eventful and thrilling part in my life, and yet I'd never really belonged. I was part of it, yet always apart. But the enforced decision had come at a cruel moment'.[14] Fay had no intention of giving up on motorsports, however, but that meant she faced a much greater financial challenge when it came to motorcar racing, a challenge that meant that she would have to beg or borrow cars, or drive for private owners. She would no longer be able to fund herself through appearance money and winnings.

By November 1930, Taylour was still unsure about what direction she wanted to take. She could repeat her two previous tours of Australasia, but the ban in the UK seems to have undermined her commitment to motorcycle speedway. Finally, she decided that she would take up a long-standing invitation from an old school-friend, Sheelagh, to visit her in India. Sheelagh was married to a British officer in the Indian Army and was part of Taylour's circle at Alexandra College in Dublin. Prior to leaving England, Taylour prevaricated about whether to send her dirt-track bike ahead to Australia and travel on from India for some racing after visiting Sheelagh. Finally, Taylour decided to simply go to India. She left London for Bombay on 19 December 1930, sailing on the P&O liner SS *Ranpura*[15] for a trip of some six months.

The *Ranpura* called at Malta when the British Mediterranean fleet was 'in', and Taylour reacquainted herself with a Royal Navy officer, Hugh, whom she had met on her last voyage from Australia to England. Hugh was serving on the aircraft carrier HMS *Eagle*, and, to Taylour's surprise, had recently married. Fortunately, Taylour and Hugh's wife struck up a good friendship. When Taylour missed the departure of the *Ranpura*, she spent three weeks living at the Imperial Hotel enjoying lunches, dinners, cocktail parties and dances, and a 'Masked Ball' at the Malta Club. She was also asked to give a demonstration of speedway riding on an extempore track at the racecourse. She borrowed a bike, removed the left footrest, and set out to demonstrate powersliding. She discovered, however, that it was not possible to broadside on a surface of wood chips, 'I'd just learnt that wood chips don't like dirt track riders'.[16]

Taylour caught the next ship to India, landing in Bombay before taking the night train to her destination of Jubbulpore in the Central Provinces of British India (now Jabalpur, Madhya Pradesh). The city was a garrison and administrative centre, with five British and Indian Army regiments stationed there. Sheelagh's husband, Pat, was a captain in the Royal Artillery. Although the Indian independence movement was active in many parts of India, life for the British military and the small number of British civil servants was still idyllic. Taylour later described what she found:

> It was a world within a world, a pleasant existence of social fun – horse shows, tennis, dancing, inter-regimental contests, football matches, horse-riding, and of course military parades and concerts. Willing native servants did all the domestic work for shillings in place of pounds, so it was no wonder that wives found it hard, after their five years spell in India with several servants, to face again a one-maid household in England. Officers' pay isn't prince-ly, but life in India was.[17]

With her upbringing, Taylour fitted easily into this upper-middle-class military life of horses and parties. In her time with her old Irish schoolfriend she seems to have put her disappointment about the UK speedway ban on women behind her. Doubtless, she talked about her motorcycle career. At one of Sheelagh's evening parties the New Zealand speedway silent film that Fay had starred in was shown. This led to her starting a platonic relationship with a young Royal Signals sub-altern, Erek. They bonded over a shared love of horses, and Fay discovered that Erek, too, was interested in motorcycles. A few years later in Taylour's life, the relationship might have developed, but at this point it remained friendly more than anything else. In Taylour's later writings there is a strong sense that this was yet another missed opportunity for a long-term relationship that she, in part, regretted.

Sheelagh and Pat had leave owing, so Taylour went to stay with another Irish army wife, Joyce, towards the end of February 1931. Then she moved on to see her old Irish governess, Miss Orr, in Calcutta. She said goodbye to Erek and was aware that this shy officer was upset that she was leaving. After Calcutta, Taylour travelled to Delhi to see Gee, an old hockey friend from her days at Burghfield. Delhi, known as 'New Delhi' since 1927, was the capital of British India, and was different again from Jubbulpore:

> The difference between a city and the country. Army life seemed less chummy, the parties more sophisticated. Bungalows were spread out, British officers didn't own the place even if they ruled it, and, although the streets were full of old-fashioned transport we went everywhere by car. Gee's husband, Peter, met me at the station and drove me to their attractive bungalow with its porch draped with jasmine. Gee was playing in a squash match.[18]

Taylour returned to Calcutta to stay with Miss Orr (now married with children) again. It was during this stay in Calcutta that Taylour learnt that there was a motorcar speed record for the 300-mile road run between Calcutta and Ranchi. The existing record was held by Captain Yates Benyon, and Taylour met with him to discuss the run. This was a significant meeting for her, as Captain Benyon had contacts with a Brooklands racing driver and promised to give Taylour a letter of recommendation for the driver if Taylour could beat his time to Ranchi. Benyon had given her just the incentive she needed. 'Brooklands! The king of all racing tracks! I just had to break the record, and I drove possessed to the terror of the motor club official who came along as observer and navigator'.[19] She had borrowed a 1931 Model Chevrolet for the attempt, and 'set up a new record for a non-stop motor-car run from Calcutta to Ranchi of 7 hours 13 minutes, beating by 40 minutes the previous record held by Captain Benyon'.[20] Benyon gave Taylour the promised letter of recommendation, and she left for a short stay at the hill station at Darjeeling before returning to Calcutta and taking a ship back to London.

Taylour was back in England by mid-July 1931. It was not a happy return. She was unable to capitalise immediately on the letter that Benyon had given her because the Brooklands driver was out of the country. Taylour was affected by a sense of anti-climax after her long holiday in India. Without racing in her life she was at a loss. Worse, London was strongly associated with speedway and Lionel Wills, neither of which she had any claim on. She decided to visit Dublin, staying with her Aunt Mabel who was still teaching at Alexandra College. Her aunt took her to lunch with some of her colleagues, Taylour's old teachers, but in the mood that she was in, even this proved unsatisfactory. 'I felt oddly remote for most of them in this Protestant college were as conservative as she [Aunt Mabel] was, and my odd career, which was no career to them, differed more than a little from the successful positions attained by other students'.[21] In fact, Taylour's 'odd career' was in the doldrums, and there was little sign at that moment that she could revive it. After the disappointing reunion with her old teachers, Taylour also spent time in Dublin at the Horse Show Week. While watching one of the jumping events, another spectator came over to her. It was Erek, whom she had last seen at Jubbulpore. They spent time at the horse show together, and he took her to the show ball a few nights later. It was here that he asked her to marry him. Later, she wrote: 'to say yes could certainly banish the lost and aimless feeling that had sent me Irelandwards, but Fate had not altered my emotions. I cared, even loved, but I wasn't in love. And so we said goodbye'.[22] After visiting more friends in Dublin, including her closest Alexandra College friend, 'Dormouse', Taylour returned to London to find the Brooklands driver and introduce herself with the letter from India.

The driver was Brian Lewis, otherwise known as 'Bug' Lewis, scion of the shipping firm Furness Withy and later Lord Essendon, part of a group of aristocratic motor-racing amateurs that characterised the sport in Britain in the inter-war period. Lewis was one of A.W. Fox's long-distance drivers. He and Hugh Eaton had driven Fox's Talbot to third place in the previous year's Le Mans 24-hours grand prix, covering 162 laps. Lewis was also motoring correspondent for the *News Chronicle*. Taylour's Calcutta to Ranchi run and her meeting with Captain Benyon had paid dividends with this introduction to Lewis. He explained to Taylour that 'he raced for Fox & Nichols who tuned a team of racing Talbots at their service station on the Kingston bypass. "I'll give you a note for Arthur Fox, he might like to enter one of the cars for the women's race".'[23] Taylour was not entirely enamoured by the sound of a 'women's race', but she knew that it was an entrée into the Brooklands world. She went immediately to see Arthur Fox and his garage of Talbot racing cars.

Fox agreed to trial Taylour with a view to entering her as driver for one of his Talbots in a Brooklands women's event. Taylour subsequently met him at Brooklands for the trial. He had brought two Talbots with him, presumably 'Brooklands specials', with highly tuned engines of greater capacity than normal, and one was warmed up ready when she arrived. Fox was keen to see how Taylour handled the car:

> 'Keep her to that white line'. He said, pointing to the line two or three feet from the inside. That meant not using the banking. The two and a half mile concrete track sloped upwards to the outer edge on the two sweeping bends to allow high speeds. At over a hundred you could use most of the steep banking, at eighty the banking helps though you would be further down. I drove as directed where it was flat on the curves.[24]

After the trial run, the mechanics asked Fox if there was anything wrong as Taylour had been driving up to 85mph but not using the banking. Fox laughed, saying that he had told Taylour not to use the banking because he did not want her going over 50mph. As Taylour noted, that had not stopped her given that she was used to unbanked speedway curves. Taylour had passed and was to race Fox's Talbot.

The women's event at Brooklands, the Brooklands Automobile Racing Club (BARC) Ladies Handicap, was run on 17 October. The race was held on the 'Mountain Circuit' at the track. Taylour's competitors included the actress, Paddie Naismith, the Hon. Victoria Worsley, Mrs Kay Petre, Elsie 'Bill' Wisdom, and 'two very business-like girls who ran a garage in London'.[25] Taylour drove Fox's Talbot 105 to win her first circuit race at Brooklands:

> Despite never having previously raced a car [...] Fay's spirited and swift driving in practice meant that she had been given only a five second start over the vastly more experienced Elsie 'Bill' Wisdom, who started from scratch. By the end of the 6½-mile race, Fay had stretched this advantage to 250 yards. Irene Schwedler, in third place, was 200 yards behind Wisdom, having started 1 minute 10 seconds before her, so it seems obvious that both 'Bill' and Fay were pushing their cars to the limit.[26]

Taylour was pleased by her performance, being told afterwards that she had lapped the circuit at 108mph. Her performance beat the previous Mountain Circuit best, which was held by Malcolm Campbell, along with the best lap record, held by Raymond Mays. Despite this success, neither Taylour nor any of the other racing women would be allowed to compete against men. BARC events at Brooklands prohibited this. Nonetheless, Taylour's victory over Elsie Wisdom was a good augur of things to come for Taylour. Wisdom had already established a reputation in rallies and hill-climbs and had competed in a mixed (men and women) race in the 1931 Junior Car Club (JCC)'s 24-hour race, run over two days because of a ban on night racing at Brooklands. The JCC event was not regarded as a BARC race, even though run at Brooklands, which enabled BARC 'prejudice against women entering its prestigious events [to] be circumvented by entering club competitions hosted at the circuit to gain valuable experience of larger races'.[27] If Fay thought that by abandoning her speedway career she had left male attempts to avoid competing with her, and other women, behind, she was wrong. The problem was something that would affect her until the very end of her motorsport career, more than two decades later. Taylour raced again for Fox, driving Talbots twice more at Brooklands during 1932. Her last race in a Talbot at Brooklands also saw her competing against Wisdom in the Ladies Handicap of 10 September 1932. Taylour again beat Wisdom, but the two rivals came in second and third behind the actress Eirane 'Paddie' Naismith, who had occasionally chauffeured the Labour Prime Minister, Ramsay MacDonald, and later became an aviatrix, most notable for her flight to Australia in 1934 in the Centenary Air Race.[28] Naismith had bested Taylour by 20 yards. Naismith, Wisdom, and Petre were the leading women car racers of their day. Although Taylour later made much of her speed at Brooklands, in fact the real speed queens at Brooklands were Petre and Gwenda Stewart-Hawkes. In 1934, they competed against each other at Brooklands for the unofficial title of the fastest woman on that track. Stewart-Hawkes drove a Derby-Miller 1600, while Petre raced in a 1924 10.7-litre Delage. Petre lapped Brooklands at 134.75mph, while Stewart-Hawkes managed 130mph. At the height of her fame in 1937, Petre was later very badly injured at Brooklands when her stationary Austin was rammed by Reg Parnell in an MG. Petre was nearly killed and it was a year before she was able to race again, although she switched to rallying.[29]

Despite her victory in the 1931 BARC Ladies Handicap, the way ahead for Taylour was far from clear. She had an allowance, along with some capital, which, typically, she was happy to draw on, but she needed more money. She applied to 'Universal Aunts', which operated under the slogan, 'Anything for Anyone at Any Time',[30] which offered, as Taylour wrote, 'jobs for gentlewomen, trained or untrained'.[31] She hoped that her Alexandra College diploma for housekeeping, and, perhaps, her driving, might lead to a job. It did, and she found herself employed as a *chauffeuse* for a Mr Cooper in Suffolk. The job involved driving the lady of the house into Ipswich for shopping and accompanying her employer when he went shooting. Her job interview had consisted of being given a rifle and asked to shoot two walnuts at the top of a tree. The racing season in the UK was over, so Taylour was able to tell herself that a return to country life was merely temporary. There was shooting and her driving tasks to occupy her, but little else. A visitor to the house, whom Taylour was attracted to, attempted to get into her bed one night, but she threw him out. Reflecting on her attitude to sex at that time, she wrote later, 'I was still a virgin and I believed in the morals built for me by my elders. Men were different, what was wrong for me wasn't wrong for them. That's why there were prostitutes. But why couldn't they all be like Cuthbert and Erek! It was disappointing.'[32] Life in Suffolk was 'leisurely' – far too leisurely – for Taylour. Although she was a good shot, and had accompanied her father on field sports as a child, she discovered that she was no longer happy to shoot game. As the winter of 1931–32 came to an end, she left Suffolk and returned to London, taking a bedsit near Putney.

Taylour was still short of money, and still wanted to race. Unlike motorcycle racing, she could not afford to buy and run her own racing car. Manufacturers did support racing owners, but one had to be able to afford a good racing car. The difficulties seemed, at times, to be insurmountable. She sold her MG sports car and bought 'a larger car of the same make, a sporty-looking 2-seater of 14 horse-power [...] it was no racer though it made a lovely noise'.[33] She also had a springer spaniel with her, called Beau or Bob. That meant that she needed a bigger home than a bedsit. After much searching she found a mews house, 'Lucerne Cottage', in Lucerne Mews, just off Church Street, Kensington.[34] This small house in the supposedly Bohemian environment of a London mews, was to be Taylour's base for the next eight years, until she was arrested and detained in 1941. It was the nearest that she ever had to her own home. She enjoyed fitting it out, and described it in some detail:

> It was called 'Lucerne Cottage' though it didn't look at all cottagy. Once inside, however, you climbed a miniature curving staircase to a little white-railed landing, and there you discovered a sitting room, two bedrooms and a WC. At one end of the sitting room was a kitchenette, and a large bath complete with geyser stood at one end of the bedrooms; and curtains, I decided, could make it private. The cobblestoned mews was L-shaped [...] and there was plenty of room to park the MG.[35]

Fay chose new furniture, 'a plain unvarnished oak for the sitting room and curtained off kitchenette [...with] something less mellow for my bedroom [...] pea-green lacquered furniture from a nearby shop', with, for the floors, 'Japanese mats until a wealthy friend, Mrs Deane, ordered wall to wall carpeting [in soft green] from Harvey Nichols.'[36] She moved into her new home in September 1931.

Taylour advertised in the personal column of *The Morning Post*, which was the leading conservative (and Conservative) newspaper. Her advertisement read, 'Lady driver available with or without car', wording that, it soon transpired, had the potential to attract unwelcome male customers. The first customers, however, were a holidaying American couple who wanted to be taken on a tour of historic English towns and graveyards; they were on a quest to find English forebears. The work was well paid at £3 a day plus expenses, which was a typical weekly wage for many people. With the husband sitting in the pop-up 'dickey' seat in the rear of the MG, the three set off on a tour that covered Stratford-upon-Avon, Stonehenge and many of the graveyards of Wiltshire. Taylour clearly enjoyed the whole business. Less so her next job, when a City man asked to be taken 'into the country' for, it transpired, a sexual attempt on Taylour. It went no further than his arm around her neck and his hand on her leg before Taylour stopped him. Telling a friend afterwards led to Taylour rewording her advertisement, which then read, 'Driving Lessons by Expert'.[37]

Taylour settled into Lucerne Cottage quickly, and began to invite friends who were visiting, or who lived in London. These included her old Alexandra College friend Alice Beary and her husband, John, who trained race horses. Alice made a habit of introducing Taylour as 'the only virgin in London'.[38] Taylour happily used Lucerne Cottage as her social centre:

> Life at Lucerne Cottage followed no pattern. Friends and acquaintances of all ilk dropped in, from mechanics to countesses. It was the era of sherry parties, and when Louise Ponsonby was in town she loved to arrange a party to which all and sundry came. We bought the best sherry for the first glass or two, and then replenished from four-and-sixpenny bottles when the guests were too merry to notice the difference.[39]

Among the visitors was the driver 'Spike' Rhiando, a famous name in speedway, especially midget car speedway, who was adept at creating myths and stories about himself. Taylour described him as 'a breezy Red-Indian American, dark and handsome'.[40] This sounds very much like Rhiando's mythologising. In fact, it may well be that he was born in Berlin in 1910 to a German mother and an English father. At various times he claimed to be American or Canadian, but there is some doubt as to whether he had ever been to North America.[41] As well as motorsports characters, Taylour's little house was filled with friends, many of whom she would keep in touch with throughout her life. One such was Joyce Pope, whom Taylour had met in India. Joyce was in the process of divorcing her Indian Army officer husband and stayed at Lucerne Cottage for a while. Although Taylour wrote that Joyce was one of her 'many tangent friends',[42] it was, none-theless, an important friendship for her, and in later years the two would share political views. In Lucerne Cottage in 1932 they 'had long talks on life, men, books and music. Her future, like mine, seemed uncertain, but unlike me although she moved as the spirit moved her she preferred to know what was around the corner. She was discovering that men were far more interested in a woman's body than in her mind'.[43] A few years later Joyce married a doctor and they moved to Switzerland, from where she corresponded with Taylour.

Taylour still wanted to race, yet was also aware that 'to live alone in London was surely a privilege and adventure', with 'Lucerne Cottage [...] like a new toy, so was London'.[44] The year passed and there was still no sign of being able to race until another friend, Dick Cole, suggested that she try driving in car rallies in order to get her name in the motor magazines. Cole encouraged her to write to the managing director of Ford in the UK, Sir Percival Perry, to see if they would support her to rally with the new V-8 model Ford that was being introduced into the country. For a while it looked as if she would be successful, but then the offer was cancelled, with no explanation, following the intervention of Ford in the USA. Nevertheless, Ford UK loaned Fay a car for the forthcoming RAC Rally. This marked the beginning of a new avenue for Taylour.

Before 1933 was out, Taylour rallied in the Ford V8, and took part in the Monte Carlo Rallye (but failed to finish). 'She also took the Ford to the JCC [Junior Car Club] Members' Day gymkhana at Brooklands and in March she finished 6th overall in the RAC Rally, following this with a bronze medal in the Scottish Six Day Trial'.[45] She raced again in the Ladies' Handicap at Brooklands in October, in a Salmson which was possibly the car that Naismith had raced with in 1932, but Taylour was unplaced in the 1933 event. She had mixed feelings about long-distance racing, writing, 'I drove in several rallies [...] though driving to a time schedule over long distances on open roads did not appeal to me as racing did'.[46] Taylour preferred the concentrated excitement of the racetrack, its cheering crowds, the short, high-speed races against opponents riding or driving close, and everything that made speedway a fantastic spectacle. Nonetheless, her move to rallying and distance racing in 1933 did, as Dick Cole predicted, keep her name in the motoring press. It did not, however, give her an opening into the motor racing 'crowd':

It did not help me to become better acquainted with the car crowd. 'You drive too hard and drink too little perhaps', someone suggested, but in any case, I was not good at tagging on, and too often those who tagged on to me were married men who were not disposed to introduce me to others. Being a loner, and a woman loner, had its disadvantages.[47]

During October 1933, Taylour visited the Olympia Motor Show, and with her new interest in rallying, found that the manager of Rover's London depot was keen to enter her in the Monte Carlo Rallye in a Rover special Speed Twenty. The famous rally was to be run over six days in January 1934, and Taylour enlisted her old Alexandra College friend, Norah, to be co-driver.

For British drivers the Monte Carlo Rallye began on 20 January at John O'Groats. Competitors from other countries started in different locations, all to meet in Monte Carlo six days later. The field was dominated by French, British, and Dutch drivers. Ahead of them, and Fay and Norah in the Rover with race number 35, were 2,352 miles of winter driving. Snow and ice were expected, but an unusually warm spell across continental Europe turned that into slush and part-frozen roads. It was a major challenge to drivers. For Taylour and Norah things were made worse by the fact that a cold with which Norah had started the race turned into flu, giving her a high temperature and limiting the amount of time she could spend at the wheel. Their first stop was Harrogate, where they checked in, ate, and checked out, only to discover they had a flat tyre. Changing this delayed their start on the next stage to London. Outside Grantham in Lincolnshire the engine blew a cylinder gasket. All the garages were closed, but a policeman woke up a mechanic he knew who fitted the spare gasket they were carrying. It was 5am and they still had about 120 miles to go before checking in at the RAC Headquarters in Pall Mall by 7am. On the outskirts of London they ran into thick fog, and only just made it to the check in. The Rover mechanics were waiting for them. The next stage was France.

The pair headed towards Paris, then Le Mans, the next check-in stop. By now, tiredness was affecting both of them, particularly the feverish Norah. Despite repeatedly checking their route before they started, they lost their way in the countryside. Two men in a car stopped and asked if they could help. Taylour showed them the route they wanted on the map, and the men told the two women to follow their car. But the further they went, the more uneasy the women became. 'Suddenly the roads became very narrow, and Norah spoke my thoughts. "I think they're playing a joke on us", and now we were in a small lane and I looked for somewhere to turn. The next second the lane dead-ended in a clearing with a shack on the right, and the men had stopped'.[48] It was clear that they were about to be attacked. Taylour threw the Rover into a 'tight, skidded turn' and accelerated back the way they had come. The men followed, but once Taylour reached a metalled road, the Rover easily outpaced them. The women were still lost, but eventually managed to pinpoint where they were. They just made the check-in at Le Mans, but only had time to eat with the other drivers. Two of these were Germans whom they had met at the start, a Captain Nord and his co-driver, Fritz Grollmann, who were in a Mercedes-Benz. Fay and Norah told the Germans about their 'adventure' with the two strange men and were gratified when the Germans expressed horror and outrage. The two sets of drivers promised to go together to the Sporting Club dinner and ball that marked the completion of the rally.

Fay and Norah stopped during the night for petrol in Nantes, then drove on towards Bordeaux, then to Bayonne near the Franco-Spanish border before their route headed east along the foothills of the Pyrenees. Darkness fell again. They were passed at speed by two other competitors, including a lone driver in a Vale Special. Leaving the foothills, the road became straight, lined by evenly spaced trees with trunks that 'resembled high poles'.[49] By this time, tiredness was really beginning to tell on both women. Taylour was driving. The combination of lack of sleep and the hypnotic effect of the tree trunks flashing past in a repeat rhythm led, inevitably, to her falling asleep at the wheel: 'we plunged off the road between two of the trees, and our landing in a frozen field five or six feet down woke me'.[50] Fortunately they had not hit a tree, nor had the car overturned, and both of them were unharmed. The Rover, however, was stuck. Farmers who had seen them crash brought an ox to drag the car back onto the road, and they started again. Not far ahead, they came across the wreckage of the Vale that had passed them.

It too had left the road, but it had crashed into a tree. There was no sign of the driver, although they later discovered that he was in hospital with a broken leg. At Toulouse they had to stop to have the front axle of the Rover straightened. There was no chance now that they would reach Monte Carlo in time to qualify as having finished, but they drove on. They did not arrive in time, but neither did the Germans in their Mercedes-Benz, which had suffered a seized gearbox after Le Mans. Taylour, Norah and the two Germans then spent several days 'dining, dancing, and lazing on the beach',[51] as well as attending the dinner and ball that marked the end of the event. Although Taylour and Norah were recorded as having 'retired' from the race, they were not alone: twenty-nine other competitors were similarly retired from the arduous event. Of the 114 who finished, one was Enid Riddell, who finished in 52nd place.[52] Riddell would later become a friend of Taylour's, both of them being detained in 1941, with Riddell being a member of the Right Club and a close friend of Anna Wolkoff.

Taylour and Norah drove back to England, stopping for a while in Paris. Back in London, Taylour made a last entry into her Monte Carlo logbook:

Lucerne Cottage: Norah sleeps and sleeps and still sleeps it off while I feel fine. But oh the depression! Back to fog and gloom and the dullness of England where nothing ever happens. When N. is awake we sit at each side of the fire and stare into space [...] But thank Goodness she's staying on with me a bit. London isn't really such a good place to live in alone without money and proper friends.[53]

In this complaint, there was a degree of anti-climax after Taylour's Monte Carlo Rallye adventures, but the bigger problem for her was that she still was not in a position to break into car racing in the same way she had made her name in motorcycle speedway. There was a realisation that she was unlikely to be able to do so, possessing neither the money nor the connections needed. She knew that she did not 'fit in with the glamorous car-racing throng, often hard-drinking rich owner drivers. The stands at a Brooklands meeting were liberally sprinkled with West-end actresses attired as fashionably as for Ascot. The drivers' lists too included stage personalities, not to mention earls, lords, counts, marquis', princes, flying aces ...'.[54] Although Taylour came from a good, established upper-middle-class family, she was not aristocratic. Class was working against her when it came to the car-racing option left to her following the motorcycle speedway ban on women. Despite Taylour's gloom in the February depths of a London winter, 1934 would turn out to be a good year for her in terms of racing.

In the early spring of 1934, Taylour convinced the competitions manager of MG, Cecil Kimber, to loan her an MG with which to enter the annual Shelsey Walsh Spring Hill Climb. This hill-climb of 1,000 yards was, and is, one of the steepest hill-climb competitions, with an average gradient of 1 in 9.14. Taylour drove an MG K3 Magnette and won the women's trophy. Cecil Kimber was pleased and told Taylour that they would further tune the car and alter the gear ratios to enable her to enter the September Shelsey Hill Climb. However, that offer was subsequently withdrawn, and Taylour was replaced as MG's woman driver by Elsie Wisdom. Taylour blamed this switch on Wisdom's husband, Tommy, who was the motoring correspondent for the *Daily Herald*, suspecting that he had engineered the change.

The Monte Carlo Rallye was not Taylour's only long-distance event in 1934. The round Italy race, the *Coppo D'Oro del Littorio* (the Lictor's Gold Cup) in May was for production sports cars. Taylour entered the competition with her co-driver, Jack Bezzant, driving a 1,500cc Aston Martin. Mussolini started the event with a speech to the competitors delivered from the balcony of the Palazzo Venezia in Rome. The competitors then started at midnight from near the Coliseum. The entire event was characteristic of the modernism of Mussolini's Fascist regime, bringing together 226 competitors, racing in three stages, each of around 1,200 miles, over 'every conceivable kind of country [...] from broad highways running dead straight over the plains, to the mountainous heights of the Apennines and the Alps'.[55] The cars were followed by a fleet of aeroplanes, with team managers dropping messages to their drivers, the air support being organised by 'a famous Italian "ace", Colonel Ferrarin'.[56] After four days of racing, only two of the five British competitors (which included Taylour) were left in the competition, and the press reported that only Bezzant and Taylour were still in the race to win. By 1 June two stages had been completed and 139 cars were left in the race. Bezzant and Taylour started the final leg but had to carry out running repairs shortly after the start, losing time at a point when they were in twelfth position in their class.[57] The problem was with the car's cooling system, but, at almost the last gasp, Bezzant and Taylour had to withdraw from the race when the Aston Martin's gearbox gave in, just as the pair was 'fast overhauling the leaders'.[58] The race was won by Pintazuda and Mardilli, driving a Lancia. The only British team remaining, Minstall and Diamond, driving a Singer, came 24th with an average speed of 50mph.

It seemed, then, by mid-1934, that Taylour had made some impression in terms of road racing, although she correctly realised that other women drivers like Kay Petre and 'Bill' Wisdom were far more well-known, better connected and more likely to continue to build their car-racing careers. Nonetheless, Taylour was 'aching for a road race'.[59] However, her next outing was not in road racing, but in midget car speedway racing. Racing small, high-powered cars of up to 1,100cc engine capacity on speedway tracks had been attempted as early as 1928 in England in an event organised by the Junior Car Club at Greenford.[60] Unlike in the USA, the sport found it difficult to gain popularity and traction in Britain, and most of the early events consisted of exhibition driving and attempts on track records. Interestingly, Taylour later claimed that motorcycle speedway promoters 'see to it that it [midget car racing] does not go over big. They have control of the speedways'.[61] In 1934, however, Taylour was involved in the beginnings of attempts to popularise midget car speedway. One of the early enthusiasts was Jean Reville of Merton Park Parade, Wimbledon. On 25 January

1934, he wrote to Taylour as 'Secretary and Manager' of the 'Speedway Racing Drivers Club':

> Dear Miss Tayleur [*sic*]
>
> In view of your close association with the Speedway in the past, it has occurred to me that you might possibly care to become a member of this club.
>
> In the near future, we hope to form a team, consisting entirely of LADY RACING DRIVERS. I have enclosed some literature which will no doubt be of interest to you, and if you wish will communicate again with you if you are interested.
>
> In your case, no subscription is of course necessary.[62]

This letter came at what can be seen as the real beginnings of midget car speed-way in the UK. The enclosed literature that Reville mentioned claimed that 'nearly 100' drivers from the UK, Australia, America and the Continent had already applied to join the club. Further, the first meeting was provisionally booked for 31 March at Crystal Palace Speedway. It appears that Taylour replied and that Reville had the idea of a 'headline grabber [event] to introduce a woman driver to the track'.[63] Taylour agreed to race Reville:

> Wembley jumped at the chance to put on a match race between Reville and Taylour. Taylour was to drive an Alto and Reville a special front wheel drive BSA-based car of his own construction. All the publicity and hype in the world could not disguise the fact that the racing wasn't very good. The press [...] were honest enough to report, 'these shows do not excite the huge crowds of spectators as the motorcycles do'.[64]

The reference to the press view of that Wembley meeting may possibly explain why Taylour mentioned her early pre-war involvement with midget car racing in England in only one of her autobiographical manuscripts.[65] By June 1934, there was a much more concerted effort, again led by Reville, to establish the sport. Reville was a builder of midget cars, as well as being a racer and a promoter. By early 1934 he had built enough cars and brought together enough interested drivers to approach Crystal Palace to host the first 'all car meeting [...] on Saturday 30 March 1934'.[66] The meeting was a success, and Crystal Palace hosted midget car races for the rest of the year. Taylour raced there on 9 June, setting a women's track record,[67] possibly the first for women at the track. On 30 June she improved on that record,[68] and she raced again on 7 July, defeating Dot Oxenden to win the British Ladies Championship.[69] Taylour went on to race that year at Lea Bridge, Dagenham and Coventry but, at some point, women were restricted in what they could compete in. The details are unclear but it seems that women were banned from taking part in midget car league racing, just as they had been in motorcycle speedway before the outright ban.

Although midget car racing lacked the glamour of road racing that attracted aristocrats and actresses to that sport, it was a spectacle. Midget car racing advertisements emphasised the 'spills and thrills' aspect of the races, with crashes being common. They were seen to be an integral part of the entertainment and were certainly used to draw crowds. In addition, midget cars were relatively affordable,[70] unlike the cars used in road racing. Both these attributes help explain why Taylour became involved in the sport, even while she was still trying to carve a niche for herself in the more glamorous field of road racing. It was fortunate that she did so as, after the Second World War, it would be in midget car racing that she built a new reputation in Sweden, the USA, Australia and New Zealand.

Taylour's next road race was to be in her native Ireland. Her participation, and victory, in the first running of the 'Skerries Race', on 4 August 1934, brought her lasting fame in Ireland. Taylour was invited to compete by the Dublin Motor Club, which asked her if she would 'race a German car for an Irish agent in the Leinster Trophy Race'.[71] The agent was Robert Briscoe, a member of the Irish Parliament, the *Dáil*, who sold Adler cars. He was entering three Adlers in the Leinster Trophy. Briscoe was of Lithuanian-Jewish descent, a notable member of Fianna Fáil, had been very active in the Irish Republican Army (IRA) and was an anti-Treaty activist during the Irish Civil War. Later, he would become a Zionist and a friend of Jewish terrorist leaders in post-war Mandate Palestine. As Taylour grew older, she, too, would become a supporter of Irish Republicanism, but also a national socialist. All that was in the future when she returned to Ireland to race. The Dublin Motor Club had 'found' Taylour for Briscoe's Adler team, but he 'wasn't so happy when he found the driver was a woman'.[72] By then it was too late.

The race was a 100-mile handicap race by engine size and practice times around a 13-mile course on difficult, twisting roads. Taylour was aware of the challenge: 'races are won on cornering, the more bends the better as far as I was concerned, and I took the trouble to learn each bend by heart, reciting them like a poem while going to sleep the night before the race'.[73] Taylour had a fantastic race, with other cars from the field of twenty-nine competitors dropping out or crashing. Her cornering-first approach paid dividends. The race was described by *The Irish Times* correspondent as being 'a much keener race than was expected on a 13-mile circuit',[74] and became a noted fixture in the Irish motorsport calendar. Taylour was presented with a silver cup and a £50 cash prize. Her victory was long remembered in Ireland. She also had further success in Ireland later that month, winning the Ulster Craigantlet hill-climb in a 1,469cc Frazer Nash.

By the end of 1934, Taylour had apparently begun to re-establish herself in motorsport after the cruel blow of the total ban on women racing in motorcycle speedway in the UK. Despite the difficulties involved in breaking into road racing, she had success at Brooklands, and had taken part in both the Monte Carlo Rallye and the nearly 4,000 miles of the round Italy race. She had also enjoyed hill-climbing successes and a move into the new sport of midget car racing. In her personal life, she was still trying to decide how to manage relationships. She also had a secure base in Lucerne Cottage. There were, then, plenty of reasons for her to believe that her career was picking up once more. However, the next few years would bring multiple challenges.

Chapter Six

Problems, a Change of Gear, and Last Years of Peace, 1935–39

Over the next few years, Taylour seems to have experienced a variety of problems. Compared to her racing life prior to 1935 she competed in relatively few races, and was far from successful. She also had problems finding owners or companies to back her racing. Without this she was unable to build her motor-racing career. By the end of 1936, it looked as if that career had come to a halt. She made no appearances in the following year. Another reason for this change in tempo was that her personal life had come to overtake her racing life.

On 31 May 1935, Taylour was convicted at Kingston on Thames Petty Sessions of a motoring offence, namely speeding, and was sentenced to a fine of £1 2s, or seven days' imprisonment.[1] The subsequent events reflected notable aspects of Taylour's public life. She made great play of her refusal to pay the fine on the basis that the 30mph speed limit was 'absurd'. Opting to serve the seven-day prison sentence, she was received into Holloway Gaol on 24 June. She posed for the cameras outside the women's prison, and the story featured in newspapers around the world. However, she did not serve her sentence. A journalist from the *Daily Express* paid the fine, and she was 'put out' of Holloway the next morning. She professed herself to be angry at the development:

'I wanted to serve the week's imprisonment as a protest against the absurd speed limit,' Miss Taylour said. 'I did not go to prison as a joke, and I realise that a week there would not have been a very pleasant experience. Paying the fine has spoiled it all [...] The point I have tried to make is that if every motorist convicted under this new speed limit refused to pay the fine and went to prison, an alteration would soon be made in the law.'[2]

As a girl, Fay had visited Holloway to see her imprisoned Suffragette aunt. That experience, and the knowledge that militant women's suffrage activists had attempted to bring about a change in the law through law-breaking, along with the acceptance of imprisonment, probably provided the reason for her speed-limit protest. Although she was deprived of the experience of imprisonment, she would no doubt have been pleased by the press coverage. Her next experience of Holloway would not be so brief, nor so satisfactory in terms of publicity.

1935 was also the year in which Taylour established a stronger link with Germany, through the German car manufacturer, Adler. Sometime during the year, she visited Germany specifically 'to talk with car manufacturers'.[3] It is likely that it was this visit that gave her access to Adlers for racing. She had, of course, driven an Adler when she won the Leinster Trophy the previous year, and would, therefore, have been in a strong position to argue that the company should back her. She was successful in this, driving 'a left-hand drive Adler Trumpf cabriolet in both the Monte Carlo and RAC Rallies – [...] without success'. The car was 'German registered IT-70539 and probably loaned by the company'.[4] She also entered the Eastbourne Rally in an Adler, and, in the month following her brief imprisonment, intended to defend her Leinster Trophy also in an Adler – a 995cc single-seater. But her attempt to reprise her 1934 victory was blighted by a series of problems. The initial announcement of drivers and cars shows that less than three weeks prior to the race, with the exception of Taylour, all entrants had cars for the race.[5] However, the week before the race, Taylour was listed with an Adler, as were two of the other contestants, E.M. Mitchell and C.H.W. Manders.[6] During practices, Manders's Adler was damaged, and Taylour had to withdraw her Adler, subsequently qualifying 'using the M.G. car entered by S.R. Sheane'.[7] But the loan of the MG was only for the qualifying run, and she was unable to find a car to race with. It was turning into a bad year for her. By the time of her close of season appearance at Brooklands, when she was unplaced, she had not enjoyed any success. Further, she had failed to build on her 1934 record in midget car racing (although she did appear at a midget car event at West Ham in August 1936). Taylour's motor-racing career had slowed down by the end of 1935.

The next two years of Fay Taylour's life saw a notable decline in racing appearances. She 'almost drop[ped] from view and does not seem to have taken part in any rallies, track or road racing events in 1936 or 1937',[8] and 'as far as motor sport is concerned 1937 seems to have been a complete blank for Fay Taylour'.[9] Given the precarious nature of Taylour's motor-racing career, and her reliance on being able to persuade car owners or manufacturers to back her, it is likely that she was simply constrained by a lack of money. However, the 'complete blank' of 1937 is explained by something a little more prosaic than difficulties associated with motor racing. Around this time Taylour's social life changed as she became sexually active.

Although Taylour had a very large circle of motorsport friends and acquaintances, most of whom were men, she seems at first to have looked elsewhere for a sexual relationship. In her papers there is a single letter from a man responding to her 'lonely hearts' advertisement in a newspaper. This letter, dated 21 March 1935, was from a rather lonely, church-going man living in the countryside. It is not clear why she kept the letter, but it is unlikely that anything came of it. Instead, she helped out a friend 'who ran a good dancing school for adults'.[10] Taylour drove clients to and from the tea dances her friend organised and took part in the dances. Taylour described this period of her life as being 'full of variation and never dull'.[11] Further, it was then that she changed her behaviour. Long attracted to men, and having conducted a number of platonic relationships, but still, as her friend Alice Beary had teased, 'the only virgin in London',[12] Taylour decided that the morality she had absorbed as a girl was redundant. 'Finally, I ask myself the question so frequently put to me: what am I keeping myself for? And I'm no longer a virgin'.[13] Taylour later explained why she thought it had taken her so long to become sexually active:

> Sex is only a word, a word that follows the adjective masculine or feminine, when I move into the London flat. Falling in love was little different from hero-worship at school except that now it is men. There were no boys at my school. I have not sorted out that this mechanism inside me producing such attraction is only a device for regenerating the species, that I can never find a man with whom it will last. I had learnt however that I couldn't make sentimental eyes at a good looking man on board ship without finding him in my cabin later. I had not learnt why a pretty girl had wanted me to spend a night with her for no apparent reason. An amusing encounter with the same girl years later enlightened me. Most of the men I fall for now are out of reach, they are married or have another girl or there is no one to introduce me. The young men who frequently come to my flat to talk cars and racing lack the background I'd wish for, but not all.[14]

In 1937, aged thirty-three, Taylour discovered that she was pregnant. A medical student she knew confirmed this, and she went to see a gynaecologist, 'England's most famous'.[15] It was, of course, illegal to procure or carry out an abortion, but the gynaecologist agreed he would, warning Taylour to say nothing. She was booked into a private nursing home in Bayswater and treated for ten days to induce an abortion. However, that treatment had no effect and the gynaecologist 'postponed his sailing holiday in the Adriatic to operate on me'.[16] The experience was unpleasant, largely because of the attitude of a nurse towards Taylour. Doubtless the financial rewards of working in what sounds like an expensive nursing home in London offset the legal and moral issues that might have troubled the nurse.

Taylour's abortion was, in all probability, expensive, probably costing much more than she could have raised herself. This opens up the question of who paid for the abortion, and the related question of whose child it was. In Taylour's papers there are two letters from a Colonel Harris, of Pinhoe, near Exeter, dated 15 June and 19 July 1937. The letters address Taylour as, 'My very dear Mischief', and 'Mischief Darling', and are signed 'Uncle'. Although the contents of the letters are innocuous in tone, one includes the line, 'I shall be alone for about 10 days after Monday next'.[17] The same letter also thanks Taylour for the photograph that she had sent of herself, saying 'I'm more than grateful for the Photograph of yourself – it is the one I wanted, & you look just ripping'. In the later letter, Harris tells Taylour that he and his wife are going to Japan, then Australia, on 8 October, not returning to England until 14 April 1938. Although these letters do not confirm a relationship between Taylour and Harris, he also loaned Taylour £400 that year (worth around £30,000 in 2022), in a single amount. As late as 1952 she was trying to get access to a legacy in order to repay the money which, she said, had been loaned to her by Colonel Harris, known as 'Uncle'.[18] Although not conclusive, the letters and the loan are suggestive. At the least, the entire business gives an insight into her non-racing life in 1937, when her personal life was 'full of variation'.

Taylour got back to racing in 1938. She drove an Opel Olympia in the JCC Members' Day and the RAC Rally, but without success. She failed to enter the 1938 Leinster Trophy race, again because she was unable to find a car.[19] Success also eluded her at Brooklands, when she drove an Alfa Romeo Monza in the Whit Monday and August Bank Holiday meetings, and a Bugatti T35B in the Dunlop Jubilee and October meetings.[20] She continued to try to take part in rallies, but, unlike other women competitors such as Betty Haig, Kay Hague and Countess Moy, she failed to appear in important events. Only in midget car racing did she seem to be able to put in regular appearances. The key problem for Taylour was a lack of finance:

> Fay's lack of further success outside the realms of speedway midgets [was] due more to a lack of opportunity caused by the lack of access to suitable machinery and – by extension – a lack of money. Her [Continental] speed-way and midget racing earnings must have provided enough to live on, but presumably were insufficient to support more than the occasional drive begged – or perhaps rented – from someone else.[21]

With the end of the 1938 season in the UK, Taylour journeyed to South Africa at the beginning of December, looking to revitalise her motorsport career there and overcome the seemingly perennial financial difficulties that had been holding her back.

Her first major race was the fifth South African Grand Prix, run on 2 January 1939. She drove a Freddie Dixon-tuned Riley, supposedly capable of 130mph.[22] Dixon paid the entrance fee of $2,000, and Taylour and the Riley sailed on the Union Castle line's MV *Warwick Castle*. The race was run at East London, east of Cape Town, and Taylour was the only woman driver in the race. Other drivers included Piero Tarrufi, Earl Howe and Luigi Villoresi. Unfortunately, engine trouble ended the race for her and the Riley about halfway through the event. Maseratis took the first three places, and *The Irish Times* reported, 'Miss Fay Taylour, who only entered at the last minute, following a telephone call from London, was never happy with her Riley. After a slow start she was eventually forced to give up on the fifth lap'.[23] In compensation, Taylour seems to have had a good time at the race ball, being much in demand as the only woman dance partner among the drivers. As she remembered later, 'the visit is one huge ball for me'.[24]

The failure to finish in the Grand Prix probably led to the abandonment of any idea of selling Dixon's Riley in South Africa. Taylour later said, 'I had been out there [in South Africa] racing in a big race, the Grand Prix in South Africa. I raced for an English designer out there. When his car went back to England I sold American cars for an English firm'.[25] As well as selling cars, she also enjoyed success in midget car racing, beating top South African driver Dennis Woodhead, and other notable local drivers, including Betty Trew and Gus Collares.[26] She also found time to race speedboats, something that she had tried before in Australia and the UK. In South Africa, she raced a 'small Johnson Outboard, the LADY LINDY, in a 12-hour record at Port Shepstone'.[27]

Taylour stayed in South Africa for six months, but her car sales job did not provide enough of an income to keep her there, and she eventually 'went broke'.[28] Her financial difficulties meant that she had to 'sell out my 1st class return fare on the Union Castle railship'[29] and take a cheaper fare on the German–Africa line's SS *Watussi*, which was sailing to Hamburg from Beira via Cape Town. Taylour arrived in Hamburg early in July and remained in Germany until a week before the outbreak of the Second World War. Those weeks in Germany, and her activities there, would cause her difficulties in the future, and help to keep her detained. During the war, pre-war visits to Germany could be regarded with suspicion by the British authorities. People travelled to Nazi Germany for a variety of reasons – some out of curiosity, some to be convinced of the positive nature of the regime, others to confirm their belief that it was a dangerous regime. But for those who came under suspicion in 1940 time spent in Nazi Germany could prove problematic, even for those who had merely holidayed there. And Fay Taylour's last visit to Germany did cause issues for her.

Taylour's 1939 visit to Germany was a result of her need to find cars to race. Given that she had gone 'broke' in South Africa, and that she had obtained a refund on her return ticket to the UK, it looks as if her decision to go to Germany was a combination of immediate financial problems and the hope that she might find cars to race. It was unlikely that Taylour had much chance of obtaining a car to race, as German racing teams typically only took on well-established, world-class, motor-racing drivers. Nonetheless, she 'arranged to visit a world-famous motor racing firm in Germany, and at the same time, one [to] the big German motor race at Nürburg Ring [*sic*] at the end of July, for which my arrival coincided'.[30] She was able to visit at least one German motor firm, Auto Union (presumably the 'world famous motor racing firm'), and talk to officials there,[31] but she was not able to convince them to give her a test drive. She also met some German officials, presumably from the Nazi Party, and, after writing to Berlin radio, she gained access to the airwaves. She benefited from the fact that someone from the African service of German radio had seen her race in South Africa and arranged for her to appear on Berlin radio.[32] For Taylour, this was an entirely normal thing to do – wherever she went, she tried to arrange broadcasts, which were part of her publicity and income-raising efforts. This time, she broadcast to South Africa about motor racing. Later, the British authorities would be particularly concerned about this, worried about the impact of radio propaganda and aware of the pro-German sympathies of sections of the Afrikaner community.

But Taylour's view was that she had only talked about motor racing, and that the programme was not unlike the BBC programme, 'In Town Tonight', which focused on famous people visiting London.[33] This would not be the view of the British authorities in 1940. Taylour's broadcast, and her new contact in German radio, did, however, open up the possibility that she might be able to make a link at the highest level of German motorsport. She explained:

> Through that [broadcast] I met a man in the Propaganda Ministry, who said that he would like, if possible, to arrange for us to meet Henlein [*sic*]. I do not know him. He is the Sports Leader. If I had met him it is possible that a test [drive] would have been taken.[34]

It is very likely that Taylour was talking about Adolf Hühnlein here, the leader of the Nazis' motor corps organisation, the *Nationalsozialistisches Kraftfahr-Korps* (NSKK). Hühnlein was himself a motorcycle enthusiast and an engineer, and may well have helped Taylour, if she had been able to meet him. Instead, she used money from the refunded *Union Castle* ticket to stay in Germany until 'war seemed imminent'.[35] She arrived back in England on 26 August 1939, a week before the outbreak of the Second World War. Two months later, on 26 October, the main newspaper of Oswald Mosley's British Union announced that Fay Taylour had joined that fascist and national socialist movement.[36]

Chapter Seven

Joining the 'Peace Campaign'

Within weeks of broadcasting from Berlin to South Africa, Fay Taylour was back in London, listening to German radio. But she also ensured that neighbours could hear the English language broadcasts from Germany. This 'upset one or two local residents'[1] who subsequently provided information to the police about Taylour's activities at this very early stage of the war. It seems that as soon as she returned to England, Taylour began to argue strongly that the war was wrong. She constantly brought the subject up in conversation in public, and in letters to friends. At this stage, she was acting by herself. There is no evidence of Taylour's active involvement in politics prior to September 1939. However, there is some evidence of her pro-German political sympathies dating back to 1938, which would later form part of the security services' case against her. The UK's declaration of war on 3 September 1939, following Germany's invasion of Poland on 1 September, was the catalyst which began her pro-German political activism.

Taylour was opposed to war, but she was specifically opposed to war on Germany. She had visited Germany repeatedly, both before the rise of Hitler and after the establishment of the Nazi regime. On a personal level, Germany was associated with her 1928 participation in the International Six Days race in partnership with Lionel Wills. In motorsport terms Germany had provided her with a sporting refuge for much of the summer of 1930, following the ban on women in UK speedway. She also had a personal link with Germany as a result of her grandparents' visits to the country, one of which resulted in her mother's birth in Dresden.[2] These personal links added extra force to her political activity in 1939/40. She later commented on her 'love' for Germany: 'I couldn't help hereditary. My grandparents must have loved Germany since they evidently couldn't drag themselves back to England in time for my mother's birth'.[3]

In her personal links with Germany and her pro-German views, Taylour was far from unique. A number of well-known British fascists had similar ties to Germany. For example, the leader of the British Union in Scotland, Richard Plathen, and the women's BU leader for Scotland, Maire Inglis, both had part-German parentage and first met each other at the German church in Edinburgh.[4] Oswald Mosley's movement underwent a number of changes of title in its short life, from British Union of Fascists to British Union of Fascists and National Socialists (BUFNS) to its final title of British Union. In East London, one of the prominent local BU leaders in Bethnal Green was also part-German. He was Clement Bruning, who was in Germany when war broke out and was later to be murdered in a Nazi concentration camp.[5] More notably, a large proportion of pro-Nazi spies and potential collaborators also had personal links with Germany. Examples included Jessie Jordan, a Scotswoman who married a German and lived in Hamburg from 1907 until 1937 when she returned to Scotland. Back in Scotland she opened a hairdressing salon and began to spy for Germany, only to be jailed in 1938 for four years for her efforts.[6] Others included a 17-year-old girl, Dorrie Knowles, whose mother was German,[7] Mitzi Round or Smythe, a German who had married a British soldier in 1923,[8] and Margaret Elizabeth Newitt, who had also married a British soldier on occupation duty in Germany after the First World War, thereby acquiring British citizenship.[9]

In addition to her personal links to Germany, Fay Taylour had established some links with the German car industry, and probably stronger ones with elements of the Nazi motor organisation, the *Nationalsozialistisches Kraftfahrkorps* (NSKK) as well as with the propaganda ministry. These ties to Germany, and her approval of the regime, led her to state in a letter of February 1940, 'I love Nazi Germany and the German people and their leader, and this war seems terribly unfair'.[10] Her turn of phrase in that letter reflected that in a German newspaper's report of her immediate pre-war visit to Germany. She had attended a 'big car race' and a German newspaper had used that to run a feature on her headed, '*Ich liebe Deutschland*' ('I love Germany').[11] This newspaper article would later form part of the security services' case against her. Fay Taylour's political sympathy for Germany can be dated back to at least the beginning of 1938, when she cut out a map of the world from *The Daily Telegraph* Colonial Supplement and marked in the extent of the British and French empires, annotating the map with, 'So we are afraid of Germany. Or are we dogs in the manger?' She later explained this note by saying, 'I meant that seeing we were so big we [the UK] did not need to be afraid of being swallowed up'.[12] This combination of sympathies lay behind her initial attempts to argue the anti-war and pro-German case. But in October 1939, a visit from the Special Branch of the Metropolitan Police galvanised Taylour's political life. She then became involved in a number of political groups dedicated to stopping the war, and to promoting fascism and national socialism. Taylour was to bring to these endeavours the same single-minded drive, determination and enthusiasm that she had brought to her motorsport career.

Fay Taylour's habit of loudly denouncing the war in public places such as restaurants, playing German radio late at night, and writing about the war in letters to friends and relations, brought her to the attention of the British security authorities. Taylour herself was convinced that the main complainant was a neighbour of hers who had reported that:

> I said Germany was a beautiful country, and that I'd told him that Poland and Czechoslovakia hadn't existed before World War I, but had been built up after that war to hem Germany in, and I didn't believe in declaring war on Germany to save the Polish corridor [...] and I'd also said that the Germans didn't want war with England, which apparently also annoyed the cockney Londoner.[13]

All this activity led, at the beginning of October 1939, to Taylour being visited at Lucerne Mews by detectives from Special Branch. After interviewing her, the detectives reported 'she could see no reason for this country being at war and did not hesitate to expound her views to anyone who would listen'.[14] This incident had a lasting effect, putting Taylour on the path to detention without trial in June 1940 as a threat to UK national security. The visit from Special Branch was seen by Taylour as a 'no', a prohibition on her doing what she wanted to do. She had always taken such attempts to prevent her from doing something as a challenge. Previously it had been men trying to stop her from racing; now it was men trying to stop her from saying what she wanted to say about the war. Taylour explained how the Special Branch interview led her to joining the British Union:

> The exact reason why I joined [BU] was that when the war broke out I felt my views were rather similar to British Union. I do not know who it was but somebody had reported to Scotland Yard that I disapproved of the Government's war policy, and I was visited by detectives. This man [*sic*] wanted to find out about me. Up to then I had not been a member of any club or anything. After speaking to him he asked me if I was a member of British Union and actually I was interested enough to go along and have a look at British Union and read their policy. Quite frankly, their views were similar to mine and I joined.[15]

Fay claimed, after her detention, that her only previous knowledge of BU was having read a copy of the movement's main newspaper, *Action*, some two years earlier. Given how much time she spent outside the UK, and her commitment to motorsports, it is likely that she had little knowledge of Mosley's movement. She said as much to the Special Branch officers, telling them that she had 'been far too busy praying to God for a race car all her life to have got involved in politics, much less join anything that isn't a motor club'.[16] Indeed, she probably had more knowledge of German National Socialism through her visits to Nazi Germany and meetings with members of the Nazi Party, than of British national socialism. Nonetheless, once the Special Branch officers had left her house, Taylour lost no time in finding out more about the BU, spending 'the whole afternoon at British Union headquarters',[17] subsequently joining the movement and, in the words of *Action*, 'putting herself at the service of the Peace Campaign'.[18] The BU had, from its inception, been marked by an isolationist and pacifistic approach to foreign policy, which was embodied in its slogan, 'Mind Britain's Business'.[19] By 1938 that approach had developed into a campaign specifically aimed at stopping war with Germany. This campaign was formalised in September 1938 as the 'National Campaign for Britain, Peace and People'. Following the outbreak of war, a dedicated women's version of the campaign was established, the Women's Peace Campaign.

Until she joined British Union, Taylour had been campaigning against the war in an *ad hoc* and isolated fashion. Joining the BU meant that she had moved into the orbit not only of partisans of Mosley's movement, but also of other ultra-right groups. She was, in fact, part of the growth of both the BU and other anti-war right-wing groups that marked the last year or so of peace and the first months of war. In the seven years since its founding in October 1932, Mosley's movement experienced changes of fortune, waxing, then waning, only to grow again prior to the war. New recruits in the period 1938–39 were often focused on Britain avoiding another world war, something that the isolationist and, indeed, pacifistic British Union movement had always advocated. As the international situation deteriorated during 1939, so those most opposed to another general European war gravitated to the political parties and groups that seemed to offer the best hope of successful opposition to war. Mosley's BU was certainly the most prominent, but it was far from being the only option, and some on the ultra-right regarded Mosley with suspicion and more. Arnold Leese, the leader of the Imperial Fascist League (IFL), had long regarded Mosley as a 'kosher fascist' who was in the pay of 'Jewish interests', while Serocold Skeels, a veteran of the Boer War and the First World War, and one-time parliamentary candidate for the short-lived United British Party, damned Mosley as 'a charlatan [...] being paid by the Jews'.[20] Leese and Skeels were not alone, and Mosley's instructions to his movement on the outbreak of war did not endear him to the most enthusiastic supporters of Nazi Germany:

> To our members my message is plain and clear. Our country is involved in war. Therefore I ask you to do nothing to injure our country, or help any other power. Our members should do what the law requires of them, and if they are members of any of the forces of the Crown, they should obey their orders, and, in particular, obey the rules of their service ... We have said a hundred times that if the life of Britain were threatened we would fight again.[21]

Nevertheless, Mosley did attempt to create some degree of unity among the ultra-right, both to oppose Britain's involvement in the war, and to prepare for possible outcomes if a war-induced political crisis brought down the government, but those attempts were fruitless.[22]

At grass-roots level there was some overlap between BU activists and others from the ultra-right. These links were largely governed by opportunism, with the more strongly pro-Hitler supporters attempting to use the BU's local structures to advance their own pro-German agendas. For example, early in 1940, MI5 reported that Charles Stephen Geary, a veteran of the First World War and the Irish War of Independence, was attempting to get his close associates to 'penetrate the British Union organisation and form in each branch cells of really reliable men who would, if necessary, actually fight', presumably if there was a breakdown in British politics leading to a civil war situation.[23] British Union was in a state of flux during the period of the 'Phoney War', with younger male members being called up for military service, some members leaving the movement, or becoming inactive because Britain was at war. New members, like Taylour, often had little knowledge of the ideology of the British Union. Taylour was particularly supportive of the 'new' Germany, increasingly anti-Semitic, and critical of what she called the 'greed' of Britain with its enormous empire. For Taylour there was also a strong sense of relief that she had found a party, and, as it transpired, a network of like-minded men and women: 'actually, it was an awful relief to me [when she 'found' the British Union]. Perhaps you cannot understand that. I mean, the war started and I thought it was wrong. It seemed so dreadful. And then I found that I was not alone in holding that opinion'.[24] Politically, she had found a 'home', but she had also firmly marked her card with the British security services, who put her under surveillance, which did not end until 19 March 1976, not long before her seventy-second birthday.[25]

Once a member of the Marylebone branch of the BU, Fay Taylour threw herself into a range of political activities, which were described by the security services as 'considerable' in frequency and scope.[26] She also came into contact with a well-known BU activist, Charlie Watts. Watts was born in January 1903, and after interrupted schooling at Alleyn's School, Dulwich, he joined the Royal Air Force as a teenager, and served for twelve years as a corporal involved in parachute testing. By the time Taylour met him he was working as a bookkeeper in his brother's chandlers' firm, spending almost of all his free time campaigning for the British Union.[27] Charlie Watts had a great deal of experience of extra-parliamentary street politics. In the opinion of the security forces, Watts 'although never officially influential in the hierarchy' of British Union, was nonetheless 'considered as one of the most efficient, active and revolutionary members of the movement'.[28] Watts was seen to be particularly dangerous because he had organised a British Union Cab Drivers' Group. It reached a peak membership of around 1,000 London cab drivers, and averaged some 700 members at any one time, between Watts starting the group in 1938 and the spring of 1940.[29] When Watts was interned, on 24 May 1940, other BU members believed that he was regarded as particularly problematic for the authorities, not just because of his activities, but also because of his contacts with cab drivers. Those cabbies who operated in the West End of London delivered prostitutes to wealthy and powerful clients. It was believed that Watts had therefore gathered a good deal of intelligence relating to this activity. This may have been an issue for the authorities, but Watts's 'pleasant personality', ability to make friends, his constant activism, and, once the war started, the belief that he was part of an underground network – the 'Home Defence Movement' (HDM) – producing anti-war propaganda, was enough to see him interned.[30] Watts was the District Leader of BU's Westminster and St George's branch, but he was well known throughout central London. He befriended Taylour, and they met every Tuesday at BU headquarters. It is likely that it was through Watts that Taylour became involved in a wider range of activities than was typical for BU members. She also became more involved with other ultra-right groupings, including a semi-informal group of women activists who formed a key part of the ultra-right anti-war campaign at the end of 1939 and the beginning of 1940.

In Britain, the coming of war in September 1939 did not, as many people feared, result in immediate large-scale air raids and high civilian casualties. Instead, the initial effects were uncertainty, dislocation, and a degree of unreality, especially once Poland had been engulfed by Germany and the Soviet Union. Young men began to be called up (a process that had already started before the invasion of Poland), men and women looked for war work, and children were evacuated from the cities. Parliamentary politics entered a period of heightened factionalism which would not be resolved until Churchill became Prime Minister in the aftermath of the failure of Allied forces to prevent the German occupation of Norway in April 1940. The home front at this early stage in the war – in the period that would become known as the Phoney War – was in a state of flux. For those involved in extra-parliamentary politics there still seemed to be much that could be done, despite the actuality of war. The Communist Party of Great Britain (CPGB), for example, opposed the war in line with the Comintern's view that the war was an 'imperialist war'. As a result, the CPGB campaigned against the war, both directly and through 'front' organisations like the 'People's Convention' movement of 1940.[31] The CPGB also made preparations to go underground should the party be banned by the government. The Communists produced cyclostyled papers as test runs for underground propaganda, prepared for police raids, and established a secret printing press. By contrast, the British Union made no comprehensive plans to offset the banning of its movement, and clandestine activity was very limited. Such clandestine action was usually carried out by people, like Fay Taylour, who were latecomers to the BU and members of other ultra-right groups. In the early wartime atmosphere, there was a sense among extra-parliamentary groups that a crisis point had arrived that might lead to revolutionary opportunities. This feeling was shared by the ultra-right as well the CPGB, and Fay Taylour was caught up in it. In some respects, her involvement in political activism at this time can be seen as a substitute for the racing that she was no longer able to undertake. In modern terms, she can be seen as an 'adrenalin junkie'. Potentially dangerous, partially illicit activism may well have had an appeal in its own right, notwithstanding her genuinely held beliefs about the war.

Taylour combined a range of political activities. She continued to talk to anyone and everyone she could about the war. She argued that Britain should not have declared war on Germany, along with the need for a rapid negotiated peace. As a member of British Union, Taylour was able to draw on its resources. She collected BU propaganda material, its main newspaper, *Action*, and leaflets and flyers, for distribution on buses, trams and in other public places. She wore a BU badge in her coat lapel and frequented BU meetings in London. She was tireless in this sort of activity, and clearly did not care who she offended. Indeed, even her relatives informed on her, with a Special Branch report noting:

> Shortly after Christmas 1939, a communication was received from a relative
> with whom Miss TAYLOUR had stayed, reporting that she was an ardent

admirer of MOSLEY, had strong pro-Nazi views, which she had expressed even to servants and local tradespeople, had distributed Fascist leaflets and wore a 'Flash and Circle' [British Union] brooch.[32]

Interestingly, later, during one of her appeals against detention, Taylour denied being a strong admirer of Mosley, stating, instead, that 'I admire British Union for sticking out for their views'.[33] This was probably the case, as she was not a long-term member of the movement. She was also drawn into the orbit of other activists on the ultra-right who were indifferent or hostile to Mosley. However, she was clearly seen by some BU leaders as being a good 'catch' for the movement, and at one stage she was added to the movement's list of women speakers, although she later adamantly denied that she had ever spoken at any meeting. Despite that claim, she admitted that the leading BU woman activist, Olive Hawks, had been keen to get her to speak; further, Special Branch reports noted that she did, in fact, speak at public meetings, although perhaps this was in an impromptu fashion.[34] But Taylour did not limit herself to British Union activity. She was quick to become part of a network of people also involved with the anti-war campaign.

From the time of her initial interview by Special Branch, Taylour had been put under surveillance, with her letters and phone calls intercepted, as well as notes made of her participation in public events. She had a wide circle of correspondents and was a frequent letter-writer. Some of these correspondents held very similar views to hers. One was her old friend, Joyce Pope, who was now living in Gstaad, Switzerland. Pope greatly concerned the security services. They suspected that Taylour was 'communicating with Germany by letters passing through Switzerland and Ireland'.[35] Given Taylour's extensive networks of contacts, including servicemen, and women in contact with diplomats, the security services feared she was an actual or possible conduit for information. No evidence was ever produced to substantiate these fears. The letters from Pope that have survived seem to indicate that Taylour wrote about her political views and concerns to a friend who was of a similar cast of mind. But to make matters worse, Taylour had also written to a friend called Box in Hamburg almost as soon as she had returned to England in August 1939. She later said that she had written merely to say thank you for his being 'particularly kind' to her when she arrived in Hamburg from South Africa.[36] It is highly unlikely that she was able to send more than one letter to Box, for although she was in better contact with Pope, even Pope's last wartime letter to Taylour, dated 10 January 1940, was intercepted by the security services.

Intercepted letters made Taylour's life particularly difficult, both for their actual content and their suspected meaning. The fear of Fifth Column activity was clearly uppermost in the minds of the security services when they intercepted a postcard from Tony Dickson, sent to Taylour around Christmas 1939. William Anthony 'Tony' Dickson was a Scot who had served in the King's (Liverpool) Regiment during the First World War. He met Fay Taylour through motor-racing before the war. They started a long-term on-off relationship that continued into the 1950s. Taylour did not have the best opinion of Tony Dickson, but, especially after her release from detention, she frequently slept with him. A post-war intelligence report on Taylour noted that she 'does not want to get married – and certainly not [to] Tony Dickson whom she regards as gutless and no business man and whose lack of education would grate on her nerves!'[37] Her somewhat trenchant views on Dickson's marriage potential notwithstanding, she was certainly closely linked to him in 1939 and 1940. Taylour encouraged him to join ultra-right groups during that period, but perhaps not British Union. Dickson had a tendency to create difficulties for Taylour, and his 'Christmas card' of 1939 did just that. The card was, in fact, a postcard of the Forth Rail Bridge, on the back of which he had written, 'Do you think using H.M. agents for propaganda worked?'. This cryptic message on the back of a picture of a key piece of the rail network[38] caused Taylour a great deal of trouble. In her first appeal against detention, on 28 August 1940, she was quizzed at length about it, and she referred to a telegram that Dickson had sent her around the same time which she said was 'wrongly worded' but appeared to be about Christmas 'in the land of poverty and plenty'. She went on to say that Dickson was particularly concerned about social issues, and 'very much feels that there is lots of poverty where there should not be'.[39] The explanation given by Taylour was that Dickson was referring to the Post Office when he had written 'H.M. agents', and that he was testing to see if political remarks could still be sent by post and telegraph. This explanation did not entirely persuade the appeals committee, which, in late summer 1940, still seemed to have been concerned that there was a Fifth Column organised and operating. This was despite the fact that the War Cabinet and the Security Intelligence Centre had recognised that this was not the case. As early as 17 May 1940, the War Cabinet was presented with a report that dismissed the idea that the rapid collapse of the Netherlands had, as popular opinion and elements of MI5 believed, been the result of Fifth Column activity by pro-Nazi elements. By June 1940, it was recognised that there was no Fifth Column in Britain either. However, the idea of a Fifth Column was a very strong one, and the sort of semi-clandestine activities that were taking place on the far left and the ultra-right fitted into that model.[40] But if the government had ceased to have genuine concerns about a Fifth Column by August 1940, for the first ten months or so of the war such activity was suspected and feared. Fay Taylour was involved in loose networks of men and women that were suspected of subversive activity.

During her pre-war sporting days, Taylour had built extensive networks in the male-dominated worlds of motorcycle and motorcar racing. Acting as her own manager and publicity agent, she had gained access to a wide range of motorsports, news outlets, manufacturers and owners to enable her to build a racing life. She was clearly at ease in men's circles. In terms of British Union, her key contacts seem to have been men, and, in addition, she appears to have built links with men in the armed forces – something that alarmed the security authorities. When her home at Lucerne Mews was searched, following her detention on

1 June 1940, a list of the names and addresses of six Scots Guards officers was found, along with the names of two men in the Royal Air Force. There were different ways in which the presence of this list of names could be interpreted, but it was difficult to imagine that Taylour had noted them down for entirely apolitical reasons. The names had been marked with an asterisk, and a note said, 'stars denote degree of possibility; but one never knows'.[41] Understandably, Fay denied any knowledge of the list, or indeed of knowing any Scots Guards. However, she did admit to knowing the RAF men, sergeants Macdonald and Rothwell. She explained that the latter was a 'fan' of hers, an Irishman whom she had met in Ireland and who had asked for a signed photograph, which is why she had his address. She had met Sergeant Macdonald in London since the outbreak of war, and she described him as a friend. Later, in her appeal against detention held in April 1942, Taylour gave a slightly different account of why there might have been a list which included the six Guards officers' names. She said then that the men might have been potential customers for a Brooklands racing experience that she advertised in 1931–32, which had been part of her attempts to make money after the speedway ban on women.[42] How accurate this was as an explanation is unclear, but, in the context of the time and Taylour's own activities since the outbreak of war, the list did her no favours with the authorities. The lack of clarity around the list of serving officers and NCOs, and whether or not it actually existed, reflects something of the atmosphere of the time. While the security services were busy trying to establish cases against many people, pro-German, anti-war political activists were increasingly switching to clandestine methods in their campaigning. Fay Taylour was involved in this activity, which was particularly concerning for the British authorities.

Chapter Eight

Going Underground – Covert Anti-War Activity

In the early months of the war, Taylour was involved not only with the overt anti-war campaigning of the British Union, but also with covert activity carried out by some BU activists, and other ultra-right groups. These groups were fluid and complex, particularly those operating in London. Their size and styles of activism differed. Some, like the inner London branch of The Link, had hundreds of members,[1] while others had only dozens of supporters. Membership of the groups overlapped. As time went by, formal organisation mattered less; instead, informal networks were formed, often based on friendships. Taylour's member-ship of the British Union, and her wide circle of friends, enabled her to become active in underground anti-war activity in a number of these groups, some led by men, others by women. It was a world of roneoed leaflets left on buses, trams, and trains, and 'sticky backs' proclaiming, for example, 'Conscript the Jews, it is their war' and 'This is a Jews' War', stuck to lampposts and other street furniture, night-time chalking of slogans on walls and pavements, and meetings with other activists. Fay Taylour entered this realm with considerable enthusiasm. She distributed roneoed propaganda, prepared such material, and undertook more public activity in her involvement in the anti-war campaign.

Fay Taylour's friendship with Charlie Watts, the leader of the BU cab drivers' group, drew her into activity with a very small group called the Home Defence Movement (HDM). This group was led by men who were members of British Union or associated with it, but its membership included women some of whom, like Taylour, were members of BU. The Home Defence Movement carried out a range of underground propaganda activities designed to reinforce an anti-Semitic, anti-war campaign, but without making any links to British Union. In 1939, Watts was against the war, believing it to be a result of Jewish hatred of Hitler and Germany. The energy which had enabled Watts to make the BU cab drivers' group so successful he also channelled into his underground activities with the Home Defence Movement. Watts was assisted by Andrew Burn, who was an official in the Ministry of Health, and Howard Hall, who was described in security files as a 'butler-secretary'. Prominent women, such as Norah Elam, *aka* Norah Dacre Fox, the former Suffragette, well-known BU figure and anti-vivisectionist, supported the HDM. Taylour, who knew both Watts and Elam, was also involved.

The informal, amorphous activism of the Home Defence Movement unsettled the security authorities. They reported that:

> The illicit literature with which WATTS is connected is of two types: Home Defence Movement leaflets, and sticky-back labels. The Home Defence Movement leaflets consist of typewritten or Roneo'd pamphlets. There is a series of 'News Commentaries', a quantity of anti-Semitic verse and a number of miscellaneous libels. It is to be observed that the 'News Commentaries' never mention the names of British Union or of Oswald MOSLEY. The policy advocated by them, however, vague though it is, is identical with that of the B.U., though couched in cruder and more scurrilous terms. Each sheet ends with the slogan: 'Join the Home Defence Movement, stop the war, and clean up Britain.' Almost every issue contains one or more libels on Mr. Winston Churchill, Mr. Hoare-Belisha and Sir John Simon. Others exhort the reader, 'Don't wait for revolution, work for it'. Others, again, warn the reader that the propaganda is illegal.[2]

MI5 also feared that Home Defence Movement members were advertising (presumably on stickers and small flyers) the frequencies on which the 'black radio' broadcasts of the 'New British Broadcasting Station' could be found. The New British Broadcasting Station was an English-language station broadcast from Germany but purporting to be an underground station operating from within the UK. It broadcast up to four times a day from 25 February 1940 until 9 April 1945. A senior BBC official later explained, 'The activities of this station caused considerable concern to the authorities of this country', and the broadcasts themselves were 'rather clever broadcasts to begin with and rather above the average'.[3] The New British Broadcasting Station's line during the early months of its life was that it was an underground station 'run by British patriots with the intention of saving their country from a potentially suicidal war'.[4] The station argued that what was needed in Britain was a 'Peace Front' to unite all those opposed to the war, from whatever political background, to campaign for a 'Peace Now' policy. The New British Broadcasting Station also offered advice in respect of clandestine activity, and how to prepare to continue an underground peace campaign should the government make such activity illegal.[5] Given the concern about the possible effectiveness of the station, this was yet another reason why the authorities wished to stop the activities of networks like the Home Defence Movement.

The security authorities were never able to prove to their complete satisfaction that Taylour's friend, Charlie Watts, was the leading light behind the activities of the HDM, but they believed that there was sufficient circumstantial evidence to assume that was the case. Watts himself consistently denied having anything to do with the Home Defence Movement, and implied that it did not exist, or that it was an example of anti-BU *provocateur* activity.[6] Immediately following his arrest on 23 May 1940, Watts wrote from Brixton Prison:

> I wish to protest most strongly against my arrest & detention in this prison.
> I am neither a German or even pro-German. I am a 100% patriotic

Englishman & would be one of the first to volunteer for services against an invasion of this country by Germany or any other country. One of the many reasons I am a follower of Sir Oswald Mosley is because I consider this country has already been extensively invaded by Jews. Nobody else seems to worry about that but the Leader so hence my support goes to him & with him I sink or swim.[7]

Watts's view of the war changed over time. He was eventually released from detention in September 1941 as the authorities accepted his argument that, with the bombing of the UK and the continuation of the war, it was necessary for all Britons to unite to fight Germany.[8]

In addition to her involvement with the male-led Home Defence Movement, Fay Taylour took part in other anti-war activities led by women. For example, she distributed a roneoed pamphlet called 'The Voice of the People', which was produced by a Mrs Hilton. Hilton was a BU activist, but was also part of the informal, cross-cutting network of anti-war activities that involved people from different groups. 'The Voice of the People' was regarded by the authorities as being particularly 'anti-British',[9] by which they meant strongly anti-war, anti-government, and probably anti-Semitic. In Taylour's first appeal against detention, she claimed that there were few of these pamphlets available, although the authorities believed that it had been 'circulated to great numbers of people'.[10] On 14 May 1940, Hilton's 'The Voice of the People' merged with the Home Defence Movement. Taylour did not limit herself to passing around clandestine publications. In May 1940 she was involved in an incident at the Newsreel Cinema in London that was regarded very seriously by the authorities. Part of the reasoning for clandestine political activity was to give the impression that opposition to the war was widespread, not confined to those groups well-known for that stance. As part of that effort, Taylour organised a group of people to attend a newsreel cinema showing film of the return of British sailors from the first Battle of Narvik. During the battle, HMS *Hardy* had been lost in heroic circumstances. Its commander was posthumously awarded the first Victoria Cross of the war. The surviving crew were met by Winston Churchill, still First Sea Lord. Taylour had previously seen the newsreel and had prepared her group, who sat in different parts of the cinema, to hiss every time Churchill appeared on the cinema screen but to clap the surviving sailors. Given the context, it is little short of astounding that Taylour thought that organising an anti-Churchill, anti-war protest at the cinema would be an effective intervention. The audience reaction was hostile, and Taylour later admitted that the hissing nearly caused a fight.[11] She was subsequently questioned closely, and at length, about why she organised this protest. She explained that she had hissed at Churchill, 'not because I am against the war, but because I felt most sincerely that Mr. Churchill's policy would not do good for the country [...] I believed most sincerely that the more the war went on, the worse it would be for us'.[12] This incident, and Taylour's subsequent defence of it, did little to help her in appeals to be released from detention.

It fitted the profile that the security services drew of her as an active, vocal, and unpredictable protestor.

Around the same time, in early April 1940, Taylour penned a piece of doggerel verse entitled, 'War Alphabet 1940'. This 'A B C' of Taylour's views can also be seen as representative of the views of the people she was working with in their anti-war campaign. It attacked Churchill, Chamberlain, Secretary of State for War (until January 1940) Leslie Hoare-Belisha, the French and British empires, Jewish financiers, the press, poverty in the UK, and Britain's 'real' war aims. By contrast, it supports Hitler, German grievances around the Versailles Treaty, those like Mosley, Lord Tavistock (the Duke of Bedford), Captain Archibald Ramsay MP, and Arnold Leese, the leader of the nazi Imperial Fascist League, working to stop the war. It is an odd but revealing document, given here in full:

War Alphabet 1940

A for the Army that started for France
    and found when it got there that it couldn't advance.
B for Belisha who waved it goodbye
    with a smile on his lips as the lads went to die.
C stands for Churchill, B better describes
    this bloodthirsty braggart, his boasts and his gibes.
C also for Chamberlain, easily persuaded
    that war with Herr Hitler could not be evaded.
D for the Day when people find out
    how these old fools betrayed them, and kick 'em all out.
E for the Empire our forefathers won
    at the point of the sword while their brave deeds were sung.
F for the French whose possessions abound,
    on the world map together we cover much ground.
G for the Germans deprived of such wealth,
    yet we're told if we don't fight they'll win all by stealth:
H for Herr Hitler, their saviour and guide
    who broke down Versailles and restored them their pride.
I the Injustices made by that peace
    so that Hitler an army must build that they'll cease.
J for those Jews whose dealings he banned
    who poured into Britain to libel him, and
K for the Knighthoods bestowed on this race;
    Lord Reading sounds British, but look at his face!
L for the Lies that those aliens told
    to mobilise armies to fight for their gold.
M stands for money, true cause of the strife;
    in England there's plenty yet poverty's rife.
M also the Morals we threw overboard
    in the form of some Mines per our worthy First Lord.

N for his Navy that lost more than men,
  was the Nickel from Narvik his real object then?
O for the Oceans we claim to control,
  But if Winston stays in then so will our coal.
P for the Poles we professed to defend
  with a Pact that was only a means to an end.
Q for the Question successfully stilled:
  is it right to make Pacts that can't be fulfilled?
R stands for Russia, the Bear of the East
  though Hitler's conveniently painted the beast.
S for the System we fight to maintain
  whereby money's kept short by Financiers who gain.
T for the 'Traitors' all working for peace
  Mosley, Lord Tavistock, Ramsay and Leese.
U for the U-boats by Winnie put under,
  that more should appear is a matter for wonder.
V for the Verdict that proved to be wrong
  that the Blockade would finish the war before long.
W the War that the Jews have controlled
  by the power of the Press and the strength of their gold.
X for the cross roads we long ago reached,
  the way was marked clearly but the war-mongers screeched.
Y for the Yanks, we're their friends they profess,
  but they like something better, it's dollars I guess!
Z stands for Zero, the hour still ahead,
  When a new England rises and the old one is dead.[13]

It is possible that Taylour's 'A B C' was intended to be a Home Defence Movement leaflet but, whatever the intention, it neatly encapsulates Taylour's ideological position in early 1940. The final couplet, anticipating a 'zero hour' when the Phoney War would be broken by some sort of ultra-right revolution, not only reflects the somewhat optimistic view of Taylour and her fellows, but also echoes the fears of the British security services.

During the period of the Phoney War, women's networks lay at the heart of ultra-right activity. Partly this was because younger men began to join the armed services, but also because women developed methods of pursuing political activity in an increasingly hostile context. As a result of the increased feminisation of ultra-right political activity during the first six months of 1940 in particular, the security services were compelled to utilise women agents and *agents provocateurs*. Recent books that cover the role of Maxwell Knight, MI5's spymaster who ran the security service's operations against the ultra-right during the early years of the war, have stressed his skills in, and preference for, running women agents. Knight's most notable inter-war success for MI5 had involved the recruitment and running of Olga Gray, whose activities took place within the Communist

Party and Comintern front organisations.[14] In the case of the ultra-right in early 1940, however, Maxwell Knight's preference for running multiple women agents was, to a large degree, a result of the dominance of women's networks in the semi-clandestine world of the ultra-right.

Fay Taylour was a member of a range of these small political groups in which women activists were to the fore. Special Branch alleged that she was a member of the Nordic League, the Angles Circle, the Anglo-Irish Friendship League, The Link and the Right Club.[15] The Right Club is an interesting example. It had a very brief existence. Founded in March 1939, it was officially closed at the outbreak of war, but members continued to meet. The brainchild of Captain Maule Ramsay, the Conservative MP for Peebles, the Club's purpose was to spread Ramsay's anti-communist, anti-Semitic message on the right. The Right Club's membership was around 235, of whom 135 were men and 100 women, and included six MPs and some members of the House of Lords.[16] However, the gender balance tipped towards women once war broke out, as a later figure for membership was 100 men and 150 women.[17] With the outbreak of war, many of those associated with the Right Club ceased to have connections with it. Its unofficial activities were largely continued by its remaining women members. They met for lunches, and were responsible for low-level anti-war and anti-Semitic propaganda involving 'sticky-backs' and leaflets. Taylour was involved in all this activity, although she later claimed that she was 'only introduced to two or three members [of the Right Club] and had not had the opportunity of getting to know them'.[18] In fact, she kept in touch with a wide circle of these women activists, including Mrs Hilton, a Mrs Winfield, whom she seems to have met at the same time as she met Charlie Watts, and Olive Hawks, the BU speaker. Although the Right Club was small, its main women activists mostly lived in London, and formed part of the extended network of groups and individuals involved in the anti-war campaign.

The exact date when Taylour joined the Right Club is unclear. Later, in a written appeal against her detention, she said that 'shortly before my detention, I joined the Right Club'.[19] This is likely to have been in an informal manner, not involving subscription fees or a membership card. Indeed, many years later, in a booklet describing her political detention experiences, Taylour gave an insight into Right Club activities and its informal membership:

> [Right] Club members seemed to me a group of well-educated people who enjoyed going to lectures given by Historians, Economic experts, scientists, etc., and I went to one lecture with a friend who was a Right Club member. He suggested I should join the club and I became a member. There was no entry form or book of regulations. I merely expressed a desire to join.[20]

As Taylour's account of joining the Right Club suggests, formal membership of such groups had lapsed. Instead, membership meant taking an active part in group activities. This was also true of other groups. At one stage, it was reported that Taylour was trying to get hold of a membership badge from another right-wing group, The Link, 'for a friend' but the badge (featuring a linked map of the UK and Germany), was not available as The Link had ostensibly been disbanded.[21] The other complicating factor around ascertaining membership of such groups was that those involved began to create innocuous-sounding front organisations to cover their activities. For example, the Nordic League (whose fourteen-strong directorate was headed by Ramsay)[22] also operated as the Holborn Public Speaking Society.[23] The Right Club's membership book was eventually held by Marjorie Mackie (agent M/Y), an MI5 spy in the group. Mackie was one of the agents run by the MI5 case officer, Maxwell Knight. Given Knight's predilection for *provocateur* activity, it may be that the membership list was inaccurate in any case.[24] Although Fay Taylour's name was not in the membership book, the security services believed her when she said she was a member.

The Right Club's greater significance for Taylour and many other political activists was in the unwitting role that it played in MI5's manoeuvring to create the conditions whereby political detention without trial could be instigated. MI5 placed three women agents in the organisation to gather intelligence and act as *agents provocateurs*. The official historian of MI5, Christopher Andrew, enthusiastically described the success of MI5's agents in the Right Club, noting that one of the agents 'codenamed M/Y [Marjorie Mackie], was so successful in posing as a pro-Nazi that [Anna] Wolkoff called her "the little Storm Trooper"'.[25] This seems like classic *provocateur* behaviour and was something that Fay Taylour became aware of once she was detained. At least one of the other MI5 women in the Right Club, Joan Miller, seems to have been as much prone to conspiratorial fantasies as any *bona fide* member of the group.[26] Whatever their motivations, the activities of these MI5 women helped to exacerbate the atmosphere of tension, the sense that there was a semi-clandestine underground working against the continuation of the war, and for Britain's neutrality, or for Nazi Germany. These tensions were not only to be found in London.

In early February 1940, Fay Taylour returned to Dublin, and added her own anti-war views to the mix of pro-German and anti-British views that could be found there. Dublin, like the rest of Éire, and Republican parts of Northern Ireland, harboured a good deal of popular support for Germany, and then the Axis in general, as first Italy, then central European countries, joined the war. At root, this support was built on the foundations of 'my enemy's enemy is my friend'; it was, in essence, an anti-British position. However, there was more to the pro-Axis stance than that. Recent work has shown that Éire produced its own brand of fascist and totalitarian politics during and after the war years. In the early 1930s, post-Irish Civil War tensions between supporters of the Free State and Fianna Fáil (the inheritors of the rejectionist elements of the IRA) had led to the creation of the Army Comrades Association under the leadership of General O'Duffy. O'Duffy's 'Blue Shirts' quickly took on the trappings, if not the complete form, of fascist politics.[27] In addition, the seemingly unstoppable rise of Hitler's Germany, the long-term success of Mussolini, and the dictatorship of

Salazar in Portugal, helped convince some in Ireland that a right-wing, authoritarian future beckoned.[28]

The exact reason for Taylour's visit to Dublin is unclear, but the trip was another stage in the development of her relationship with her home country. Taylour left Liverpool for Dublin on Sunday 4 February, embarking on the SS *Innisfallen*. She was closely watched by the British security service. A report by a Sergeant A. Kay (presumably of Special Branch) on her movements was sent to MI5, noting:

> She is now going for a few weeks' holiday to Dublin to Miss Webb [FT's Aunt Ella] 61, Palmerston Road, Dublin. She was travelling alone and the only luggage she had was a small travelling case which was thoroughly but discreetly searched. Nothing of an incriminating nature was found. From her demeanour during the casual conversation I had with her, I am of the opinion she is anti-British in her feelings and cunning.[29]

Sergeant Kay's distrust of Fay Taylour's 'cunning' notwithstanding, she had already greatly assisted British security by writing a letter, dated 2 February, to H.T. 'Bertie' Mills of Queen's Gate, London, SW7, telling him just what she intended to do in Éire. Bertie Mills was not a member of British Union, although he was later detained for 'furthering the cause' of the movement.[30] From Taylour's letter it appears that he was also connected to The Link, and it is known that he was involved with the Nordic League, the Imperial Fascist League (IFL) and the Right Club.[31] Mills provides another example of the *ad hoc*, informal and interlocking nature of support and membership of the fascist and anti-war groups during this period. In her letter to Mills, Taylour outlined her views on the war: 'To me the only thing that really matters these days is that a brave nation [Germany] who has been forced to fight must not be anhiliated [*sic*] – a nation upon whom we have done the dirty'.[32] In her letter, Taylour wrote that she was returning to Mills 'the U.D.C. Newsletter [... which] gives one useful facts in such a way that one can draw one's own conclusions'.[33] This appears to have been a copy of the Union of Democratic Control's Newsletter. It is likely that Mills was, in fact, a pacifist supporter of the UDC, the organisation that had opposed the First World War, and which by the late 1930s was an anti-fascist and pacifist group. This is another example of the way in which fascists, pro-Nazis and pacifists found themselves in the same camp in the period of the Phoney War. She continued, in the letter, to ask about Mills's likes and dislikes, which suggests that they had only recently met, and enquired about his obtaining more UDC literature for her. Finally, she told Mills that she intended to meet up with the Catholic priest, 'Father F.' while in Dublin. An annotation to the security services' copy of the letter notes that this was Fr Fahey. Father Denis Fahey was a prolific Catholic author, monetary reformer, and anti-Semite, who, during the war, set up the Irish group *Maria Duce* – a Catholic Irish 'extremist movement [...] which regarded the Irish Constitution as illegitimate because of its affirmation of the legality of sects other than the Catholic Church, and because it failed explicitly to acknowledge the kingship of Christ over the island of Ireland'.[34] This was just the type of contact that was regarded as potentially dangerous by the British and Irish security services, both of which were alive to the potential threat of anti-war and pro-German networks that could be conduits for espionage or sabotage.

The other concern of British security was that Taylour's trip to Dublin was prompted by a plan to access radio broadcasting for the anti-war message. By this time, British renegades like Dorothy Eckersley and Margaret Bothamley,[35] both of whom had been active in the Imperial Fascist League and The Link, were broadcasting into the UK from Berlin, along with William Joyce – 'Lord Haw Haw' – and his wife, Margaret. Consequently, there was concern over any prospect of an anti-war, pro-German broadcasting station based in Éire. MI5 feared that Taylour's visit represented another attempt by Mosley to find a base for radio broadcasts. Mosley had already attempted to enter the commercial radio market in order to provide his fascist movement, British Union, with a steady, reliable stream of income. His inspiration was the English language station *Radio Normandie*, which was owned by the Conservative MP Captain Leonard Plugge.[36] The only way to break the BBC's monopoly of broadcasting in the UK was to broadcast from outside the country. The popularity of music-based radio stations like *Radio Normandie* and *Radio Luxembourg* meant that there was money to be made in commercial radio. For a time in 1937, it had looked as if Mosley would be able to base a radio station on the island of Sark, then, when legal difficulties arose, from German territory in the Baltic.[37] Neither scheme came to fruition, but the secrecy with which Mosley had pursued the attempts, using holding companies and intermediaries, meant that, despite the financial incentive behind the idea, the British authorities were concerned that there was also a propaganda impetus. Such an impetus would be understandable, as the National Government had, in agreement with the BBC, secretly banned Mosley from speaking on the BBC,[38] and British Union members often chalked the slogan 'Let Mosley Speak' on walls and pavements. Further, British fascists, such as the leading BU officer, Ian Hope Dundas, the movement's liaison officer with its Italian counterpart, had broadcast from Italy numerous times during the mid-1930s.[39] So too had James Strachey Barnes, the author of *The Universal Aspects of Fascism* (1928), which had a preface by Mussolini.[40] Against this background, and given Taylour's own history of radio broadcasting around the world, including from Dublin in February 1939, it is perhaps not surprising that there were concerns about the possibility of more radio propaganda being beamed into the UK. German broadcasting included not only the Berlin station, but also 'black' radio stations purporting to be clandestine anti-war stations operating from within the UK, such as the New British Broadcasting Station and the 'Workers' Challenge' station.[41] The Berlin centre for black radio broadcasting was the Villa Concordia, which was a secret operation, so much so that James Clark, the son of the renegade British broadcaster Dorothy Eckersley, was threatened with execution should he reveal that he had been voice tested there.[42] Questioned after her detention, Taylour denied having anything to do with any such radio plans and repeated that before the war she had always sought to broadcast about motor-racing wherever she was, as a matter of course. But if she took no part in radio activism in Dublin, she did continue to push the anti-war message.

On Taylour's return from Dublin, writing again to Bertie Mills, she told him of her assessment of the Irish mood, and of a visit and talk she had given at her old school, Alexandra College. This letter was also intercepted by the security services and became part of the case that led to her detention. The British authorities seem to have taken her comments, which they regarded as anti-British, as evidence that she was hostile to the war effort because she was Irish. During her appeal against detention in August 1940, the chairman of the appeals committee, Mr A.T. Miller KC, drew Taylour's attention to the letter and its contents:

> In this letter of the 9th February we are told that you commented on the anti-British feeling in Ireland, and told him – that is Mr. Mills – that some remarks in a lecture given by you to your old college went down well as the head of the department was very anti British [...] That is rather awkward, is it not, if that is in your own letter.[43]

Taylour's response to this was to become caught up in the question of her own nationality. She immediately said 'I am Irish, you know'. The chairman said that he had not realised that, and Taylour went on to say, 'that does not mean I have to be anti-British'. But she then said, untruthfully, that 'I was born in England and I belong to Britain'. She used that statement to explain why she was unhappy about people outside Britain thinking the country was, in the words of the Alexandra College teacher, 'very greedy', and that in her view the only way that impression could be dispelled was if Britain 'lost' the mandated territories, the former German colonies. The whole exchange was rather confused and gives the sense of Taylour attempting to manoeuvre around questions of her loyalty and nationality. However, she came partially unstuck when she wrongly claimed to have been born in England.

Following her brief visit to Ireland, Taylour returned to London and continued her political activity within her pro-Nazi, anti-war networks. It was February 1940, and Europe was in the grip of a fierce winter. The war was still a matter of sea warfare, occasional aerial alarms, and little activity on the western front. The 'Winter War' between the Soviet Union and Finland continued, with Britain supplying equipment to the beleaguered Finns. It seemed to those opposed to the war that there was still time to stop the war. During this time Taylour also began to write more, explaining her views with respect to the war and Nazi Germany.

It is difficult to track the pre-war development of Taylour's political views, although it is very likely that her repeated visits to Germany, both before and after the Nazi rise to power, were highly influential and gave her a pronounced sympathy for the regime. Her racing in Germany, her visits, and her numerous friendships with Germans involved with motorsport may well have been the source of her political views, which emerged in late 1939. Taylour's eclectic views certainly went beyond the official 'line' of Mosley's British Union. Her links with other groups meant that she 'was not in very good odour at [British Union] National Headquarters owing to her habit of voicing violently pro-German views too openly'.[44] Taylour's political development in the early months of the war (September 1939 until she was detained in June 1940) represented a range of influences from all the political groups in which she was involved, along with her own idiosyncratic interpretation of events.

At the beginning of 1940 Taylour wrote a document that was designed as an underground pamphlet. It was sent out by post but does not appear to have been widely circulated. There is no surviving copy of the pamphlet, entitled 'The Two Conflicting Economic Systems Which Caused the War in 1939', but Taylour discussed its contents in August 1940 in her first appeal against internment. In that appeal, Taylour stated that her views on economics were the basis of her anti-war stance and of her support for Germany: 'I do sincerely believe that the war is not so much a war of boundaries and things, but a war of economic systems; because, I mean, economics is the life of the nation'.[45] In response to this statement, a member of the appeals panel, Mrs Cockburn, asked Taylour what her statement meant in terms of Taylour's preference between the economic systems of 'England' (i.e. the UK) and Germany. Taylour replied:

> In my opinion the system of the English was a system whereby individuals could make profits to the detriment of the people – or not to the detriment; whereas under the other system [Nazi Germany] individuals were not allowed to make profits. Is that not right? That is more or less the gist of it.[46]

Taylour further commented that she preferred a system which 'did not fill the pocket of the individual'. Later, she would characterise the core of the economic problem, at both an individual and national level, as one of 'greed'. Taylour saw the war as a clash of two economic systems, which had been exacerbated by the UK pursuing its economic and imperial interests. A negotiated peace was the 'solution' that she supported. Although Taylour's understanding of the operation of the Nazi economic system was somewhat lacking, her standpoint was clear and reflected other statements she made regarding economic and social questions. She made favourable comment about people she knew who showed concern about economic and social injustice. That had, for instance, been one of the major points she valued about her friend, Tony Dickson. She was also aware that some of the anti-war people she came into contact with were unhappy about her focus on social issues. For example, Taylour remembered that at a lunch in February 1940, she was talking 'about war and economic conditions between England and Germany. And after the lunch, the woman who gave the lunch told me later that somebody said to her, "My dear, the girl is a socialist", in a most horrified tone'.[47]

Taylour stuck with her concept of 'the two conflicting economic systems' as the explanation for the outbreak of war throughout her subsequent life. She linked Hitler's economic policies to the idea of contrasting systems, arguing that the war had been forced on Hitler by international financial circumstances, in which she saw Jewish influence. In 1962, she wrote: 'I thought it was right that Hitler should alter the age-long system of world finance and get away with it, that he was indeed correct to make sweeping changes by which financial manipulators were swept away ...'.[48] Writing to a relative in February 1974, she returned to her economic concept and contrasted her view of the two war leaders: 'WAR WAS INEVITABLE BECAUSE OF THE TWO IRREVOCABLE FACTS: (1) Totally opposing economic systems of both countries which set the spark, and (2) The fact that Hitler and Churchill were the leaders'.[49] Firstly, she explained her 'conflicting systems' concept, linking that to Hitler's policies, which, she argued, led inevitably to a worldwide conspiracy against the new Germany:

> Hitler's socialism could have run parallel and even at angle to the economic systems of the capitalistic Democracies. And, whether or not, he was forced to wipe out Trades Unions, the Stock Exchange, Free Masonry, and the power of the Jews in the overall control of the running of the country, in order to give the recovery from World War I which she (or the 'father' land) so starvingly needed, the plain hard bare fact is that in taking those measures he raised against himself what proved to be, and would surely seem probable at the time, antagonists that were more powerful than any other source in the world. And who possessed the money and international influence to control, through the Press and every other media, including business interests, the thoughts of the mass millions in the Democracies.[50]

Taylour also believed that Churchill's personality partly explained the UK's involvement in the war. For Taylour, Hitler was a man of peace, and Churchill was a war leader. This fundamental difference, she argued, was responsible for the war between Britain and Germany:

> Churchill was a war leader – in his finest element conducting a war. That was his forte. Previously big assignments had been denied him. He just stepped into that leadership as Chamberlain was easily ousted – and, no doubt, had there been an election he would have been elected, for to 'stop Hitler' was the war cry – and Churchill was a brilliant orator at that time. He would 'down' Hitler no matter what – blood, sweat, tears and all the maudlin word tools, as well as the hardware from his friend Roosevelt, would do the job, and he would show that he was greater than Hitler. He'd stop at nothing. [...] But, and I add again that this is my view from me – propaganda facts, HITLER WAS NO WAR LEADER. He wanted peace – above all, peace with England. He was committed, fanatically committed to undoing the injustices of Versailles, to dissolving the guns pointed at him from the newly formed Czechoslovakia, to dissolving the also newly-made corridor

that separated Germany's Prussia into two parts by the newly made Poland, to reclaiming the Rhineland, to establishing his sea outlets, to union with Austria, and no doubt reclamation of German colonies. [...] Wouldn't we want to do the same?[51]

Taylour reiterated her view that Churchill 'gloried in war', while Hitler merely wished to right unjust wrongs to Germany, and, of course, develop a new economic system. For Taylour, it was Hitler whose 'hand was forced'[52] and it was Churchill, driven by personal ambition, who ensured that the war continued, even after the defeat of France. These views had clearly motivated her orchestration of the 'hissing Churchill' cinema incident around April 1940.

It was also Taylour's view that the UK and France, the two leading imperial powers, were unnecessarily 'greedy' in their desire to maintain their empires while preventing Germany from accessing similar advantage. She summed up this view at the appeal hearing, saying, 'we [the UK] have got so much of the world [...] there is no need to interfere in Europe'.[53] She was, in fact, an isolationist in this context, and regarded 'small nationalities' in central Europe as not 'in our sphere of interest'[54] – a view that was very much in line with British Union's long-held policy stance, expressed in its slogan 'Mind Britain's Business'.

One important aspect of Taylour's ideological outlook that was not directly addressed in her appeal hearings was her anti-Semitism. Yet she was an anti-Semite. Her contacts in the 1940s with the Irish anti-Semitic activist, Fr Fahey, suggest that she had adopted such a stance early in the war. Fahey founded the extremist *Maria Duce* (neatly combining Catholic and Italian Fascist themes in the group's title) group in 1942, but it was through his 'prolific anti-Semitic' writings that he had the wider influence.[55] In a briefing report that the British authorities later sent to the Defence Ministry in Dublin in October 1943, as part of the preparations for Taylour's release from detention, it was noted that, prior to the outbreak of war: 'Miss TAYLOUR appears to have been particularly impressed by German hospitality, and become greatly concerned with the perils of Jewish world domination, Free-Masonry and "international finance".'[56] Her letters over several decades following the war also confirm that she continued to attribute international plotting to financial interests that she often equated with Jewish interests. Even when in her seventies, Taylour rehearsed these views in letters to the former British Union Northern Inspector, R.R. 'Dick' Bellamy, giving a detailed account of how she felt the 'Jewish conspiracy' had operated, and still operated, in the 1970s. For example, in a letter of 4 March 1974, Taylour wrote:

I think one has to have lived in USA in the last [two and a half] decades and have all points of view to understand their 'use' of Communism. They as well as us put Soviet Russia in the saddle after World War II, and all their seemingly valiant anti-communism has been the convenient cudgel for all that Mosley, Hitler, and the few other enlightened and idealist men fought against – i.e. control of the masses the world over by International Finance –

control by the Jews. It cannot ever be accounted as co-incidence that out of 388 members of the new Bolshevik government in Petrograd in Dec. 1918 only 17 were non-jews one of those being a negro, & the remaining 16 were the only real Russians. 265 of those Jews (according to the Rev. Mr. Simons who served in Petrograd from 1907 to Oct 1918) came from the Lower East Side of New York [...] When one considers that the Jews were just and are a mere minority in numbers, the coincidence cannot carry! And especially when one considers the part they played in past centuries & the setting up of Freemasonry.[57]

Taylour's allegations concerning absurdly large numbers of Jews being involved in the Bolshevik Revolution was staple fare for anti-Semitic conspiracy theorists. Key figures in the first revolutionary movement in Imperial Russia, 'Proletariat', had been Jews, as had members of the later Bolsheviks, but it was not the case that only Jews were involved.[58]

During the Phoney War, Taylour's ideological standpoint rested primarily on concerns about social conditions, her view of economics, a strong sympathy for Nazi Germany, and anti-Semitism. These were the core views that underpinned her activism in late 1939 and the early months of 1940. But the war was soon to accelerate dramatically in the west, and Taylour's activism would be stopped by the British authorities.

Chapter Nine

Last Days of Freedom –
Arrest and Detention

Once Germany began its campaign in the west – first in Denmark and Norway in April 1940, then against Belgium and France in May – the domestic situation in the UK underwent a transformation. The anti-war campaign, even though it was made up of widely disparate groups and individuals, began to be regarded by some within the government as a real threat to Britain's war effort. The larger background to this potential threat was the fear of the Fifth Column. The idea of the Fifth Column had emerged during the Spanish Civil War, when the nationalist General Mola announced that, in addition to four military columns advancing on Madrid, he had a 'fifth column' inside the capital, poised to rise against the defenders. A Fifth Column was therefore an extensive underground organisation capable of carrying out effective actions, such as sabotage and killings, at the behest and in support of an attacking enemy. In the UK in the spring of 1940 fear of a Fifth Column gained a new lease of life as country after country fell to the Germans – an 'ill-assorted hotchpotch of aliens, native fascists, communists, pacifists, and religious dissenters under Nazi control [...] were deemed responsible for the collapse of the dominoes following the blitzkrieg in western Europe'.[1] In the UK, those in the security services who wanted tough action to counter any potential Fifth Column focused primarily on two groups – enemy aliens (citizens of countries at war with the UK, which included large numbers of anti-Nazi refugees), and political opponents of the war. The security services' view was that the government should use the internment powers under Defence Regulation 18b that it had possessed since the outset of the war. MI5 wished not only to see the widespread internment of enemy aliens, but also the detention of fascists and communists. However, the Home Office resisted this call, arguing that such a move would not be in accord with traditional British civil liberties, might create a difficult underground situation among political activists left at large, could inflame fears of a Fifth Column, and make martyrs of those interned. The issue became an extended tussle between MI5 and the Home Office, with the latter remaining sceptical of the security services' claims. On 22 May 1940, for example, the Home Secretary, Sir John Anderson, reported to the War Cabinet that although MI5 believed that large numbers of BU members would 'go to any lengths on behalf of Germany' there was 'no concrete evidence' that this was the case.[2] Much of the drive to convince the government that there was a Fifth Column appears to have come from MI5's Maxwell Knight. His efforts against the various anti-war groups and individuals seem to have been driven by the determination to prove the Fifth Column threat. In the most recent biography of Knight, it is noted that even though his women agents had 'penetrated to the heart of the Right Club', by early 1940 Knight had not been able to bring about any arrests, nor had he 'yet found the fabled Fifth Column'.[3] The task that MI5 faced, therefore, was not only to gather sufficient evidence against those it wished to see interned, but also to create a situation in which the government could be convinced that there was a real threat of an organised Fifth Column at large. The security services therefore increased *provocateur* activity to exaggerate the threat posed by pro-German groups and individuals.

Fay Taylour was part of a network of anti-war, pro-German activists who were involved in a range of semi-clandestine activities. She was just the sort of person that the security services wished to stop, and her activism was reasonably easy to evidence. But she was also the target of MI5 *provocateur* activity, certainly once she was detained and probably also prior to that. In addition to intercepting her mail and monitoring her movements and conversations, it is possible that Taylour was, as she believed, the victim of *provocateur* activity just a week before she was detained. Following an incident in Hyde Park on 26 May 1940, Taylour was arrested by police. She described the occasion later:

> My arrest [her internment], apart from my views, could well have been prompted by a Communist frame-up to which I was a victim six days earlier. British Union was anathema to the Communists just as Communism was corrosive venom and openly opposed by British Union. It was Sunday afternoon and I'd been walking through Hyde Park with friends reaching Marble Arch about 4.30pm where we intended to exit and find a tea shop. Suddenly, in front of me, out of the crowds gathered to hear the soap box orators at the corner, sprang a disreputable-looking man and woman, and the man tore the little British Union brooch I was wearing out of my rain coat. Immediately, two policemen from behind grabbed the man [Taylour's friend] who was walking beside me, but at that moment the disreputable man and woman who had receded popped up again from the front and pointed at me. The policemen then transferred their grip to me, jogging my elbows and marching me off to the police station in the middle of the park, disregarding protests from me and my friends.[4]

Taylour believed that the 'disreputable' man and woman had been working with the police. She was charged with 'struggling with a man in Hyde Park, causing a breach of the peace and public speaking'.[5] She appeared before Marlborough Street Police Court the next day, but the magistrate dismissed the case on the grounds that as no one 'could give an accurate account of what had actually happened the prisoner must be acquitted'.[6] For Taylour, the Hyde Park incident took on great significance. She attributed her subsequent detention to being primarily a result of the 'frame up' and the collusion between communists, police and the security service. Writing twenty-two years later, she still maintained that it was 'because of the 26 May 1940 Hyde Park incident' that MI5 was able to ensure that she would be detained.[7] Although the incident did form part of the case against her, it was just a minor part. It is odd that she did not appreciate that her activities with the Home Defence Movement, the Right Club, and on her own initiative, might be the explanation for her subsequent detention. Whatever the truth of the incident in Hyde Park, it was one element in the case that MI5 brought to detain Taylour on 1 June 1940.

MI5 used a variety of *provocateur* tactics, from placing its agents at the heart of groups like the Right Club to effectively 'framing' its targets. The most infamous of the latter forms of MI5 action were in relation to Ben Greene, the former Labour Party activist, Quaker, pacifist, and treasurer of the British People's Party (BPP). Ben Greene was the target of a honey-trap and blackmail attempt by MI5 using a woman agent who called herself 'Mrs Pope'. When this and other attempts had failed, Maxwell Knight simply framed Greene in order to have him detained.[8] To achieve this, Knight used two German refugees, Friedl Gaertner and Harald Kurtz, as *provocateurs*. Failing to get Greene to rise to various baits, they concocted a story against Greene, and subsequently, on Knight's orders, attempted to entrap Greene's brother, Edward. Although Maxwell Knight's attempts to entrap Greene had failed, Ben Greene 'was one of the first men to be rounded up in May 1940 after the introduction of Defence Regulation 18b(1a)'.[9] Greene was held for a year and a half. On release, he took a libel and false imprisonment case against the Home Office. He was unsuccessful, but the case had implications for Maxwell Knight's MI5 career. In Knight's and MI5's defence, it might be said that, given the fears of the time, and the backdrop of German military success, both 'could plead national security in justification of their dirty tricks, but neither [MI5 nor Greene] emerged with their reputation unscathed'.[10] The Greene example showed the length to which MI5 (in particular Maxwell Knight) went to ensure the arrest and detention of targets that Knight had identified. Greene was not in any way another Taylour, yet he was the victim of MI5's *provocateur* tactics.

Maxwell Knight and MI5 also used *provocateur* tactics in their drive to have political internment introduced on a comparatively large scale. For Knight, the aim was to defeat those in government, who argued for the maintenance of civil liberties, even in time of war. Despite Knight's best efforts, by the spring of 1940 he had failed to provide any hard evidence that the various right-wing groups and parties represented a real Fifth Column threat to the UK. What was more, Knight's primary target – Mosley and British Union – was not regarded by the Home Secretary, Sir John Anderson, as representing a dangerous threat. As late as 18 May, Anderson told the War Cabinet:

> Although the policy of the British Union of Fascists is to oppose the war and to condemn the Government, there is no evidence that they would be likely to assist the enemy. Their public propaganda strikes a patriotic note ... In my view it would be a mistake to strike at this organization at this stage by interning the leaders. Apart from the fact that there is no evidence on which

such action would be justified, it is to be borne in mind that premature action would leave the organization itself in being and other leaders could be appointed to take the place of those who had been apprehended. In my view we should hold our hand.[11]

Yet within a month, Mosley and over 1,000 of his supporters were detained without trial, and British Union proscribed. That drastic change was brought about by what became known as 'the Tyler Kent–Anna Wolkoff affair' involving MI5 entrapment of Wolkoff, a Right Club member, and fears over secret Anglo-American communications taken by Kent from the US Embassy. Knight used this 'affair' to convince the government to make an amendment to the Defence Regulation 18b, and to act 'against Mosley and his party [...] although neither Kent, Wolkoff, nor indeed Ramsay had any direct connection with the BU'.[12]

By the spring of 1940, the mainspring of Right Club activity was provided by its women adherents. Fay Taylour was active within this network, as was her friend and fellow woman racing driver, Enid Riddell. Riddell, in turn, was a long-term friend of Anna Wolkoff. But among the Right Club women were MI5 agents, planted by Maxwell Knight. Those agents were Joan Miller, Hélène Louise de Munck and Marjory Amor.[13] Of these women, the key agents were Miller and Amor. They enabled Knight and MI5 to ensure that the links between Anna Wolkoff and her friend, the US Embassy cipher clerk Tyler Kent, could be exploited successfully, and lead to the implementation of political detention in the early summer of 1940; hence its relevance to Taylour's life.

Anna Wolkoff was the daughter of the Imperial Russian naval attaché at its London embassy. After the Bolshevik Revolution, Admiral Wolkoff and his immediate family had remained in London as refugees, later setting up a business – the Russian Tea Rooms – on Harrington Road, near South Kensington Underground Station. Anna became a dress designer and was naturalised as a British citizen in 1935. By the outbreak of war, she was active in the Right Club, and was part of an informal group of friends and political activists who opposed the war, believing it to be a 'Jewish conspiracy'. One of her friends was Tyler Kent, who joined the US Embassy in London in October 1939. He had previously held a posting in Moscow and was fluent in Russian. His role was to code and decode radio traffic to and from the Embassy, and as 'London acted as a hub for Embassy traffic within Europe, he was able to read many exchanges between the White House and its various European outposts'.[14] As the Nazis advanced across western Europe, Kent read secret cables between Churchill and the US President Roosevelt. Those cables showed that President Roosevelt was involved in negotiations to support the UK and, probably, to bring the USA into the war, despite the fact that he was fighting a re-election campaign pledging:

I hope the United States will keep out of this war. I believe it will, and I give you assurance and reassurance that every effort of your government will be directed to that end. As long as it remains within my power to prevent, there will be no blackout of peace in the United States.[15]

Not only was Kent reading these cables, and in contact with various anti-war activists, but he was also making copies of the cables and taking them to his flat. Knight and MI5 feared that he was passing information to members of the Right Club who could then pass this on to contacts in enemy countries. Kent's friendship with Wolkoff opened up the potential for a further leak of information. Wolkoff claimed that she knew Colonel Francisco Marigliano, the Assistant Military Attaché at the Italian embassy, well enough to get him to pass messages out of the UK by Italian diplomatic bag. But Knight's agents – Miller and Amor – were well placed to prevent anything like this happening, and, crucially, were also placed to entrap Wolkoff. Knight arranged for one of his agents in the Right Club to feed Wolkoff with a letter supposedly for William Joyce in Berlin. Wolkoff passed it on to another Right Club woman (in fact an MI5 agent). By doing so, Wolkoff had shown her willingness to use her friendship network to enable the passing of secret information to the enemy. That opened the door to the arrest of her friend, Tyler Kent, the US Embassy cipher clerk and Right Club associate. Wolkoff and Kent were both arrested, tried in secret and found guilty of acting with the intention of assisting an enemy. Wolkoff received ten years penal servitude and Kent seven years. Wolkoff served five years. Released in June 1946, she then returned to the Russian Tea Rooms. When they closed after her father's death, she moved to a Bohemian lodging house in Tite Street, Chelsea. In the febrile atmosphere of May 1940, the Kent-Wolkoff affair led 'inexorably to the internment of British fascists',[16] one of whom was Fay Taylour.

On 1 June 1940, Taylour was arrested at her home, Lucerne Cottage, Lucerne Mews, Kensington, which was then searched. She was there for at least part of the time while the search was carried out. Particular attention was paid to Taylour's papers, and she later came to believe that the searchers were looking for a copy of cables taken by Tyler Kent: 'they started going through all my papers with almost feverish activity. Later, I had the explanation. It wasn't until I got to jail that I heard about the decoded messages [the Tyler Kent-Anna Wolkoff messages]. Three copies had been made. The police recovered two. They were madly searching for the third.'[17] From Lucerne Cottage Fay was taken to Holloway Prison by Inspector J.W. Pearson of Special Branch on a 'Home Office Order dated 30th May 1940, issued by the Under Secretary of State, Sir John Anderson, under Defence Regulations 1939, 18.B.'[18] It was Taylour's third time at Holloway, after her childhood visit to her imprisoned Suffragette aunt, and her own one-night stay in connection with the speeding offence. This time, as prisoner 4634, she would be held there for over two years, before being moved to the Women's Internment Camp in the former Imperial Hotel, Port Erin, on the Isle of Man. She was released in October 1943 after more than three years of detention without trial. The order that began this imprisonment was issued by Sir John Anderson, and stated:

> Paragraph 1. The Secretary of State has reasonable cause to believe that you have been a member of the organisation now known as British Union; or

have been active in the furtherance of its objects; and that it is necessary to exercise control over you.

Particulars: You, Frances H. TAYLOUR, were at the time of your detention a member of the British Union and have been active in the furtherance of the objects of the said organisation by attending and speaking at public meetings, writing and distributing propaganda, and publicly disseminating pro-Nazi and anti-British views.

Paragraph 2. (relating to the organisation known as 'British Union' and contained in the formal 'Reasons for order'.)

(3) Miss Taylour is the daughter of an ex-senior officer in the Royal Irish Constabulary, and a racing motorist of some distinction. Shortly before the war, having completed a six months' racing trip in South Africa, she proceeded to Germany, and while there broadcast to the motoring public of South Africa from the short-wave station at Berlin. She stayed in Germany until war seemed imminent, and then crossed to England. About a month after the war started Miss TAYLOUR was questioned by detectives, who asked whether she was a member of the British Union. After the interview Miss TAYLOUR, on the same day, joined the British Union, and wrote a letter, which was published in 'Action' announcing that she had placed her services at the disposal of the Peace Campaign.[19]

This bare statement outlined the formal reasons for Taylour's detention – her membership of British Union (which was, up until she was detained, a legal political party), her visit to Germany, broadcasting from Berlin prior to the war, and her part in the anti-war campaign. Of these four reasons, the most interesting, putting on one side being involved in legal political activity, are the citing of Taylour's visit to Germany and her radio broadcasts to South Africa. Taylour had a long history of visiting and racing in Germany, both before and after the Nazis' rise to power, but it is suggestive of the concern that the security services had that such a visit so close to the outbreak of war might in fact have been in some way concerned with preparations for Fifth Column activity. The concern over radio broadcasting was a constant, reflecting not only the immediate fears raised by the operation of English language broadcasting into the UK from Germany (including the black stations purporting to come from inside the UK), but also the fear that British fascists would attempt to broadcast from outside the UK, perhaps from Éire. Given that Taylour had a strong Irish connection, had visited Dublin in February 1940, and had a history of radio broadcasting from a range of countries, it was perhaps feared that she would be involved in such an attempt.

The stated reasons for Taylour's detention did not present all the authorities' reasons for arresting her. Prior to the first hearing against her interment on 28 August 1940, the appeal Advisory Committee was sent a 'Statement of [the] Case Against Frances Helen Taylour'. This provided details of why the security services believed that she should be detained. It focused on points which were felt to be particularly concerning. While acknowledging that Taylour's own written appeal of 16 July was 'as far as actual facts go [...] accurate [...] it should be added, however, that whilst in Germany [in 1939] she apparently became very friendly with a number of German officials, and that her pro-German feelings dated some way back'.[19] These links with Germany were to the fore in the case against Taylour, as were her contacts with her London friend, Joyce Pope, then in Switzerland, plus information that Tony Dickson had informed Special Branch that Taylour was 'communicating with Germany by letters passing through Switzerland and Ireland'.[20] The Popes were regarded as being pro-German. MI5 noted that it had intercepted letters from them to other addressees in the UK. The focus on external links continued, with much being made of Taylour's February 1940 trip to Dublin, and her links with Fr Fahey. MI5 continued to insist that her trip to Ireland was 'in some way connected with a project of MOSLEY's for broadcasting from Éire to England', despite apparently having no evidence for this. It was also stated that she was a member of a number of groups other than British Union, including the Nordic League (in its 'Holborn Public Speaking Society' guise), the Right Club, the Angles-Circle, the Anglo-Irish Friendship Society, and The Link. It is likely, however, that Taylour was a 'member' of these groups simply on the grounds of her contacts, friendships, and shared activities. Her political activities were described as 'considerable'. Among her dangerous contacts were a mix of activists from various groups, but particularly those associated with clandestine activity: Mrs Hilton, Captain Ramsay, Mrs Winfield, and Charlie Watts. The list of Scots Guards officers and two RAF men found in Fay's house was also seen to be sinister. This, then, was the case against Taylour – she was seen to be potentially dangerous, very active, connected with a variety of groups and people, had contacts abroad, and might in some way be involved with radio broadcasting on behalf of BU. It is difficult to assess the full validity of this case. Certainly some were worried by her foreign contacts, the speculative link with a possible broadcasting venture, and her frenetic, though probably not very effective, activism. More broadly, the case seems indicative of the general picture that MI5 was attempting to build up to push for political detention. In the context of the rapid collapse of Western Europe, and the widespread assumption that the dramatic events in Norway, the Netherlands, France and Belgium were, in part, to be explained by a German-controlled Fifth Column, the case against Taylour assumes greater potency, though it is still sparse. To some extent, however, Taylour was her own worst enemy. The fact that she was detained for an unusually long time (certainly longer than almost all other BU members and supporters) was, in part, due to her behaviour record while in detention.

Chapter Ten

Women Detained

Political detention and the proscription of British Union effectively finished Mosley's movement but, for the few remaining fascist activists, the fate of the '18b' detainees became a propaganda tool for many years. During the war, 'The 18B Publicity Council' published a pamphlet, *Persecuted Women in Britain To-Day*, outlining the fate of women detainees. Years later, Taylour also published her account of internment, *Your Attention is Arrested under Defence Regulation 18-B*. Both sought to establish not only the illegality of detention, but also the privations suffered by the women detainees. The 18B Publicity Council's pamphlet stressed the fact that the interned women 'have never been charged with any offence'[1] and went on to outline the circumstances of the arrests of the women, the conditions – particularly in Holloway Prison – that they were held in, and the consequent health problems. The government's decisions in 1940 to intern large numbers of foreign nationals and refugees, and to detain certain political activists, led to an immediate problem of where to hold these people. As a result, some of the camps used were barely habitable; for example, under the stands at York racecourse, or in a previously abandoned wing of Brixton Prison. For women detainees, the primary place of detention in 1940 was Holloway Prison, where Taylour spent over two years. Here, too, there were not enough cells to cope with numbers, and, as at Brixton, a previously abandoned wing ('F') had to be re-opened, and cleaned by detainees: 'in "F" Wing conditions of extreme filth were prevailing. Stacks of dirty mattresses and dirty utensils had to be carried away, before even a start could be made at cleaning; [...] despite the shortage of cleaning materials'.[2] Shortages of soap, cleaning materials, and sanitary products marked the women's imprisonment, all impacting on health. As a result, women experienced hair loss, skin disorders, and menstrual dysfunction. In these poor conditions, three women also gave birth. Taylour herself was in a good state of health when arrested; in detention, her main health problem seems to have been recurring and increasingly severe headaches.[3] When the London Blitz started in September 1940, the raids added an extra aspect to detention. Holloway had no air-raid shelters. At first, the women were locked in their cells during raids, although later the doors remained unlocked. Taylour described experiencing the Blitz from inside Holloway:

> During the blitz, we had to remain in the dark because the black-out curtains were no good [...] we had no shelters, and so I could watch London burning through my cell window, and the angry red glow would afford quite a lot of

light. When the bombs were very close, perhaps trying to knock out the nearby railway stations, and the flares that dropped in advance lighting up the whole place, I would get out of bed and put on some undies and a sweater – just in case. [...] At first we were locked in, and one detainee who was nervous got hysterical during bombing. Who could blame her? Her cell was on the high top floor, and it was quite queer to feel that great solid building rocking from ground wave repercussions for seconds at a time. I was only on the third floor, so it must have been pretty bad on top![4]

Holloway was hit at least once, with part of a wing (holding criminal prisoners) collapsing. Prisoners attempted to escape, but were prevented by warders.[5]

Taylour later summed up the experience of detention in 'F' Wing in a piece of verse, 'Holloway Jail, by One of the Graces of 18B', the penultimate stanza of which read:

Ailments came through bad detention,
Rheumatics, thyroid, not to mention
Dental troubles, failing sight
From sloppy food and rotten light.
Not least of them the lack of man
Since our detention days began –
'Preventative'! Yes, that was true!
Not punitive! Odd point of view.[6]

Taylour's doggerel makes light of conditions but, given her pre-war life surrounded by the male racing fraternity and her various relationships in the late 1930s, she clearly did miss men. Taylour described the various women detainees as 'a motley bunch':

There were women from England's oldest and highest families – titles and all – and charwomen from the slums. There were Colonel's, Captain's wives, and more than one Admiral's wife. There were typists, artists, racing drivers, and London socialites. School teachers, women doctors, musicians, clerks, and even a famous boxer's wife. We fought – sometimes. But I think we were a good crowd. And we had much in common.[7]

As a memento of her detention in Holloway, Taylour kept a small piece of paper headed 'H.M. Prison. Holloway. 20.IV.1941'[8] with signatures of twenty-one fellow-detainees, including those of Lady Diana Mosley, Norah Elam, the former Suffragette, the 61-year-old First World War ambulance driver Diana de Laessoe, and some who became Fay Taylour's friends: Ann Good, Flo Hayes, Judy Whitham, Tula Henham and her daughter Lolita.[9] Later, Taylour wrote about the impact of internment on some of the women detainees. She said that she believed that some detained women had become 'fanatical' in various, sometimes surprising, ways: 'as with many women with unusual and hard circumstances behind them, they become bitter or fanatical in some new direction. Joan Evans let me read a letter from another woman 18B [i.e. a fellow-detainee] who had become a water diviner and could write of nothing else!'.[10] In fact, the impact of detention was felt by detainees in different ways, with some being particularly badly affected. Family breakdown was not uncommon – this was the fate of Charlie Watts's family[11] for example – while others faced long-term problems, often health related. Richard Thurlow's assessment of the impact of internment on some of the detainees was that their 'smearing as "fifth column" and potential traitors caused personal trauma and destroyed lives. Suicide, physical and mental breakdown, divorce and the splitting of families were some of the results, and some became embittered'.[12]

During the early months of her detention, Taylour was the target of MI5 *provocateur* activity, with Maxwell Knight's agent, Marjorie Amor, being the antagonist. Fay Taylour's papers, letters and her booklet, *Your Attention is Arrested under Defence Regulation 18-B*, provide a convincing account of the role of Marjorie Amor as an MI5 plant (MI5's agent M/Y) in the Right Club, both before and after the detentions of late May and early June 1940. MI5 continued to develop their case against the Right Club and its members, even once they were detained. The focus on the Right Club suggests that Maxwell Knight saw this comparatively small group of mostly women activists as a useful tool in the development of his strategy. Marjorie Amor's role in this has been overshadowed by that of Joan Millar, whose own subsequent accounts, particularly her book, *One Girl's War*, reinforced her image as a lynchpin in the events of 1940.[13] However, Marjorie Amor appears to have been of more continuous importance to Maxwell Knight. She had been placed by MI5 as the Right Club's secretary, where her role included accepting membership applications. She probably helped compile the Right Club's membership ledger, which was subsequently found in the search of Tyler Kent's flat. When the political detentions started in earnest in summer 1940, Amor was one of the first to be imprisoned in Holloway. A week later, Fay Taylour was also detained there. She was quickly informed by another detainee, a 'Mrs N', that Amor was, in fact, a spy. After her first night in Holloway, Taylour was lying on her bunk when:

> The woman who was accused of being a spy [Amor] walked in and sat on the end of my bunk. 'Ridiculous, isn't it', she cried, 'calling ME a spy!'. I knew her as being a member of the Right Club, and she continued to tell me that she was not only secretary of the club but also founder and organiser. Therefore she should be one of the first people to be put in Holloway [...] it was perfectly natural for her to be amongst us, she continued. And, as if to convince me further, told me that no one could join the club without her sanction. 'Why', she said, 'I sanctioned you for membership!'[14]

Amor followed this up by telling Taylour 'fantastic tales of how the club would take over key positions when Hitler won the war',[15] and that in the event of an invasion, the club members would seize radio stations and other key points. Taylour's reaction was: 'suddenly, in spite of my headache and the first day in such gloomy and frightening surroundings, I had a barely controllable desire to laugh. In my mind was conjured up a picture of fat-ish well-heeled coffee-drinking women marching on government bastions'.[16] As Amor continued to embroider her story, Taylour remembered that, at one meeting of the Right Club, Captain Ramsay had made a surprise appearance, and that the door had been opened by Amor, who had announced, 'the Leader!'.[17] The next day in Holloway, Taylour was visited by two men who asked her a series of questions about the Right Club designed to elicit the very information that Amor had fed Taylour the day before. When the two visitors asked Taylour whether she had ever heard Captain Ramsay referred to as 'the Leader', she said, 'no, discounting Amor's tea party'.[18] This incident was later described by Taylour as being part of the fictitious and 'atrocious supposed plans of the Right Club (as invented by MI5 or the Jews).'[19] Taylour subsequently referred to the 41-year-old, 'short and stout' Amor,[20] with heavy irony, as 'Mata Hari'. Writing over thirty years later, Taylour still did not know for certain that Amor was an MI5 agent, referring to her as 'that crack-pot woman'.[21] In all her time in detention, Taylour did not change her mind about 'MI5 or the Jews', nor about the struggle between Germany and the Allies. Detention in Holloway certainly did not change her mind, as another of her verse compositions, written in the jail in 1942, made clear. Entitled, *A Dream. Prisoner No. 4634 18B has a dream in her prison cell E 1/10,*[22] it was a strange, slightly surreal versification of a dream featuring two fellow detainees: the racing driver, Enid Riddell, and Lady Diana Mosley. In fifteen stanzas, Taylour recounted her dream of the two women in the Western Desert meeting up with a German panzer commander who smuggles the two to a meeting with Taylour. The verse refers to meals, a fast MG sports car, Churchill, and aerial bombing, all mixed together as in a dream. A refrain from the verse composition can be taken to be an accurate summary of the women's standpoint: 'Britain First! Hail Mosley! P.J.! Amen!' ('P.J.' was an anti-Semitic slogan, 'Perish Judah').

Taylour's account of Amor's role among women detainees in Holloway rings true, as this combination of intelligence-gathering and *provocateur* activity characterised all of Maxwell Knight's tactics during this period. He had been successful in convincing the Home Office and war cabinet that political detention without trial was necessary. However, he failed to establish that there was anything approaching a Fifth Column under orders and capable of carrying out any effective or widespread action in support of a German invasion. Despite the wishful imaginings of some pro-Germans, there was no armed and prepared organisation able to seize power at a crucial moment. Individual actions, such as the sabotaging of public phone boxes, the passing of German radio station frequencies, and putting up anti-Semitic stickers, were more characteristic.

Some of Taylour's letters from Holloway survive, including one she wrote to her Aunt Evelyn six months after being arrested. All prison letters were censored, and Taylour's letter largely deals with mundane matters of prison life, detailing how between sixty and seventy women detainees had to share the same gas stove, that food was alright, but that the 10 shillings that her aunt had sent her would be spent on buying more food, and how the lighting was poor (25-watt bulbs were used). She also wrote about the Blitz and how Holloway was hit by bombs. At the heart of the letter, however, is a plea that her few remaining relatives attempt to understand her viewpoint:

> My first prayer is that you and Enid [Fay's sister] and Daddy will not worry about me and that it will be given to you to understand my point of view. And please stop thinking I am unpatriotic! I have done nothing seditious or traitorous. I merely belonged to a movement whose activities were legal till July 10th, a purely British movement, and I voiced their policy which I sincerely believed was best for my country.[23]

But Taylour was not content with submitting her letters to prison censors. She managed to smuggle out at least one uncensored letter to her friend, Freddie Dixon, the ex-motorcyclist and expert engine-tuner, around the same time as her letter to Aunt Evelyn. Dixon received the letter on 14 December 1940 but, unsettled by the contents, he took it to the police in Reigate. In her letter to Dixon, Taylour once again stressed that she had been imprisoned because 'my [...] crime is that I disapproved of the war. I have done nothing illegal or traitorous in any way shape or form'.[24] She went on to say that she had been detained for the duration of the war, but 'that won't be long however'.[25] At the time, the UK was the last country in Europe still fighting against the Axis, albeit supported by the Empire and Commonwealth, and invasion by Germany still seemed a real possibility. It is likely that she thought that either a negotiated peace or a German invasion would end her detention but, whichever option she thought most likely, putting that phrase into a smuggled letter did her no favours with the authorities. To make matters worse, the rest of her letter attempted to get Dixon, whose own attitude to the war was far from enthusiastic, to begin a coded form of communications with her.

Taylour was held for much longer than others who had been primarily detained for membership of British Union. Her friend Charlie Watts was released as soon as he established his support for the war effort – something that coincided with the beginning of German air attacks on British cities. However, Taylour did not move from her position of opposing the war, and regarding Germany favourably. On 19 May 1942, for example, the Home Secretary recommended Taylour's continued detention, largely as a result of reports from the governor of Holloway, who wrote of Taylour that 'at visits she does not hesitate to speak scathingly of the Government'.[26] Further, it was feared that if she were released then it was possible that she would re-engage with a women's network:

> In another report sent to us the Governor [of Holloway] deals with the point [about Taylour's likely activism] from a somewhat different aspect. 'It is likely' he writes 'that she would remain passive both as regards the war effort and speaking about her political views, unless and until she came under the

influence of women hostile to the war effort. Then she might become active in speech against the Government.' In our opinion it is almost a certainty that TAYLOUR would fail to control her tongue if she were at liberty.[27]

This is a rather revealing note, not only about Taylour's views. It shows a surprising degree of fear of the impact of unidentified 'women' who might influence Taylour and others to such an extent that they might speak out against the government – or, as the report put it in respect of Fay Taylour, 'fail to control her tongue'. That fear led to Taylour being imprisoned for a further year and a half. In fact, the governor of Holloway's reports had been damning in other ways too, noting that although she associated largely with other Right Club women, she had not made close friendships with any of them. Given the activities of MI5 within Holloway this would not have been surprising – but it was probably an inaccurate assessment, as Taylour maintained friendships with other women detainees after the war. Most revealingly, however, in March 1942, the governor of Holloway complained: 'She [Taylour] is a selfish type of woman and one feels that she can never be trusted. She has been suspected of breaking prison regulations on more than one occasion, but she has been too cunning for me to get sufficient evidence to report her'.[28] It appears that, in some respects, the governor had met his match in Fay Taylour. He had to wait several more months before he was rid of her.

In autumn 1942, Fay Taylour was moved from Holloway prison to an internment camp on the Isle of Man, where she continued to irritate the authorities and espouse her politics. In her unpublished manuscript, *The Political Experience in Detail*, written in California in 1962, Fay provided an account of the time she spent detained on the Isle of Man. During the First World War, the island was used to hold interned aliens (nationals of enemy countries), but during the Second World War it was also used to hold political detainees, including Irish Republicans, communists, fascists and pro-Nazis. The many boarding houses that served holidaymakers in peacetime were surrounded by barbed wire and used to hold the detainees. Taylour was held in such a camp in Port Erin on the south-west coast of the island. She gave an account of the boredom, and the lives of detained women, including lesbianism, the absence of men, attempts to get round the petty regulations, and their efforts to amuse themselves and give some meaning to daily life.

Taylour's first impressions of her new 'home' in Port Erin in 'Camp W' were marked by relief, and by freedoms that she had not enjoyed in Holloway, 'the fresh air and sea, and comparative freedom after prison, blew away many cobwebs – unlike the poor cobwebs that hung from the chicken wire spanning the floors in F Wing'.[29] She described the small seaside town, which was entirely occupied by detainees, internees, government officials and police:

> The camp comprised the little town, and the long hill beside the sea cliff that ran to the cliff-top café, which was also a dance hall. The hill was lined with boarding houses and hotels on one side, the cliffs and sea on the other. These

houses and hotels, which were now our billets, would be full of vacationers in peace time. I lived in the largest, near the top of the hill. It was just a step further along the cliff road to the café, and then the barrier. The café and dance floor were ours. With our guarding policewomen and various government officials we made up the total population of Port Erin, except for the landladies or hotel owners. There must have been several hundred internees and detainees, and all women![30]

Once installed in the former boarding house, one of her first visitors was a young German woman who asked if Taylour was a lesbian:

Lesbianism had sprung up, and a mischievous internee sneaked into my room at my billet one night soon after I arrived to ascertain my status. A lot are curious about you, she said. 'They think you might be a lesbian the way you wear that old sweater and slacks'. That gave me the heartiest laugh I'd had in ages, and this very normal German girl became my ally.[31]

Taylour put camp lesbianism, which she called an 'abnormal state', down to the authorities being 'starchy' and insisting that men and women be held in different camps. Fay Taylour had many relationships with men, and her racing life was characterised by being one of the few women in a male-dominated world. By the time she was moved to the Isle of Man she had been without male company for over two years. She thought it was time to put an end to the enforced 'starchiness' of the authorities who kept all the male detainees elsewhere on the small island, or as Taylour said, 'their camp was so near – yet so far!'.[32] Putting aside the possibility of finding 'a secret fisherman like one or two internees found',[33] she took advantage of a camp regulation that allowed brothers and sisters or married or affianced prisoners to meet up once a month. Taylour did not, of course, have a brother, husband, or fiancé, but another inmate said that all she needed to do was know the name of a male detainee, and write to him suggesting they should apply to be allowed to meet up. The tricky aspect of this was writing to a supposed fiancé in a way such that the recipient would understand what was happening, but the camp authorities would not realise that Taylour and the male detainee were not engaged to be married:

I did have a friend in the Men's camp, and he was wifeless. But I couldn't write and say 'let's be engaged so that we can meet'. Letters were all read by our officials before mailing. And I'd have to wait three weeks to smuggle a letter to him, because the next meeting was three weeks away. It would be another month then before he could see me. 'Just write to him as if you WERE engaged,' my informer said. 'He can't be a dope if he's in that camp'. I wrote, telling him I was putting in a request for visits, and then I had to answer all sorts of questions, hoping his answers, if questioned, would synchronise. It was touch and go, but permission was granted. I was informed that my fiancé would be on the next visit.[34]

The visit day, which was held in the café at the top of the seaside road in Port Erin, was a day of great activity. All those women who were expecting visitors were taken to the café, while all the other women detainees were locked inside their billets. Taylour commented: 'But *what* harm could it do to allow the women to remain outside and wave? Did the officials believe that the men-starved women might stop the bus by force, and commit rape! Starchy, I said! That isn't even the word'.[35]

Fay Taylour greatly enjoyed her meeting in the café, with biscuits and tea provided by the women inmates:

> I enjoyed the meeting so much that I laughed. The next time I laughed a policewoman tapped me on the shoulder and said: Less noise please! Prison camp laughter was regulated. From then on I had meetings once a month. The stay-in-your-billets rule for the others was finally relaxed, and they would gather outside the café to wave. It was really pathetic how some of them would shed their sportswear and doll up to the nines just for that split-minute glimpse of the opposite sex.[36]

Besides plotting to meet men, Taylour and her fellow detainees enjoyed trying to get around the various camp regulations. An attempt to avoid morning roll call failed when the detainee who was meant to answer Fay Taylour's name shouted out 'Yes', instead of Taylour's habitual 'Present'. The detainees also smuggled candles to each other's rooms to beat 'lights out', when the electricity was cut off and inmates were supposed to be in their own rooms. The proprietor of the building Taylour was in patrolled the corridors to check that there were no lights, while the women used bedclothes to shade the candles. The atmosphere among the inmates in Port Erin camp seems to have been lighter than in the confines of Holloway prison. Taylour described a much freer, and healthier, existence:

> As all camps do, we organised plays, concerts, and dancing lessons and contests. We walked on the cliffs and sand, and the back room behind the billets was open for us too. It was heaven after prison for all its abnormality. I shall never forget it as long as I hear seagulls crying. In that camp was a comradeship never found outside. People are too busy 'outside' to get together. Friendships made up for the jealousies, heartaches, irritations, and discomforts that one couldn't run away from. It was unique.[37]

Many of the files relating to Taylour's time on the Isle of Man were destroyed in the 1950s,[38] but from those that remain, it is clear that her lengthy imprisonment did not change her views. A report on Taylour written by a P.M. Burke, dated 15 June 1943, stated:

> TAYLOUR is one of the worst pro-Nazis in Port Erin [camp]. You will see from 1216 [file, now destroyed] that in January 1943 she wrote to Tony DICKSON 'I am never downhearted. I always know it will end all right one day. Like the outside [*sic*] (who are so cheered up with Libyan news)

I too think the coming season's campaigns will finish it for us. I think the Germans have built a Siegfried line in Russia to which they are retiring and in which they can stay while they turn their attention in the other direction.' It is, I think, reasonable to assume that she was here conveying to DICK-SON that she hoped for a successful German invasion of Britain.

Miss Pinching tells me that the camp authorities looked on TAYLOUR as one of their blackest cases. Mrs SKENE's report at 104a [file, now destroyed] shows that she is in the habit of hoarding pictures of Hitler and had in her possession a hymn in which his name was substituted for God's.[39]

This is the most damning report on Taylour that still exists. It seems to confirm that, even as late as the beginning of 1943, she was resolutely pro-Nazi. There is, perhaps, an element of belligerent defiance in her words and behaviour that may well have been partly her tactic to maintain her morale despite lengthy imprisonment with no date for release. Nonetheless, her buoyancy on hearing of Axis success in 'Libya' (in fact, by January 1943, the fighting in North Africa was in Tunisia, where German and Italian forces were enjoying a brief resurgence) illustrates that she had moved a long way, from merely opposing the war to hoping for an Axis victory. In fact, previously, in her second appeal against internment, in April 1942, she had told the advisory board that, whereas she had initially hoped that there could be a negotiated peace between the UK and Germany, by 1942 she believed that the war 'has to be fought to a conclusion'.[40] There was an implication then that she thought that the UK and its allies might win, but her later letter to Dickson suggests otherwise. It was that intransigent standpoint, combined with her strong personality, which meant that she was detained for so long.

Fay Taylour was not kept much longer in Camp W on the Isle of Man, however, as the authorities were considering ways in which they could release her.

Chapter Eleven

Released from Detention,
and a Refuge in Dublin

By the summer of 1943, the authorities were beginning to think about how Taylour's release from detention could be managed. She had been before two advisory committees – in July 1940, and in April and May 1942 – and was by then arguing that the emergency conditions that had prevailed in the early summer of 1940 had passed, and that, in consequence, she should be released even though 'I have not changed my views' on the 'war policy'.[1] The Home Office and the security authorities could not agree what to do with Taylour. They feared that she would continue to be outspoken against the war, that she might re-engage with other women of similar views, and that she could be, in some way, influential. It is difficult now to imagine that Taylour really would have been a threat, especially so late in the war when it was clear that Germany's fortunes were on the wane. Although there were still conflicting views within the security and Home Office ranks about the best course to follow in relation to Taylour, on 6 July 1943 an order for her release was signed by the Home Office. The letter reminded Taylour that:

> The Secretary of State desires me to call your attention to the Order made by him on the 10th July, 1940, in pursuance of Defence Regulations 18AA. The effect of that Order is that activities on behalf of or in connection with the British Union specified in paragraph (3) of that Regulation are now unlawful and if you should be found to be engaging in such activities you will be liable not only to prosecution but to further detention.[2]

That paragraph expressed the authorities' central concern that Fay Taylour would simply carry on where she had left off three years earlier.

The Home Office letter of 6 July did not, however, lead to Taylour's immediate release. The next step was for her to provide an address where she would live on release. She gave an address in Dublin, and when that was refused she protested that Ireland was 'my native land, and I would refuse to leave the camp for any other address'.[3] Even after three years of detention, Fay Taylour was not going to take the easy way out. She wrote to the Home Secretary. Her best friend in Port Erin 'felt that she would not be saying goodbye'.[4]

Fay Taylour's refusal to be released to anywhere but Ireland left the authorities with a dilemma. By August 1943, the options had been reduced to not releasing Taylour, releasing her to Dublin, or releasing her to Dublin and not allowing her to return to the UK. In the end, she was released from detention on 5 October 1943 on the understanding that she would live in Dublin. Before she left the detention camp, she had an interview with the Camp Commandant. In later years she would attribute great significance to what was said to her in that meeting:

> I received an invitation to visit the Commandant in his private house. He was the only man official. He wanted me to sign a statement of retraction before leaving the camp. It didn't seem to matter that if I signed such a statement my views would remain the same. He wanted a retraction – period! He did his best to persuade me. It didn't matter that I had nothing to retract, or that such a paper would be a lie ... as long as I signed. I refused. I would have refused anyway – even if I know what I know now [1962]. I could not sign any paper denying my sincere convictions.
>
> I know now that the Commandant's words, when he couldn't persuade me, had real meaning, a meaning he would like to have explained but couldn't. It was top secret. It wasn't a secret that he was attached to MI-5, and would also work with FBI, but as it turned out it was very significant. His words were: if you don't sign you will always be an outcast. And I brushed them off. He repeated them, but to myself I thought: that's what YOU think, and then forgot them ... until years later when I was forced to remember, and understand. And I am still understanding, though such should be *un*-understandable in the so-called Free World.[5]

Taylour came to believe that the Commandant was, in effect, warning her that even when the war was over, those who had opposed it and who were pro-Nazi, would still face sanctions. She became sure that her later struggles to make a living in the United States, relating to publishing her autobiography, having a film made of her life, and finding employment, were because the British and American security services had ensured that she was blacklisted. Just as she gave great significance to the Hyde Park incident that had preceded her detention in 1940, so she came to give significance to the interview with the Camp Commandant at Camp W on the Isle of Man.

Following her interview with the Commandant, Taylour was released. She was given a police escort to Liverpool, the first stage of her journey to Ireland. Together, Taylour and the policewoman walked down the cliff road at Port Erin, Taylour feeling numb about the change: 'this walk with the policewoman towards freedom meant nothing. I could see nothing ahead. My friends were behind, but I didn't look back'.[6] After a rough sea passage, they reached Liverpool, made their way to Lime Street Station and found the platform for the London train. The plan was for Taylour to spend a few days in London before leaving for Dublin. The police escort left her, and for the first time in over three years she was free of supervision. She remembered later that, 'it was odd, almost frightening, to be off the leash. I found myself trying to feel natural'.[7] There then followed an incident that Taylour came to see as setting a pattern for future years, of being tailed and surreptitiously questioned by either Special Branch or the security services. She called these events 'pick-ups'.

The first 'pick-up' was a result of a delay to the loading of her baggage, which meant that she missed the London train and had to wait several hours for the next one. Taylour decided to find a cinema, watch a film, then look for a café. As she left the station she was picked up by a soldier, asking if he could walk with her. He asked her where she had come from and what she thought of the war, then the soldier 'got on to social and economic questions with amazing rapidity. Again I gave him natural answers, feeling sure I was being quizzed. No doubt I was expected to advise him to quit the Forces, to try and influence him! But I assumed his job was merely to record answers'.[8] She shook off her questioner, and went to a cinema for two hours, before finding a cafe where a woman joined her at the table, 'and led into the same sort of conversation that was introduced by the soldier. Again I answered without details or trimming. The reports would coincide!'.[9] It might be thought that Fay Taylour's suspicions were merely the result of having been detained for more than three years, having already been targeted by the security services. However, given the concern of the security services regarding Taylour, which, in part, focused on her willingness to speak out about her views, and the fact that she was of interest to MI5 for many years after her release, it is likely that the 'soldier' and the woman in the café were indeed checking on the newly released prisoner.

By the second week of October 1943, Fay Taylour was in Dublin, living with her uncle (her mother's brother) and his wife, Dr Ella Webb. Taylour luxuriated in the comforts of the Webbs' home, which she described as providing her with 'a comfortable guest bedroom and home cooking'.[10] But it was very much a temporary situation, as Taylour was a far from welcome guest. Her family in Dublin were strongly pro-British, and even on the horse cab journey from the docks to the Webbs' home, a cousin who had come to meet her made it clear how much he disapproved of her views on the war:

> As we jogged to my aunt's house his [the cousin] pro-British sentiments got the better of him. He told me severely that I would have to report to the police every week. This I would have had to do if living in England while the war was still on. I told him that I had instructions from English government authorities in London, which was final release from police supervision in the matter of reporting. And I reminded him that HIS country, Ireland, was neutral![11]

Clearly, Taylour had not been chastened by over three years in detention.

The situation in Ireland was marked by divisions between pro and anti-Nazi, or pro and anti-British (depending on one's standpoint) views. These divisions boiled over in Dublin following the death of Hitler and the defeat of Germany. On Victory in Europe Day, 8 May 1945, pro-British students at Trinity College celebrated by raising the Union flag above the Irish tricolour over College Green. This led to days of rioting by Irish Republican, pro-German and anti-British elements. Stones and fireworks were thrown at the Irish Police, the *Gardai*, who responded with baton-charges. The demonstrators included those who, according to the newly appointed Italian minister to Ireland, 'wore swastika badges in their button-holes and a few Nazi flags were waved around'.[12] In October 1943 there was no rioting, but it would not be hard for Taylour to find a milieu that suited her politics. She was quick to notice the difference between Britain at war and Ireland in the Emergency (as the war was termed by Dublin), 'you could jump on a Dublin bus and see swastikas pinned to the coats of passengers, while Churchill's V sign would be displayed by others!'.[13] Unsurprisingly, her aunt, who was pro-British, or in the eyes of Republicans, a 'West Briton', wanted Fay Taylour out of her house as soon as possible.

Taylour had 15 shillings to her name when she left the Webbs' house. She found a room to rent and started to look for a job. She felt 'terribly lonely', and although 'it was good to be back in Ireland, [...] I couldn't enjoy it, not yet'.[14] Taylour went to an employment agency run by two women. She was asked about her recent employment history and for references and had to explain where she had been for the previous three years. The two women agreed that they would not mention this but would still help Taylour to find work. Just then a 'smartly dressed young woman' came into the office, looking for a cook. Taylour said she could cook, and the employment agency women asked her to go to the next room while they talked to the potential employer. Much to Taylour's amusement, 'the moment the door shut behind me, in fact almost before it shut, the two middle-aged ladies said with an eager whisper that was bursting from them: "She's been in a British concentration camp!"'.[15] However, this revelation did not have quite the same impact in Ireland as it would have had in Britain, and Taylour's soon-to-be employer simply said, '"Oh", disinterestingly'.[16] In fact, the young woman:

> Told me laughingly that she was thrilled when she heard about the camp. She was governess in this house that needed a cook, and her special man friend was one of the German fliers that had been shot down in Ireland and was held in detention till the end of the war, by arrangement with England. There were quite a number of these fliers. They lived in camp but had full freedom. Some worked on farms, others worked for themselves, making art products. Her friend was an artist and sold his paintings. They were having their annual pre-Christmas party soon, and if I would take the job she would be free to go to the party![17]

Taylour's new employer was a widower, 'a quiet unassuming car dealer'.[18] She saw little of him and found her job as a cook uninteresting and was soon looking for a new post.

Taylour then had a number of short-term jobs. Following the cook's job, she took a job in rural Wexford, looking after an old brewery house. For a while there she thought she had found a new man. He was 'so good looking – so attractive – but an alcoholic', and her hopes in that direction evaporated.[19] That was followed by a job in Galway as a secretary to 'an eccentric Anglo-Irish landowner whose

Income Tax Returns were in a muddle like everything else around the place. He hadn't paid any taxes for eleven years, and my job was to find the forms and fill them up. I never found them'.[20] But none of these jobs did anything except help Taylour 'mark time', as she put it.

Fay moved back to Dublin after the atomic attacks on Japan, and the end of the war. Her new address was 31 Lad Lane, off Baggot Street, Dublin 2. She would be based there until late 1948. She applied for an Irish passport, although it was to be some time before she was successful in the application. Applying for the passport was a result of her realisation that a non-British passport would be useful for her. She erroneously thought that had she possessed one in 1940 then she would not have been detained. But her desire for an Irish passport was also motivated by her sense that she was no longer British, or British and Irish, but just Irish. While waiting for, and wrangling over, the new passport, she began to create a new circle of friends, usually of similar political views to herself. This, of course, led to renewed interest in her by both the Irish and British security services.

The Irish government had been alerted to the arrival of Taylour[21] and its security services kept a watch on her, as did British intelligence. She was aware of this, noting that 'Secret police were busy with my mail again, and one letter I wrote disappeared altogether'.[22] Tony Dickson, who had been released from internment at the beginning of 1941,[23] joined Taylour in Dublin, and the two renewed their relationship but, as before, he was responsible for causing her problems when he arranged for some members of the IRA to meet her. This caused immediate difficulties, as the Irish police sent detectives to interview her about the meeting. What took place at either meeting is unknown. It may be that Taylour's later enthusiasm for Irish Republicanism dated from this period. A British Intelligence report on Taylour from May 1946 noted that:

> In Fay TAYLOUR's view, despite Communist infiltration and the efforts of the de Valera police to discredit the I.R.A., the bulk of that movement was bitterly anti-English and pro-Nazi. She thinks that the I.R.A. have plenty of pluck, one instance of this being the shooting of an Irishman who had dared to serve in the Royal Navy during the war. It is understood that he was shot in the back.[24]

This seems to be more evidence of how Taylour's years in imprisonment and her continuing pro-Nazism had led to her seeing herself much less as British, and far more as Irish. She was undoubtedly a supporter of Irish Republicanism by the late 1960s, and the common anti-British, pro-German sympathies of most Republicans in 1940s Ireland in all probability reinforced both her sense of Irishness and her sympathy for armed militancy.

Taylour also renewed her links with Fr Fahey, the ultra-right cleric she had met at the beginning of 1940, and they kept up a constant correspondence. Unfortunately for the Irish security services, Fahey and Taylour were able to circumvent attempts to intercept their letters as Fahey used one of his student priests as a courier.[25] As well as revitalising old links, Taylour made new ones, becoming friends with Moira O'Byrne, who was later described by an intelligence source as 'an extremely active pro-German [who] did a great deal for the Germans in Dublin during the war [and whose] father is COUNT O'BYRNE, a Papal Count, and quite a big noise'.[26]

Ireland had to contend with the arrival of a disparate stream of political refugees from Europe. Foremost among these refugees were Breton and Flemish nationalists who had collaborated with Germany in the occupation of France and Belgium, hoping that a German victory would enable nationalist governments to be established in Brittany and Flanders.[27] The Dublin government was less than happy with these developments, and the Breton nationalists were surprised to find that their dreams of pan-Celtic solidarity did not extend very far into the corridors of power in the Irish capital. Other refugees also made their, usually temporary, home in Éire. Taylour became part of a new network of women and men on the ultra-right. For example, it was recorded that at the beginning of 1946 she was visited 'by a French Nazi sympathiser and his wife',[28] and that other associates included 'a young Luftwaffe man [... and] a half-German, one of two pro-Nazi sisters'.[29] Despite the defeat of Nazism in Europe, and the revelations of genocidal Nazi policy, it was reported that Taylour's 'enthusiasm for Germany is unlimited [...] and there is no doubt that it is the main interest in her mind'.[30] Given this, and her background in the UK, it is not surprising that, while in Dublin, she also linked up with Mrs MacNab, who acted as another go-between for Taylour and Fr Fahey. Mrs MacNab was the wife of an anti-Semite, John Angus MacNab, who had written an anti-Jewish column – 'Jolly Judah' – for the British Union's press prior to 1937, when he left the BU to help William Joyce and John Beckett establish the National Socialist League (NSL).[31] MacNab had also been detained under Regulation 18B. The MacNabs were in Dublin hoping to leave for a more congenial home than the post-war UK. In fact, they were smuggled from Cork to Spain on a Portuguese fishing boat. Once in Spain, MacNab carried on some political activity, eventually translating into English selected writings of the executed Falangist leader José-Antonio Primo de Rivera.

Friendships such as these sustained Taylour, and confirmed her political outlook, during these years spent in Dublin. She later described her friendships and social life at this time with fondness:

> The circle of friends I'd made in Dublin came to the cottage for tea or coffee, and I would visit them. What talks and debates we had! They comprised the sort of interesting people you find in Ireland's capital. Artists, writers, rebel dreamers (who fought for Ireland's freedom before becoming dreamers), scientists, philosophers, and the famous Dublin bachelors whose rooms are so full of books that the arms of the armchairs are book shelves. And indeed, what matter? For when they're at home, after an intellectual session at their favourite pub, 'tis the tay-pot they be squazing [...] Such gatherings in my cottage, usually from 8pm into the night, comprised many

of the interesting nationalities found in Ireland then, and maybe also today: French, German, Hungarian, Italian, Austrian, Scot, English, Irish and, as the Americans say: what have you. I was no longer lonely or alone.[32]

Fay Taylour's new-found circle represented, in fact, some of the flotsam from the wreck of Axis Europe, temporarily washed up in a neutral capital.

Fay also began to take an interest in domestic Irish politics. She attended at least one public meeting addressed by the Irish *Taoiseach* (Prime Minister), Éamon de Valera. He, of course, was one of the surviving Republican rebel leaders from the Easter Rising in 1916, avoiding execution, but being subsequently imprisoned in England. Later he would be a leader of anti-Treaty forces during the Irish Civil War, only to abandon armed struggle in 1926 to help create *Fianna Fáil*, which he led to electoral victory, becoming *Taoiseach* in 1937, a post he held until 1948, and again from 1951–54 and 1957–59. He was a strong social and economic conservative. With his background of armed militancy and imprisonment, he was the type of political leader that Taylour admired. In a letter to her father, 'Dordy', in October 1947, Taylour enthusiastically described de Valera's speech 'to a large street audience' in the run-up to the February 1948 general election, 'I went to hear him with great interest. His speech was quiet and restrained. He talked as if he were talking to children. The mud-slinging came from the other parties'.[33] Fascinatingly, in the same letter, Taylour claimed that she had previously met de Valera in person: 'it was the first time I heard him speaking in public though I had a private talk, or should I say audience, with him in his office at Leinster House once (not *so* many people have had tête-á-tête talks with their Prime Minster!).[34] By now, Taylour was very strongly identifying with Ireland, and went on to write of her admiration for the country in comparison with England: 'the healthy dislike and intolerance of Communism over here is good! Also of Freemasonry and Jewry, though not to such a great extent'.[35] De Valera's action in offering formal condolences to the German ambassador on the death of Hitler was, in all probability, something that Taylour agreed with. The fact that she wrote in this way to her father, a former British Army officer, and senior member of the Royal Irish Constabulary, who was strongly pro-British, shows a remarkable degree of insensitivity on Fay Taylour's part. Not to mention forbearance on the part of her father.

In the same letter to her father, she outlined her political views at that time. They were a mix of her wartime views with a renewed sense of anti-democratic politics which may well have been a product of the long discussions and debates with her post-war Dublin friendship circle of exiles from Axis Europe. Her starting point was that democracy was impossible:

> I am firmer than ever in my belief that no matter how fine an ideal Democracy may be, it just *cannot* work; and the people en masse in every country will always be just so much putty for the politicians and then cannon fodder for the politicians' generals.

The only hope to my way of thinking is in leaders like Hitler who will be strong enough and sufficiently unafraid to challenge and conquer the Money Power and all its attendant evils such as slums, unemployment, under-nourishment, ill-health, slumps, etc., and the biggest evil of all – Bolshevism, which anyway could not thrive and would automatically die if the other evils mentioned were cured.

But this 'only hope' after all isn't a hope, because even if such leaders were to be found, the Money Power could always crush them, as it has crushed them in the past, and will always rule.[36]

This is a very clear example of the way in which, for some of the ultra-right political detainees, detention had hardened their attitudes. Fay Taylour was not alone in her response to detention. In re-entering extremist politics in post-war Dublin and briefly in London, Taylour was stepping into a world that was, if anything, murkier than it had been in 1939–40. The ultra-right activists that emerged in London towards the end of the war, and in the late 1940s, were a hardened distillation from detention; more profoundly pro-Nazi than many of their pre-war colleagues and just as effectively infiltrated by the security services. Taylour's re-engagement with ultra-right politics seems to have been a reflection of her political convictions, her view that the Nazis had been creating a different, more equal, economic system, and her anti-Semitism. This was all reinforced by Taylour's experience of detention, and by her personality, which undoubtedly attracted her strongly to extremes of experience. The reborn 'movement' that emerged in 1944–45 and developed over the next few years in Britain, formed 'a somewhat bedraggled and shabby multi-headed phoenix struggling to re-emerge from the flames after 1945 in a deeply hostile society'.[37] The real driving force behind this struggling re-emergence was provided by younger men, and a few women, who had been detained.[38] These were detainees who had reacted to that experience by intensifying their pre-war beliefs and taking on board specifically wartime developments – largely related to the Nazi idea of a 'New Europe', characterised by pan-Europeanism – that enabled them to commit to a doomed, and increasingly isolated cause. Paradoxically, detention underpinned this small resurgence – 'that British fascism survived at all is largely due to internment, and to the sense of martyrdom it engendered within a hardened minority of internees'.[39] Fay Taylour was certainly a member of that 'hardened minority'.

Even in Dublin, Taylour was aware of the re-forming of small groups of ultra-right 'die-hards', with her papers containing an unsigned typescript, apparently by an Irish reporter, entitled, 'What of England's Pre-War Fascists?'. The report described a situation in London's East End that was depressingly familiar, with clashes between communists and the re-emerging fascists who operated a number of different, but small, groups. The unknown writer, 'S.D.', asked, 'But what of their future ... these lone [neo-fascist] fighters, each with their own small following ...? Shall they find themselves behind bars again? Or, in a world where anything might happen next, shall their day come at last?'.[40] Taylour seems to have kept herself abreast of these developments. In 1947 she met up with some fellow former detainees, and what she called 'another woman spy who looked me up with the usual questions', in Dublin.[41] It may well have been these ex-detainees who brought her more news of the revived ultra-right in London. The following year, 1948, Fay spent January, part of February, and from October onwards in London, picking up old acquaintances and reigniting her love life. She also used the opportunity to see for herself what ultra-right militants were involved in.

Taylour's return to London for six weeks from 28 December 1947[42] coincided with a number of small, pro-Mosley groups coming together to form what was to become the main Mosleyite effort in the post-war period – Union Movement (UM). The new movement was officially formed on 7 February 1948. However, in the few years immediately prior to that there had been a range of activities, often anti-Semitic, carried out by small, disparate groups.[43] One of these groups was the British League of ex-Servicemen and Women (BLeSW). This came under the direction of Jeffrey Hamm, a former British Union member who had been arrested in the Falklands and detained in South Africa where he had developed a strong pro-Nazi stance. Hamm led the League in a series of vicious clashes with Jewish ex-servicemen and others in the '43 Group'. This violent struggle became known as the 'Battle of Ridley Road', and ran from spring to autumn 1947, by which time people like Hamm had managed to draw Sir Oswald Mosley back into politics with a meeting in Farringdon.

It is unclear why Taylour chose this time to return to London, but it is certain that she had developed new contacts with the small circles of post-war Mosley-ites. For example, on 13 January 1948, an MI5 telephone intercept on Jeffrey Hamm noted that Taylour's name came up,[44] and in his autobiography, Hamm wrote about Taylour's rather flamboyant presence on the ultra-right scene at the time. Taylour developed a new network of political contacts in England during this period, yet she does not appear to have joined Union Movement,[45] although telephone intercepts of Mosleyites showed that her name was mentioned often. This activity was monitored by the security services, and it may well have been that MI5 was also, again, involved in *provocateur* activity. However, politics was not a sufficient interest for Taylour, and she had lost time to make up, both in personal and sporting terms.

Chapter Twelve

Rebuilding her Life

By 1947, Fay Taylour had had enough of 'marking time' in temporary employment and was thinking now of her future beyond Ireland, possibly in America. First, she was determined to gain Irish citizenship and an Irish passport and to find motorsport-related work. She was also keen to enjoy an enhanced social life, including re-engaging with some of her London-based lovers and friends. By the end of 1948, she had succeeded on all counts.

Fay believed that having an Irish passport would give her freedom from British government interference and would be a statement of her intensified sense of Irishness. She thought that gaining Irish citizenship and an Irish passport would be little more than a formality, having been born in Ireland to a long-established family. Yet it proved difficult. At first, she was told that she was not eligible for citizenship. She put that refusal down to British interference, and to de Valera's willingness to accept that. *The Irish Times* heard of the refusal, and wanted to run the story, but Taylour refused. She believed that the editor of that newspaper was in the pay of MI5 and she did not want it to exploit her story in order, she thought, to harm de Valera. Instead, she:

> talked with an influential senator of the government party, who was also a lawyer. I felt it best to insist without being antagonistic. I wanted that passport. The senator looked grave, and said my problem could be a test question in the House. He didn't want that, and sent me to a lawyer called Fitzgerald.[1]

Taylour's perseverance paid off. She received her Irish passport on 24 December 1947, more than two years after applying.

While living in Lad Lane, Dublin, awaiting the outcome of her passport application, Fay renewed her relationship with one of her pre-detention lovers, Tony Dickson. Tony had been detained too, until late December 1940, or early January 1941, but was in Dublin by 1945. Although Taylour had a low opinion of Tony Dickson's character, and did not view him as a potential husband, they had an on-off relationship as lovers. He had a history of making difficulties for her with the security services, including sending her the troublesome Forth Rail Bridge postcard in 1939, passing on information about her to Special Branch (something that she was very unlikely to have known about), and, in Dublin, arranging a meeting with IRA members. Three letters from Dickson to Taylour have survived, dating from July to August 1947. These give some impression of the relationship, and paint a rather poor picture of Dickson himself. Fay visited

Dickson in London in the summer of 1947. His surviving letters to her are dated during and after that visit. In the first letter, dated 9 July 1947, written while Taylour was in London, Dickson refers to what he felt was 'evident by your remarks on Monday, while in my room',[2] which seems to have been Fay Taylour attempting to end the relationship. Dickson claimed that he would prefer a 'death blow' to their relationship, rather than 'continual evasion' on Taylour's part.[3] He went on to blame himself for the failed relationship, in a rather self-pitying tone:

> I have naturally been a bitter disappointment to you, but I'm myself, and it does not finish – just disappointment – because I am mentally and physically sick – now weighing less than I have done since I can remember, almost – mainly due to worry – [illegible] by my inability to say No! No! No![4]

Interestingly, the tone of the letter agrees with the British security services' note on Fay Taylour's view of Dickson as 'gutless'.[5] He finishes by begging her to spend an afternoon or evening with him or at least to go to a show with him, before returning to Ireland. The content of this small batch of letters continues in a similar vein. They attest to Dickson's lack of business sense, his arguments with others, and his self-reproach over the failure of his relationship with Fay. He talked about emigrating to Spain or Kenya, where he claimed to have 'something definite',[6] and, interestingly, he said that he wanted no more to do with politics, asking Taylour not to mention him in relation to politics to anyone else. This seems to confirm that his initial involvement with the ultra-right in 1939–40 might well have been a result of Fay Taylour's personal influence. Although the letters only reveal some aspects of the relationship, it is, nonetheless, difficult to imagine the strong-willed Taylour with the very downbeat Tony Dickson.

Despite the precarious nature of their relationship, on Fay's next visit to London in January 1948, Tony was the first man she looked up. Her diary entry for 6 January 1948 notes, 'Plucked up courage look up T. but his day away'.[7] The following day she visited her Aunt Maud, then bought a green suit at the Saks sales in Bond Street. The next day she looked up Tony and they 'spent the evg. [evening] & night together'.[8] The next morning, they were still in bed when someone called and she 'had to hide T. in the bathroom. Awkward!'.[9] Her relationship with Tony was not what she wanted, and many of her friends who knew them both could not understand what she saw in him. For example, another of Taylour's lovers, Sandy, later described Tony as 'a weakly sap'.[10] Much later in her life, Fay Taylour wrote that she had never been able to find the right mix of sex and personality in one man, the only combination that would have enticed her to marry. The defect in Tony's case appears to have been in terms of his personality.

Although Taylour and Tony Dickson continued to meet and spend nights together, he was not the only man in her life at this time. The entries in her small pocket diary for 1948[11] attest that Taylour also met other men, sleeping with some of them. Of the men she slept with while in London, another long-term lover, 'Tufty' (never named in her writings), was perhaps the one to whom she was closest. On 20 January they met up and spent the night together. When Fay and Tufty first met is unclear, but there is a sense in her notes that she knew him from before the war. Tufty features repeatedly in the little 1948 diary, eight times up until she left London for Dublin on 12 February, including a record of particularly exciting sexual encounters with him. The two of them had a euphemism for such times, which they called 'getting the Boom!'.[12] The last week of January and the first of February appear to have largely been spent with Tufty. On 8 February, 'Tufty came evg. [evening] & stayed night & was discovered by maid next morning!'.[13] None of this meant that Taylour saw herself as permanently linked to Tufty. She was well aware that he had other lovers.[14] Tufty left London on 11 February, after calling on Taylour to say goodbye. After he had gone, she met up with Tony Dickson before she began her journey back to Dublin the next day, stopping off in Manchester to be interviewed by the Manchester *Sunday Chronicle*. She arrived in Dublin on 15 February and spent the afternoon with other male friends, a 'Captain J' and Sandy Proctor.

Alexander 'Sandy' Proctor, the 'Inventor & Patentee of The Tripod "All Weather" Harvesting System'[15] had been a captain during the First World War, and 'British Military Representative in Archangel' until 1919, and had liaised with the Bolsheviks in 1918 and 1919.[16] It is probable that Fay and Sandy were in a relationship, but what is clear is that Sandy had offered her a job in his firm on one of her earlier visits to London. She had understood that:

> I would be saleswoman and demonstrator in the field [...] I felt I could put my heart into it ... especially as I would be working for someone who thought our way 100% [i.e., a Fascist]! One of us! And I had no great wish to amalgamate with old racing acquaintances who had fought in the R.A.F. mostly. Also I hadn't raced since 1939.[17]

Unfortunately for Taylour, working for Sandy turned out to involve working as 'office boy in his cellar!',[18] which was his basement office at 58 Merrion Square, Dublin. Sandy was, nonetheless, obviously 'keen' on Fay, whom he always addressed as 'My dear Bold "Courageous"', or 'My dear Bonnie "Courageous"' in his letters to her.[19] Writing to Fay not long before she left for the United States in early 1949, Sandy wished her every success in America, and looked forward to seeing her return 'successful & triumphant'. He also predicted, incorrectly, that Taylour would be married in the USA, remarking that she possessed all the attributes to make any man the best wife. His comment suggests that they had a physical relationship: 'you will always be a dandy wife, worthy of a real good fellow to grace his home and table, not to mention the most important place!'.[20]

Meanwhile, Fay met and corresponded with some of her long-term women friends, including her old school friend, Amy, always referred to as 'Dormouse'; a friend from Lucerne Cottage days, Joyce Pope; her fellow detainee, Hildegarde Gooch ('Goochie'); and someone who only signed her letters with the nickname 'Enemy No. 1'. Taylour kept an exchange of letters from 'Enemy No. 1' from late 1947, all addressed from 16 Kensington Park Gardens, London, and all hailing Taylour as 'Dear Rebel'. The choice of nicknames suggests that Fay's friend may also have been involved in political activity, but the letters are chatty letters between friends, thanking each other for small gifts like new stockings and handkerchiefs. Fay Taylour tells her friend about her new office job with Alexander Proctor (i.e. Sandy) in Dublin, and problems with neighbours. She also writes about unformed plans to resume racing, or to move to South Africa. Her thoughts about reviving a racing career led 'Enemy No. 1' to respond, 'please don't go and kill yourself racing [...] please do not risk breaking your neck, for you're quite a nice person and there aren't too many of them going about'.[21]

In 1940, Fay Taylour's correspondence with Joyce Pope had caused her problems with the British security services. Joyce, a friend made in pre-war London, had moved to Gstaad, Switzerland. The security services were concerned that Pope was a 'cut out' between Taylour and others, perhaps in Germany. There does not, however, seem to have been any evidence for that suspicion, but the resumed Taylour–Pope correspondence confirms that they were friends with a similar political outlook. A card from Pope, featuring a painting of a lion by the minor German artist Hans Molfenter, dated 14 December 1947, Zürich, seems to be a reply to a letter from Fay. Pope explained that both she and her husband 'have just done 6 years psychoanalysis now and I teach. I also write and have published several things here and I hope to do the same with books later'; she went on to note that it was eight years since they had been in England and had 'lost touch and become central European in outlook'.[22]

Taylour also renewed contact with Hildegarde Gooch ('Goochie') who had been a fellow detainee in Holloway and had moved to Austria after the war. There Gooch had started a letting business, but post-war conditions in Austria were difficult, and Fay became involved in sending aid to her. Gooch had sent a £2 cheque to a mutual London-based friend to pay for an overcoat and a suit for Gooch's brothers in Austria. This mutual friend (Mary) wrote to Taylour, asking her to pass on the £2 cheque to Tony Dickson so that he could buy the menswear requested. The same letter also updates Taylour on family matters, and notes that 'I have terrible news from a friend of mine in Berlin and the poor thing expects a baby in Nov[ember 1948]. What a rotten world'.[23] There is, perhaps, some suggestion here that the pregnancy was the result of rape, which would be unsurprising in post-war Berlin.

One of Fay Taylour's oldest friends, whom she kept in touch with all her life, was her school friend 'Dormouse'. In a letter to Fay, dated 1 April 1948, from Marlborough Park South, Belfast, Dormouse chatted about her family – her husband, a surgeon at the Royal Victoria Hospital in Belfast, and their three sons – and their activities and plans. She also writes, clearly in response to a letter from Fay in which Fay had mentioned a possible future in the USA:

I do hope you managed to contact some big American business man to help you get your visa and so on. It's a perfect curse to be held up at the eleventh hour like that. I really do think you'd do well in U.S.A. and it's an excellent idea to lecture there and give demonstrations. Actually you'd be good giving talks. You have a nice voice, easy to listen to, and you know your subject well. You'd have to prepare notes but you'd soon get used to that.[24]

Although Fay Taylour's detention did not prevent her renewing many of her pre-war friendships, relationships with some members of her family were negatively affected. Her father and eldest sister, Hilda, seem to have been forgiving. Fay's first port of call on arriving in England on 29 December 1947 was her father and stepmother in Lymington, Hampshire. She spent time with 'Dordy', as she called her father, and met her sister, Hilda, for tea in Bournemouth on 3 January. But a short series of letters reveals the extent to which Taylour's politics and her war-time history had alienated other family members. For example, a visit made by Taylour to Dorothy Macardle, a Dublin aunt, led to a letter from Miss M.E. Carre, a relative living in London, saying how outraged Macardle had been by Taylour daring to visit her, and that Macardle wanted nothing to do with her. Taylour replied to Carre, who returned the letter unopened, writing on the envelope, 'Unread. Don't write letters to me. I have no intention of corresponding with you. If you upset your Aunt I will put the matter into the doctors hands'.[25] It was perhaps as well that Carre did not open the letter from Taylour, which began, 'You have written the biggest lot of bunk I have ever come across'.[26] The letter went on to say, among other things, that:

I can't see what the Nazis have to do with it! Dozens of my friends use the democratic privilege of thinking differently to each other. I don't confine my social circle in Dublin to the Luftwaffe. I don't refuse to speak to those who were drinking the health of Bolsheviks not so long ago, no matter what I thought of it! Many of my friends do not agree or think the same as I do politically. But we are good friends all the same. Those who would have us draw down an iron curtain between us because we differ politically are worse than the Bolsheviks themselves – far worse. They pose as Democrats, but are nothing less than loathsome hypocrits [*sic*]'.[27]

This was vintage Taylour, outspoken and impossible to browbeat. Miss Carre was probably wise to have returned the letter unopened.

Taylour's disappointment about how her job in Sandy Proctor's firm had turned out furthered her determination to make a fresh start in the United States. As she said at the time, 'I have been working, slowly but doggedly, since last November almost, to try and make the American idea come true'.[28] Her struggle to obtain a visa for the United States was occupying a good deal of her time, and was, to some degree, a replay of her difficulties in getting Irish citizenship. Her wartime past was already beginning to make itself felt. To make life more difficult, Taylour was given notice to quit her tenancy of Lad Lane, something that she thought she could legally challenge. That did not prove to be the case and she was subsequently evicted, leaving at one o'clock in the morning of 23 June.[29] This was a sad occurrence for her, as she said, 'I was so happy in that little cottage when things were going all right'.[30] Taylour then began a period of temporary stays with friends[31] until she moved into a hostel in Sandymount which she nick-named 'the Dump'. Despite this, other aspects of her life flourished. Following 'one hell of a good party at the O'Gs! [the O'Gormans] over after 4 AM!!' on 3 July she attended a midget car racing meet the next day at Santry.[32] Santry was at that time a greyhound racing track which, from 1948 until 1951, was also a speedway venue, used for both motorbike and midget car races. Fay had raced with midget cars before the war, and she appears to have taken the opportunity to reacquaint herself with the sport, saying in a letter a few months later, 'I did some training on the car speedway in Dublin recently, and satisfied myself that my hand is well in!'[33]

In between hard partying, and Fay's slow but determined efforts to find an opening in the US, and to gain a visa, she had brief relationships with other men. One of these was 'Michael', who featured several times in her 1948 diary, includ-ing for visits to a Dublin club called 'The Dungeon' (although this may have been Taylour's nickname for the place). Towards the end of July, however, she met Richard St Barbe Baker, more famously known as 'The Man of the Trees'. He was a botanist and biologist, and a pioneer in the promotion of reforestation around the world. He founded the Men of the Trees organisation which continues to this day under the title of the International Tree Foundation.[34] Directly responsible for planting millions of trees, he was also a prolific author and campaigner and in the post-war period gave numerous lectures on ecology and reforestation. Taylour attended one of these lectures on 21 July 1948, held by the Arts Club in Dublin at Trinity College. It was, in fact, part of a short summer school held by Men of the Trees at Trinity College. Taylour was greatly impressed by Baker, and on the 24th she had lunch with him, and they spent the afternoon together before he left Dublin.[35] It seems as if Baker was impressed by Fay Taylour, and that he asked her if she would be the 'correspondent' in Ireland for Men of the Trees. She declined the offer, explaining that she intended to move to the USA, and, in a subsequent letter, Baker regretted that but complimented Taylour:

> I admire your splendid enthusiasm and feel sure you would make a fine fist of anything you undertake – for that reason I am sorry you will not be able to act as correspondent for Men of the Trees in Ireland. However perhaps on your return from America you may be able to help us.[36]

For several months Fay Taylour made every effort to restart her automotive career, and make plans to leave for the United States, while enjoying parties, friendships and relationships. She continued to see her close male friends, Sandy Proctor and Tony Dickson, but also saw a man called 'Tommy', and spent the night with another called 'Peter'.[37] She also went shopping and met with women friends. As well as continuing her somewhat hectic social life, a new element entered Taylour's life in the summer of 1948. Although she was an inveterate letter writer, and often appears to have penned amusing 'doggerel' verse, on 1 August her diary entry was 'writing all day'. During that month she spent eight days writing a short story, or, as Taylour saw it, a novella, entitled *Rectified*.[38]

The manuscript remained unpublished, although she sent it to a woman friend, L. McGlynn, probably for critical feedback. What is of note is that writing became an increasingly important part of her life as time went on, and would, eventually become her primary activity.

For the remainder of 1948, Fay Taylour struggled with the plan to restart her career in the USA. She faced two tasks: firstly she had to find some occupation, preferably involving motorcars, and secondly she had to obtain a visa. Her focus on the USA was largely due to her recognising that getting a motor-industry or motor-racing job in the UK was unlikely, not least because of her detention during the war. In order to obtain a visa for the USA, she had to fulfil a variety of criteria, most notably having the firm offer of a job or self-employment that would pay her way. The US embassy in Dublin refused her a visa outright, and she was finally compelled to obtain one from the embassy in London. As for an occupation, Taylour pursued a number of ideas that she thought might bring employment, including giving lectures, radio talks, motor sales work and demonstrating cars, or a combination of all four. In June, for example, she wrote to the Director of Lectures, Columbia Concerts Inc, 113 West 57th Street, New York, outlining her suggestions for a lecture series 'putting my motoring career to some use [...] combined if possible with appearances at motor showrooms and speedways'.[39] She had also sent Columbia Concerts press cuttings about her racing career, and explained that, 'I raced and made records in Australia, New Zealand, India, South Africa and Europe, [although] my tours never touched America as women were not permitted to race there. And so this will be my first visit to your country'.[40] However, she soon discovered that lecture tours were booked years in advance, and there was little likelihood that this would be a way forward. An American correspondent called Dixon also suggested that she think even more widely, and in a letter of 8 August said that she might consider looking for a job as 'a personnel manager in some industry – automotive perhaps – or textiles'.[41]

Matters changed suddenly in October 1948, however, when Taylour visited the London Motor Show. This was the first post-war International Motor Exhibition and was held at Earls Court between 27 October and 6 November. It was the thirty-third such show, which had been scheduled for 1939. The show was attended by the many UK car manufacturers, all of whom were firmly in the business of 'export or die', as the government sought to pull the country out of the crippling debt that fighting the war had entailed. Taylour later recalled:

> At the London Motor Show, at the eleventh hour, I struck lucky. A London dealer, for whom I'd sold cars, introduced me to a Hollywood dealer who specialised in sports cars! The Hollywood man engaged me, though he really didn't mean it. American males were too prejudiced to stomach a woman selling sports cars.[42]

The dealer might not have 'meant it', but he had given sufficient of an opening for Fay to exploit. She immediately wrote to Mr L. Van Dyke, the vice-president of the company, International Motors, who were the agents in California for MG and Jaguar,[43] explaining that she had been engaged by his man in London. He passed her on to the President, Mr Roger Barlow, based in Los Angeles, and she wrote to him on 24 November. In that letter she rehearsed her various motor racing successes and skills and suggested that in addition to selling British sports cars for the company, she would be able to demonstrate those cars even if she, as a woman, was not permitted to race them. She finished by asking Barlow to provide her with the documentation needed to obtain the visa from the US Embassy in London: 'it is to be a letter to me confirming that you have engaged me to work for you in the sales etc. of automobiles, and specifying the terms, and period of engagement'.[44] Those terms had, she said, been agreed with Van Dyke as £20 per week, plus commission, with an initial three-month contract with the possibility of extension. She subsequently met the company vice-president in London towards the end of November, writing to him a few weeks later to remind him that a completed contract was needed for the visa. In the same letter, dated 10 December, she said that she had booked a passage to San Pedro, Los Angeles, on the Royal Mail Lines ship *Loch Ryan*, scheduled to sail on 12 March 1949.

Taylour now began preparations for her move to California. This involved selling personal items to raise funds to pay for her passage to America and saying her goodbyes to friends. Sandy Proctor wrote to her from Ireland to 'hope & pray for your success & future happiness' and again, not long before she sailed, to say that he hoped to be able to see her off to wish 'you "Bon Voyage" & a successful & triumphant return at least in my lifetime, so that I may share in both your joy & victory!'. Interestingly, Proctor also promised to send her 'a booklet or two & probably a few leaflets which might prove of interest to someone someday'. It is likely that these were political leaflets, given Proctor and Taylour's shared views.[45] From Austria, Fay's friend, Hildegard Gooch, wrote to wish her well, writing, 'I am so very glad that your departure is fixed at last! It must have been dreadful this suspense! And what a triumph for you, after all the doubting! Now all that remains for me to hope is, that you will find life over there to your liking!'. She went on to urge Fay to write from the USA as soon as she could.[46] While booking her passage, Fay met up with Lionel Wills, who was still working in his family's shipping firm. His office was only a few doors from the Royal Mail Line's offices. Wills was the one man whom she felt that she might have married, had he asked her. Misunderstanding between the two of them in the late 1920s meant that Wills had married someone else, yet they remained in touch. It is not clear who initiated the meeting in 1949, but Fay Taylour later wrote of the meeting that, 'his marriage has cracked up, and he is in the throes of getting a divorce'.[47] In between seeing friends and her father and writing to others, she sold possessions such as her radio, which raised £40, and a pendant-brooch for £100, both of which went to a friend, Ethel, on the Isle of Man.

By March 1949, Fay was ready. The planned sailing from London was delayed from the 12th until the 16th.[48] At last the time came, and she posed for a professional photograph of her stepping into a large car, surrounded by baggage, on the first step to her new life in America.

Chapter Thirteen

To the United States – Hollywood

Fay Taylour arrived in San Pedro, Los Angeles' port district, in May 1949. Paul Barlow, her manager at International Motors, met her and the next day took her to the showroom at 5670 Sunset Boulevard. There International Motors sold British sports cars by MG, Jaguar, Morris, Talbot, and Healey. Taylour worked alongside another salesperson, the former silent film star Pat Aherne. Like Taylour he was an expatriate, but from England, as well as being a motorcyclist and former boxer. By the late 1940s, Pat Aherne was still doing some film work, mostly in uncredited parts, and his main source of income was motor sales. His younger brother Brian became a much more successful actor in film and television. Taylour relished this new milieu – a mixture of motorsports and film. British sports cars were popular with moneyed actors as their small size and weight and comparatively large engines meant that they were much more fun to drive than heavier American cars.

Soon after starting work in the dealers, Taylour wrote a long and detailed letter to 'Bert' Henly of Jaguar Cars Distribution in London. The letter gives a fascinating picture of Los Angeles, and the car business, from the informed view of a newly arrived Fay. She began by describing her excitement at the standard of the showroom, and her enchantment at the high material standards:

> What a beautiful showroom! On the best strip in Hollywood ... Sunset Strip. It's like a large ballroom with a nice polished wooden floor, and from the large window across the back is a beautiful panoramic view, which looks like fairyland at night with all the coloured lights of the boulevards, the advertisements, and the floodlit buildings, and the searchlights chasing each other across the sky (the latter advertising not military!).[1]

Coming from the UK, which was in the process of post-war reconstruction, exporting most consumer goods to pay war debt, and with a population still facing rationing, Taylour was amazed by the high standards of Los Angeles:

> It is unthinkable here to offer anyone a flat, or even a room, without a bath attached. That is still a luxury in England! It is unthinkable, even in the cheapest snack bar, that the cream and sugar shall not be covered, or that the cakes are exposed for the flies to sample! It is unthinkable that the poor man who dines in a drug store shall be given less food than the richer man [...] The food at some of the restaurants here is stupendous! I still can't believe it![2]

It was a far cry from Taylour's 'bread and cheese' days in Dublin, or the rationing and shortages of the UK. It also shows that she was alive to the daily realities of economics, something that had long been a part of her world view.

Taylour's letter to Henly then turned to car sales and Jaguar cars. She explains why British sports cars were popular, especially the latest Jaguar, the XK 120:

> Our small English cars intrigue them, but the Jaguar intrigues them most of all! The sports job, the XK '120', which decorates one side of our large window attracts much attention and brings many in. Sporting motorists brake hard when it catches their eye from outside, and pull up and come in. There are plenty of sporting motorists even though the industry does not give them sports cars. They comprise those who build or have built 'hot rods' (as hotted-up motor cars are called), and also those who appreciate well-built automobiles. It is good to see their enthusiasm for the Jaguar chassis Mark V, to see them purring over details of British workmanship.[3]

The XK 120 was Jaguar's first post-war sports car, which the company began to produce in 1948. At the time it was the fastest production sports car anywhere, with a top speed of 120mph. Quantity production had just begun at Jaguar's works in Coventry. Taylour realised how important this car was to Jaguar's sales fortunes in California and lamented that the XK 120 was about to be returned to England. Her letter to Henly also included a list of comments and criticisms of details that could be improved on with regard to the XK 120 for the American market. These included seats, steering wheel position, gear lever angle, door height, bumpers, body metal, hood, and seat piping. Taylour asked Henly to pass on her comments 'to Coventry'.[4] Interestingly, under 'body' Taylour suggested that the aluminum body of the car be changed for steel, something that Jaguar did in 1950.

The Jaguar XK 120 was not, however, returned to England, for the very next day Fay Taylour sold the car to Clark Gable. The sales record card she completed for the deal shows that Taylour's sale was the first Jaguar XK 120 sold, chassis number 670003, and the car still exists.[5] Fay noted on the Clark Gable sales card:

> Talked enthusiastically about sports cars, and I told him I'd raced them. I didn't recognise him and he didn't give his name – but before he left I asked for his name and he said 'Gable'. I said: 'not Clark by any chance'? and immediately I felt silly because every man in the short time I've been here has been telling me he is some film star. So when Mr Gable said 'yes', he was Clark, I stared him severely in the eye and asked, 'are you *sure*'? Then he smiled and I recognised the dimples. And then he stayed and talked about the racing film 'TO PLEASE A LADY' now being made.[6]

That film, released six months later, featured Clark Gable as Mike Brannan, a midget car racing driver at loggerheads with influential newspaper columnist Regina Forbes, who was played by Barbara Stanwyck. Brannan's career appears to be wrecked by adverse comments in the press made by Forbes, but, in a true

The Taylour family before the First World War. Herbert and Helen with their three children. Fay is in the centre in a hat, with her elder sister, Hilda, on her left, and her younger sister, Enid, with her mother.

Last year at Alexandra College, Dublin. Fay behind a school friend, Iris Crozier, in 1922.

With the family car in England. Fay Taylour at the wheel of the Taylours' green 10hp Singer car.

Broadside Queen. Fay Taylour at speed, demonstrating the 'leg trailing' style of dirt-track cornering.

Lionel Wills during the International Six Days Trial, 1928. Wills was instrumental in helping Fay Taylour break into speedway motorcycle racing. He was also an important man in her emotional life.

On tour, Perth, Australia, 1929. Studio portrait of Fay Taylour taken during her first speedway tour of Australia and New Zealand. Note the steel-capped left boot, necessary for broadsiding.

Early years of midget car racing in England. Fay Taylour broadsiding in a midget car race at Lea Bridge, 1936.

Fay Taylour on the water. In South Africa, with Dick Cole, 1939. Taylour won a 12-hour race in this boat, powered by an 8hp outboard.

(*Above*) Pre-race publicity. Fay Taylour advertising for the midget car races at Malvern, Johannesburg, 1939.

(*Opposite, above left*) Dublin, 1946. Dreaming about a return to the racetrack.

(*Opposite, above right*) 'Tufty'. One of Fay Taylour's long-term lovers. Her flat in Lad Lane, Dublin, was full of photographs of him.

(*Opposite, below*) Leaving for the USA. London, 1949, and Fay Taylour leaves England, hoping to build a new life in America.

A Jaguar for Clark Gable. Selling British sports cars in Hollywood, Fay Taylour sold the first Jaguar XK120 in the USA to Clark Gable.

On the US midget car circuit. Fay Taylour in a midget racer, 1950.

An Irish woman driving an English car. Fay Taylour by a pre-race decorated Austin in the US, advertising 'Fay Taylour. The World's Fastest Woman Driver'.

Midget car racing, Portland, Oregon, 1951. Just another stage in her US coast-to-coast midget racing tour.

Trouble ahead. Happy racing in the USA, unaware that soon she would be banned from the country.

Racing in Sweden. Following her ban from the USA, Fay Taylour had to restart her career yet again, racing a 500cc Cooper in Sweden, September 1952.

Brands Hatch, 1953.

Midget car racing in Australia, 1953. After her motorcycle speedway success over two decades before, Fay Taylour returned to Australia to race for Empire Speedways. An advertisement, highlighting her successes in Sweden.

Miss Fay Taylour

World's Champion Woman
Speedcar Driver

Racing in Australia for:
EMPIRE SPEEDWAYS PTY. LTD.

1953

Fay in her 500 "Cooper" during her recent
successful Swedish Tour, Sept. 1952

Broadsiding, in a midget car.
Fay Taylour in a Ford V-8 60
at Tracey's Speedway,
Melbourne, 1953.

Publicity shot,
Australia, 1953.

Mercedes-Benz advertising car, Melbourne, 1953. 'World's Fastest Woman Driver'.

The 50-year-old speed queen. Publicity shot taken in South Africa, 1954.

Back in the USA, 1955. Fay Taylour's motorsports career was drawing to a close. After this tour, she would have only one more midget racing tour left before retiring from the track.

Retired from racing, 1959. A self-portrait taken at 'the Shack' in California. Fay Taylour was writing her autobiography and trying to come to terms with the end of her life in motorsports.

Hollywood romance, all ends well between Brannan and Forbes. What is interesting is that around the time Clark Gable was telling Fay Taylour about this midget car racing film, she was thinking about racing with midget cars in the United States and would also face plenty of difficulties.

Some of the opening sequences of *To Please A Lady* feature scenes from actual midget car races. With a high power-to-weight ratio, racing with these cars was, and is, a dangerous affair. The sport had originated in the US, with cars initially racing on indoor cycle racing tracks, but by the late 1940s both outdoor and indoor tracks were in use. For a former motorbike speedway racer like Fay Taylour, midget car racing must have seemed both familiar and different, a form of speedway on four wheels. Still waiting to sit her California driving test, Fay was taken to a midget car race at Gilmore Stadium by a mechanic for her firm, Phil Hill. He drove her to the race in his 'hot rod'. The sounds and sight of the cars awoke her desire to race again:

> The sound and smell of the racing cars make me restless. I beg for a ride. These midgets, powersliding the curves on the oval dirt track, take me back to the days when I pleaded for a ride on the London Speedways ... and the answer is now the same: 'What! A woman on the DIRT track! Impossible! She'd never have the nerve'.[7]

Such a response was, to Fay Taylour, 'still the same challenge'.[8] She had to wait a while before she started racing midget cars, but her first car race in the US came on 24 July 1949. A new racing venture focused on foreign cars was started by dealers and drivers involved in the promotion of foreign-built sports cars. Taylour duly appeared at the California Sports Car Club's first 'foreign car' race at Carrell Speedway, where she raced an MG against Frank Early.[9] Taylour's racing led to John Edgar, owner of a 'stable of fast racing cars', asking her to race for him.[10] She was delighted. But, yet again, she ran into the problem that women would not be allowed to race. At first, the official response was 'no women' could enter the foreign car racing, and this prohibition was further strengthened by the banning of professional drivers, which Taylour was. She was faced 'with the fact that America's auto world is a man's world'.[11] The disappointment led her to resign from her car sales job to focus on two things: racing, and an attempt to write her sporting story for a Hollywood film. The first of these was a familiar challenge, and one that she was determined to meet – 'to convince the promoters that I would have the nerve to throw these cars on full throttle into a powerslide, and that a woman would also have the skill to stay on the gas pedal and control that slide, was a battle more powerful than the cars themselves!'[12] That determination to return to racing was her primary goal, but she also began her long, and eventually unsuccessful, attempt to publicise her racing career in print or on the screen. It may have been that the conversation with Clark Gable about his midget car racing film *To Please A Lady* put the idea of a film of her racing life into her head, or perhaps it was simply living in Hollywood. Whatever the reason, she realised that a film of her life would provide her with ammunition to break down the anti-women prejudice in racing and provide her with sufficient financial security to enable her to race without bothering about the money concerns that plagued her life.

Shortly after leaving the car sales post, and starting to write her racing auto-biography, Fay met an old track adversary from her pre-war racing. This was the Australian racer Frank Brewer, who was in California racing midget cars. Brewer knew how skilled Taylour was and arranged a trial midget car race for her to show what she was capable of. The exhibition drive was held at the El Monte speedway, and Taylour made the best time, leading to 'my first write-up in an American auto paper'.[13] She had already had several 'write-ups' in the Californian press, with, for example, an article entitled, 'British hurry up gal here to throw exhaust and dust at speedy males', which appeared in the *Daily News*, Los Angeles, on 9 December 1949. That piece gave a potted history of Taylour's motorcycle and car racing career before the war. It went on to say, 'over here, she's willing to start at the bottom, and has. Always the sole woman against a field of men, she has won twice and placed twice in her only four starts since she came to this city from England early last summer'.[14] The article has all the signs of having been written from an interview that the journalist, Norman Frisch, conducted with Taylour. She was an old hand at publicity, which was important to her as she knew that if she did not sell her story at every opportunity then no one would. She had also featured in columns in the California press on 23 July, 24 July, and 14 November 1949. Although the general press was important, her appearance in the US auto-sport press after her exhibition race at El Monte speedway was more so, for that was a way to reach promoters. She was back on the track and beginning to get the attention that she knew was essential to staying there. That year, 1950, saw her racing on various speedway tracks, including Culver City, Gardena, Balboa Stadium, and Carrell Speedway, where she raced in August and November 1950, and again in March 1951.[15] Midget car racing was dangerous, highly skilled, and, for the promoters, a great crowd-pleaser. Taylour, who was now in her mid-forties, still possessed the nerve and skill, and still thrilled at the experience:

> Power-sliding fast midget cars round these tracks takes infinitely more skill and nerves than driving a sports car at twice the speed on a road circuit. But the easier and more suitable racing is closed to me. If it wasn't, I would still hanker after the thrill of that daring controlled skid – not always controlled. That fight on the curves for mastery … the challenge of tackling the harder job. I'm happy on the dirt tracks.[16]

As well as racing midget cars in 1950, Taylour also began competing in 'jalopy' races (stock car racing). If midget car racing was seen as dangerous, it still was not enough in the eyes of the promoters to keep paying crowds pouring into the stadiums. This profit impetus meant that, as Taylour put it, the 'public must be fed on something new [...] drivers have become more skilled, and crashes fewer. Something must be done to renew interest'.[17] That something was 'jalopy' racing, for, as Taylour realised, the cars 'turned over easily since they were not built for racing. They are cheaper than real race cars. There is enough tin all around to protect the boys when they crash. Safety belts and re-enforced tops are the rule. The boys drive for less money'.[18] Her first jalopy race was at Culver City:

> I line up for my race and stab that gas pedal same as I do a thoroughbred racer. For one lap I am out in front. On the second I go clean through the fence. The heavy protective crash fender on the car is stronger than the safety fence. I am pulled back on the track. If the wheels are hanging on, even by a thread, I can continue.
>
> They are! I line up once more, and finish second.
>
> When the races are over we climb out of these chariots through a hole in the roof. Some have no roofs, just the protective steel bar for when they roll over. Paint, and fittings such as windows and wheel fenders, have been torn off. The doors are strapped so they won't warp open during the hectic broadside skid on the bends.
>
> They look to me like bombed-out houses, the blackened skeletons visible in many parts of London still. And the bizarre advertising adds to the illusion. Every car has writing on it. So have the bombed-out houses.
>
> But you don't need to be handsome to be liked. The public are getting fond of these mongrels.[19]

These races brought the 1950 race season to a close, and Taylour returned to Hollywood to focus on turning her racing story into a film.

From 1949 onwards, Fay Taylour wrote numerous versions of her autobiography. Some of these were semi-fictionalised, in others the names used for her friends, lovers and others were pseudonyms, while further versions were straight autobiography. Her aim in this writing and rewriting of her life story was two-fold. Firstly, she hoped to generate an income that would underpin her earnings from racing, which were unreliable and often cancelled out by the costs associated with competing. Secondly, as time went on, and especially after she finally retired from the race track, she sought to establish her legacy. There was also a more personal aspect to her autobiographical writings, which included many of her later letters to friends. There was a sense that she was ordering her life, taking stock of her experiences and her choices. But in 1950 her immediate hope was that she would be able to sell her racing story to Hollywood.

Car racing films have been a perennial genre for the Hollywood movie industry since Fatty Arbuckle appeared in the short 1913 car racing comedy, *The Speed Kings*. In 1941, the film *Blonde Comet* featured the actress Virginia Vale, whose character, Beverly Blake, races against men all over Europe before returning to the US where she falls in love with a male driver. This film may well have had some resonance with Fay Taylour as she was careful to write into her film proposal a romantic ending, something that in her own life she avoided. At some point earlier in 1950, Taylour had given Gil Stewart, a part-time actor and car salesman, a file of material relating to her racing career in the hope that he might find someone in the film world interested in her story. Taylour had lost touch with Stewart, so drove to Studio City in a secondhand car which had cost her $25. She knew that Stewart had a friend at Universal-International studios, so she went there and was sent to the Story Department. Nobody there knew Stewart's address, but she found herself in conversation with an editor, Lee Phillips. He was interested in Fay's racing story as he said that Universal was looking for a film idea to offset the Clark Gable film, *To Please A Lady*, released by MGM. However, Phillips told Taylour that the studio could only accept material through an agent.

The next day, Fay Taylour left an 82-page synopsis entitled *One Thing Lasted* or *One Love Lasted*, along with press cuttings about her career, with Hollywood agent Laura Wilck of 6715 Hollywood Boulevard. The synopsis was prefaced by a statement summarising the main theme of the story:

> The main theme is the pull between the man and the racing machine. Men who interested her meant more till they were conquered.
>
> Auto racing was never conquered because there were always fresh races to be won.
>
> One man also was never conquered.
>
> These two loves clash in the final chapter, when her effort to master racing masters the man, and a choice has to be made between the two.[20]

Fay Taylour was astute enough to realise that no story of a woman conquering racing would sell to Hollywood unless it was shot through with romance and the eventual triumph of that romance over her sporting career.

While Taylour waited to hear from Laura Wilck, she continued to try and improve the 'shack' that she had rented. She was in dire financial straits and was forced to obtain a few weeks of social security payments. A good deal depended on the film proposal. A few days later, Wilck telephoned Taylour with the news that Universal Studios' story editor had accepted the story for filming. Wilck had also brokered a four-part contract for Fay:

> It will be a studio deal, their scenario writers will put it in order, and one of the producers attached to the lot will handle it. Rosalind Russell and Ann Blythe are ready for the story. One of them will be the star.
>
> For me, it will be a four-way deal, she [Wilck] says. They will pay me for the story, engage me as technical advisor during the shooting, use me to cover for the star in the driving sequences; and last but not least they will use me for the publicity tour preceding showing, since it will be the story of my racing.[21]

Wilck went on to say that she would call again to arrange the trip to Universal studios to sign the contract. It was amazing news for Taylour, with the clear potential to solve her constant financial worries, give her worldwide publicity, and, in all probability, open new doors for her.

Taylour immediately went out to celebrate, dining at a good restaurant and 'living on red steaks for the next few days, happily and confidently awaiting the call'.[22] She also enjoyed a moment of revenge against a group of 'foreign car' male racing drivers, the people she, in part, blamed for being banned from that racing. Coming out of the Gotham Restaurant she met a group of the men, who told her that they had heard that she was racing 'jalopies', which they thought amusing. She knew that these part-time racers were all desperate to be involved in making road sports films, particularly about road racing. Taylour enjoyed herself telling them her news, thinking, 'that'll teach 'em to put me out of the racing!'.[23] The next day, Laura Wilck telephoned Taylour again, saying that preparations were going ahead and that the contract would be ready in the next few days. Ten days later, Taylour received another telephone call, this time from the story editor, Lee Phillips, who had bad news for her:

> The producer, slated to do the picture, will not do it. But why, I ask. I thought it was all set. I'm dumbfounded.
> So did I, Phillips replies, but he just won't do it, and gives no explanations. I have tried and tried to arrange a meeting between you and him, Phillips continues, but without success.[24]

This was a real setback for Taylour. She attributed it to the influence of the group of male drivers who had engineered her exclusion from foreign car racing. That group included the dealer she had worked for on Sunset Boulevard, who also knew of her political life and detention during the war.[25] The dealer had connections with many people in Hollywood and had also written stories for the studios. Universal did, however, make a film about road racing a few years later which featured a red-headed female protagonist, though not a driver. That film was *Johnny Dark*, and starred Tony Curtis and Piper Laurie. According to Fay, the film also featured sports cars provided by the dealer, with many of the drivers being the men whom she blamed for the loss of her film opportunity.

At the beginning of 1951, Taylour was faced with the realisation that, 'I seem no better off than when I arrived in California nearly two years earlier'.[26] She had no races lined up for the forthcoming season, the great hope of a film of her racing had gone, and the local midget car race promoters had built upon using women drivers by organising women-only races for unpaid amateurs, rather than paying women like Taylour $25 a race. In this difficult situation, Taylour accepted an invitation from a race drivers' club to speak at one of their meetings. Afterwards, the club president, Joe Vollkommer, suggested to Fay that she advertise in one of the US-wide speedway newspapers saying that she was looking for races for the 1951 season. With no other obvious avenues in front of her, Taylour spent almost her last $10 on an advertisement. There were only three replies, but one of them looked promising.

The opening was from a promoter in Seattle who sent her travelling expenses to fly to the city. Instead, she spent most of the money on buying a new suit, then took the coach to Portland where she joined the aeroplane for its final hop to Seattle where she was able to 'trip down the gangway in my new suit to a reception at the Press Club'.[27] The promoters clearly knew how to publicise their racing, and their new female driver, as Taylour was greeted at the airport by state senator Wayne Morse, and a 'beautiful sign-painted car'[28] was loaned to her for daily driving. The signage probably headlined her name and the dates and times of her races. Later in the year, a contract with other promoters included details of signage on another such car. Drawings of the correct details of the sign were included, stating: 'Although the words "Fay Taylour" should be the largest, and stand out alone, it is the time place and date of the racing, that the public must be reminded of, that is important. But the public will take all that in once the car attracts them'. The 'Fay Taylour' signage was accompanied by the legend, 'World's Champion Woman Racer'.[29]

Taylour was also delighted to discover that 'Shorty' Templeman's 'very fast racing car had been hired for my track appearances'.[30] It was Templeman's No. 6 car, and as Templeman was one of the great midget car drivers of Oregon and Washington State, where he was five times state champion before his death in a midget car race in 1962, it was just the car that Taylour needed. She was back in her racing element, and her racing career, with its attendant publicity and attention, was alive once more.

Chapter Fourteen

Racing from Coast to Coast

The day after landing in Seattle Taylour was taken to see the track, which turned out to be asphalt and not a dirt track. This was a new surface as far as Taylour's midget car racing experience went and she had to master a new technique quickly. After practice runs, she was taken on a rapid promotional tour, 'from radio station to newspaper offices. From a boxing match to a dance hall. Any interview or introduction that will publicise the racing is not overlooked by speedway manager Joe Woelfert'.[1] Taylour was just as much in her element with publicity efforts as she was on the track. She was an outgoing, confident woman, and a striking figure in a world dominated by male promoters, managers, car dealers and drivers. Nevertheless, with so much depending on this new opening, and the issue of the asphalt track, she confessed that as the first race on the Friday night approached, she was 'nervy'. But she need not have worried. She won her race on the Friday night and, despite losing on the Saturday night (which she attributed to the winner having a faster car), the finish was close, and, more importantly, she claimed it was a record crowd at the track. Fay Taylour was forty-seven years old and still winning races and drawing crowds.

Fay's performance in Seattle led directly to a new engagement. A 'promoter from Portland [Oregon] with a 10-gallon hat and a fat cigar'[2] stopped her after the second race to ask her to race for him in Oregon. This cigar-smoking promoter was probably Paul Ail, President of Northwest Sports Inc., Portland, Oregon. After telephone conversations between Ail and Taylour, Northwest Sports sent her a letter of confirmation (to all intents a contract) on 29 June 1951.[3] The letter is of interest as it details the earnings she could expect racing midget cars in Seattle at the Jantzen Beach Arena, Portland, on 12 July:

> Northwest Sports, Inc., guarantees you $100 against 10 per cent of the gross gate receipts, less taxes, above the average gate. For example, if the average gate is $3,000 and the gate for your appearance is $5,000, you will receive $200 or 10 per cent of the difference which will include the $100 guarantee.[4]

All her travelling expenses and a three-night stay at the Multnomah Hotel would be paid by Northwest Sports. Also, if Taylour could arrive early then Northwest Sports would 'make arrangements for meeting the press and all other appearances – radio, theatre, etc – that can be worked in. We also will try to arrange a sponsorship [...] with a local motor car company'.[5] Finally, the letter asked Fay to send publicity material to start advertising her appearance. A week later, Taylour was in Portland, making the fastest time in a midget car race, then, the following week, beating a well-known driver who had not long won the Mexican Road Race.

These successes in Seattle and Portland enabled Taylour to begin touring under her own management: 'I sell myself by long distance telephone, following the calls with the dispatch of photographs and clippings from previous appearances. Then I get on a train and view the new terrain out of the window when I'm not busy with the typewriter'.[6] She raced at tracks in Washington State, Oregon, and back in California at San Diego. She raced midget cars and stock cars, having her first somersault in San Diego during a 300-lap event:

> I experience my first somersault in a stock car. But it was not unexpected. The car I should have driven was taken by the mechanic who unfortunately had full charge of preparations. He left me with the lighter, and quite unsuitable 'Henry J' sedan ... and when the track became too rough and bumpy for it, it turned over!
>
> I am then left hanging upside down by the safety belt till the red light stops the other cars temporarily.
>
> After the officials push me back on the wheels, and pull a bent fender away from the tire, I continue in the race. The roof, which was not reinforced, dented in to within half an inch of my head! Finally a broken axle retires the car.[7]

By this time it was September 1951, and there were only a few weeks left of the season. Fay returned to Hollywood, where she seems to have been propositioned by two managers, not for her racing, but for herself. But Taylour was not going to give up racing, and travelled instead to Kansas City.

Racing appearances enabled Taylour to earn enough money to make more appearances, but there was little left over. Her financial security depended on continual racing. This proved more difficult in the mid-Western states, where her racing in the Pacific coast states was not well known. She went to the tracks, talked her way into being allowed to demonstrate her driving skills and convinced the promoters. That way she raced midget cars in Kansas City, then at St Louis, Springfield, Cincinnati and Chicago. Where insufficient promotion efforts were made, Taylour undertook her own promotion again, visiting the press, radio, and television studios. In Chicago she appeared on the famous 'Welcome Traveler' radio show, hosted by Tommy Bartlett, which the following year became a television show. It was on this radio show that she was presented with a new way of advertising herself. In the autumn of 1950, a new fashion in bras was taking hold of the US lingerie industry – the 'bullet bra'. Although the first 'bullet bra' was sold in 1941, the fashion became widespread and popular in the 1950s. By then, bullet bras were also padded and reinforced to add extra size.[8] Fay Taylour was wearing a bullet bra and a tight sweater when she was interviewed by Bartlett on 'Welcome Traveler', along with other guests. He focused on Taylour's love life, both with racing and with men. She went along with this and read a poem she had written to a racing driver who had loaned her a car. There was a studio audience present who applauded her, with a member of the audience shouting out, 'we saw her race'. At the end of the show, Bartlett awarded Taylour the prize. Afterwards, he remarked to one of his colleagues, 'she won that by 5 inches', and, to Fay, 'You were way out in front [...] even though the other women also wore sweaters'.[9] Taylour took all this in her stride and was very quick to see the promotional potential: 'the sweater angle had become a label. An accomplishment in fact comparable with my accomplishments on the track!'.[10] Her promotional material now featured photographs of Taylour in her bullet bra and tight sweater, as well as her racing helmet. Newspapers used her photographs and entitled them, 'Shapely Racer...', 'Sweater Girl', 'Lana Turner of the Speedways', and 'Jane Russel on Wheels'.[11] The original 'Sweater Girl' was in fact Lana Turner, after her appearance 'in the 1937 film, *They Won't Forget*. In that movie Turner was not wearing a bullet bra, but she was wearing a very tight sweater'.[12] Taking advantage of the fashion and reflecting on quite the opposite fashion for flat chests in her 1920s youth, Taylour wryly commented, 'I am certainly glad now that my efforts to stop my chest growing didn't succeed'.[13]

Being in Chicago, Taylour was a few hours' drive away from Indianapolis, home of the famous 'Brickyard' track and, since 1911, the Indy 500 race. Taylour wanted to see the track, which was unique in its demands, 'the length of this race in relation to the size of the cars (big cars) and the size and shape of the track, imposes abnormal conditions, not found at any other racing track'.[14] In Indianapolis she met up with a local journalist who borrowed a Jaguar sportscar to take her to see the track. Their conversation turned to the dangers of the 500-mile race, and she talked about the particular need for strong muscles that even many men did not possess. The journalist said that surely Fay, too, needed muscle power in her dirt track racing, and she wondered whether 'my driving skill always compensates for the inequality in muscle?'[15] She also thought that having to race cars new to her on strange tracks was even more of a dangerous handicap, especially as promoters were often unwilling to open tracks for practice runs.

As Taylour and the journalist arrived at the track, stopping under the sign 'Indianapolis Speedway', a car left. The car was being driven by Wilbur Shaw, president of the Indianapolis Motor Speedway and three times winner of the 500. It was due to the efforts of Shaw that the track survived the Second World War. Wartime measures meant that the track had been closed but, while testing synthetic rubber tyres at Indianapolis, Shaw realised that the track would not survive years of closure. He contacted the track's owner at that point, Eddie Rickenbacker, the famous racing driver, First World War fighter pilot, and president of Eastern Air Lines. Rickenbacker told Shaw that the track was to be demolished to make way for a housing development, which, of course, would have meant the end of racing there. Shaw convinced a millionaire businessman, Tony Hulman, to buy the track from Rickenbacker, and the track and its famous racing survived the war, while Hulman made Wilbur Shaw president.

As Shaw's car drew away, Taylour's Jaguar stopped by a hut inside the gates. The journalist introduced her to a man who was probably the janitor and asked if it was okay for them to go on the track. The janitor joined them and, with Taylour driving, they drove around the track, and Taylour let the tuned-up Jaguar out to its top speed of nearly 120mph. The joyride over, the reporter dropped her back at her hotel, where she got ready to have dinner with a midget car fan before some of his racing friends collected her to take her to catch a midnight train. At 10pm the drivers and mechanics arrived, full of the news that Wilbur Shaw was looking for her: 'Wilbur Shaw is tearing his hair out and has been looking for me in the bigger hotels. Lucky I couldn't get a room there!'.[16] Taylour was 'wanted' because she had unwittingly broken the total ban on women driving on the track. Not only were women barred from driving on the track, they were not allowed anywhere near it. For example, it was not until 1971 that women journalists were permitted in the pit area. Taylour was then told that the source of the ban was the American Automobile Association. She had fallen foul of the 'Triple A' before, when they had banned her, and all other women, from the foreign car races in California. As Taylour knew, the AAA's Contest Board 'did not "recognise" women, to use their own expression'.[17] The Indianapolis jaunt, in unwitting opposition to the AAA, greatly amused her: 'I had invaded the holy of holies. Had shattered the most sacred and cherished rules of the hierarchy. And, worse still, could not be punished because of their very own rule – they do not recognise women!'.[18]

The 1951 season was drawing to a close, but there was still a track holding midget car races in Newark, New York. Fay spoke to the promoter and arranged to take part in the final race of the season in October. This enabled her to complete her 1951 racing and claim a coast-to-coast tour. She was also able to visit New York city and fulfill an ambition of seeing the city's skyline. Arriving in New York she was met by Bill Schindler, whom she described as 'the greatest American dirt track driver, and still the greatest after he lost a leg'.[19] Schindler had been one of the very first midget car racers in the USA. He lost his leg in a race crash in 1936. He was part of a group of drivers who fought to keep the 'Triple A' out of East Coast racing. Post-war, he won fifty-three midget car races in 1947 and 1948. When he met Fay to show her around New York City he had less than a year left to live, being killed in a car sprint race in Allentown, Pennsylvania, aged forty-three.[20] Schindler drove her round the city. They ate at several restaurants, having each course at a different one, starting at Jack Dempsey's famous restaurant on Broadway. They were joined by the racing promoter later at a night club, where Taylour was asked what she thought of the skyscrapers by the night club host. She said she had not seen them, at least not the tops, which were in cloud, and that, in any case, she thought she would be scared to be so high up. A few minutes later, the race promoter took the nightclub microphone and announced that he had just booked Taylour a room on the top floor of the Hotel New Yorker, the tallest hotel in the city. She spent the next four nights there while she did all the tourist things, and went on her usual promotion tour of radio, television and newspapers.

The race at the Newark track was to be a difficult race because of the track itself, 'instead of the conventional oval, this track has about four irregular turns. To show one's best would require some concentrated practice. To go on without is asking for trouble'.[21] Taylour only saw her car when her race was called, which meant practice was limited to 'a few exhibition laps to get the feel of it'.[22] This race, like all the other races in the US, was about the show, about the promoters making money, and giving the crowd what they came for – thrills. Taylour later gave a fairly detailed account of the race, which was unusual. In her writings she tended to assume that the reader would know all there was to know about the races themselves. It may be that this race, in particular, was more difficult than others, or more dangerous, but it is an interesting view of a midget car race from her perspective:

> That exhibition [the initial laps] puts my opponent on his metal. Using everything I have, except the brakes, I manage to stay on the track and clock a faster time than the majority of the drivers. But it is touch and go. Each turn requires a special technique.
>
> Then, without a pause, I'm circling the track in a rolling start alongside my opponent. I'm on the inside, and if I get round the first bend first, maybe I can stay in front. The race is over four laps.
>
> My opponent settles it right from the start. No, before the start. He jumps the line, which is only a few yards from the first curve, and then puts his car clean across mine.
>
> He has guts – no doubt about that. I could have hit him. But somehow I manage to take the infield instead, and when I'm back on the track he's so far ahead that the race is already lost.
>
> The promoter is only interested for me to put up a show. He has a long program that must be finished in limited time, so the foul is allowed to pass.
>
> I reduce the gap between us before the race ends, and the hand from the crowd, as I climb out of the car in front of the stands, compensates me but not all the spectators.[23]

The disappointment of the lost race was compensated by two further bookings from promoters at the race. They were Taylour's final races of the 1951 season, one at Pittsburg, Pennsylvania, and the other at Richmond, Virginia. At Pittsburg, Taylour was loaned a car from the stable of the legendary midget car racer Roscoe 'Pappy' Hough, and she raced on 'a beautifully-shaped fast half-mile track',[24] which was more rewarding and less disturbing than the Newark track. She won her bout in two straight heats.

At the end of the season, Taylour returned to New York. She needed to find a new source of income to tide her over until the 1952 season, and wanted to keep press, radio and television interest in her alive. She had already been a guest on Steve Allen's show while in Hollywood, and she contacted him again. Steve Allen was the creator of the first television late-night chat show, 'The Tonight Show'. He would later, in 1956, host NBC's flagship 'Steve Allen Show', becoming one of the most famous and popular stars of US television. Allen invited Taylour onto 'The Tonight Show', and afterwards one of his staff told her that she should get onto the equally well-known 'What's My Line?'. She had, in fact, been asked to appear on that show when she was in California, but thinking that she would never be in New York, it was not likely to happen. Now she was in New York. The day after appearing on 'The Tonight Show' she went to the offices of 'What's My Line?'. She remembered that she 'was wearing a smart tight-fitting winter suit' and took with her 'my best clippings with action photographs'.[25] The 'tight-fitting suit' was doubtless designed to enhance her 'sweater girl' appearance and shows that Taylour was quite happy to take all the advantage she had. At first, she had little response from the staff, who said that while they had asked her before, they now had plenty of contestants for the show. She met the producer, Bert Bach, but he was no more encouraging. However, before leaving the offices, another woman employee looked at the clippings and photographs and told Fay to leave them with her. A few days later she was given a date for her appearance on the show.

'What's My Line?' was already something of a television institution in the US. The format was successfully exported, notably to the UK where it was first hosted by Eamonn Andrews from 1951 to 1963, later being revived again. The format involved a panel of well-known figures asking questions to try and establish the occupations of guests. One guest would be a celebrity guest, and the panel would be blindfolded for the questions. Fay Taylour appeared on the show on 11 November 1951. She used her father's second name and was introduced to the panel as Helen Fetherstonhaugh. Part of the appeal of the programme was its semi-formal presentation, with women members of the panel wearing evening dress and opera gloves. Taylour had prepared, wearing 'a woollen suit that I bought in Richmond [which] fits me like a glove', as well as a broad-brimmed hat with a veil. She had also had her nails manicured. This was, in part, a disguise for a woman who raced motorbikes, midget cars and stock cars. There were two other guests, and the mystery guest was the well-known film star, Adolphe Menjou. Taylour was scheduled to be last on, after the mystery guest. Menjou was 'guessed', and it was Taylour's turn. The host, John Daly, announced her as an international contestant, from Dublin, Ireland. The first panellist to question Taylour was the journalist, Dorothy Kilgallen, who, after a few questions, asked her: 'Is it a sport? Does it take place on a track? Is the track built inside a field?'. Taylour thought it was all over, but then Kilgallen asked, 'Is it Horse Racing?'.[26] 'Her colleagues now question me. They try athletics. The questioning goes back to her. She gropes. She stares at me. There is nothing in my appearance or speech to suggest a tough sport'.[27] At the end of the show, Taylour's occupation was still a mystery. She was given a huge round of applause, her $50 cheque, and 'outside the theatre, a large group waits for my autograph'.[28]

Fay Taylour clearly enjoyed the show, as well as the attention and the knowledge that she did not look like a dirt track racer, nor even what people might have expected a woman driver to look like. The media appearances also had a valuable place in her overall strategy to remain a business opportunity for race promoters. She knew that it was up to her to generate and continue to maintain a media profile if she was to be able to race. 'What's My Line?' was a good example of this. After her appearance on the show, transmitted across the entire CBS network, she received letters from fans, and importantly, from people like Lee Philips, story editor at Universal-International Pictures, who had wanted to make her racing story into a film. In a letter telling Taylour that 'despite the rough treatment accorded you here in Hollywood', it looked as if she might find much more success in New York. He praised her 'hard work and perseverance' proving 'that real talent cannot be hidden', before writing of her 'What's My Line?' appearance, 'you looked perfectly wonderful, and I enjoyed the broadcast'.[29] Phillips also noted that he would try to see the Don Ameche show, which suggests that Fay Taylour also appeared on that actor's show. In a similar vein, a letter from Laura Wilck, the Hollywood agent, to Fay at the New Yorker Hotel provided her with names and contact details of agents in New York that Taylour could approach. Wilck wrote, 'we're enormously impressed and delighted with the publicity you've received and with your great success', with a postscript adding that 'I heard you on the radio from Chicago, and on Breakfast Club, and you were most charming'.[30]

Taylour's 'What's My Line?' appearance also provided her later with a political footnote. Dorothy Kilgallen, the panellist who had come closest to working out Taylour's occupation, was a journalist with a history of breaking dramatic news stories. This included President John F. Kennedy's assassination. In the aftermath of the shooting of Lee Harvey Oswald by Jack Ruby, Kilgallen had been able to manage an interview with Ruby, and it was known that she believed that she had obtained vital information about the whole affair. It was shortly after the interview with Ruby that Kilgallen was found dead in her apartment, on 8 November 1965, in supposedly mysterious circumstances.[31] For Taylour, the death of Kilgallen came to represent more evidence of the operation of conspiratorial forces. Writing later about the death of Kennedy, whom Taylour admired as a 'national socialist', she said:

> The big interests who arranged for him [President Kennedy] to be liquidated wanted their hired killer alone to be blamed, and then that killer [Oswald] was liquidated, so that he could not speak … and many others, including Dorothy Kilgallon [*sic*], the famous writer and broadcaster, were also liquidated because they knew too much and were about to speak.[32]

Taylour later returned to the fate of Dorothy Kilgallen in another letter:

> Dorothy Killgallon [*sic*] the famous columnist was bumped off in her hey-day of popularity and wealth because she had been able to get into the prison and interview Ruby, and was about to reveal some truths. Oswald's land lady was bumped off – she knew too much. Many others too, as I've told you about.[33]

What was more, Kilgallen had also broken the story that the CIA had hired Mafia killers to assassinate Fidel Castro. Castro was yet another of Taylour's post-war heroes: 'the CIA ran the Bay of Pigs invasion in the interests of the sugar kings and other big business that kept the Cubans as slaves, and Kennedy who had just been elected and did not want that invasion was blamed for it, for its failure'.[34] For Taylour these links were sufficient to suggest that Kilgallen was murdered.

1951 was drawing to a close, and for Taylour it was ending on a high note. She still faced long-term financial problems and remained dependent on constantly being able to race. But 1951 had shown her, and others, that she could still make a success of racing, and that, as before the war, she still had a knack for winning the publicity that was so important to her racing. Before the year was finished, she had one more self-imposed task in front of her. She wanted to challenge the AAA Contest Board's blanket ban on women racing in any of the events run under its rules. The Triple A's dismissal of Fay and other women with the phrase 'we don't recognise women' clearly infuriated her. In a letter to a friend, John, written on 10 December, she explained:

> Have just arrived in Chicago to tackle perhaps the biggest proposition of my life. It should not be so – but it is.
> In this advanced year of the twentieth century, in this advanced country, I have come to ask recognition for women in my work ... to plead before a Board [...] against a discrimination which does not exist in other countries, and which hinders and hurts my work, and sport.[35]

This was a clear feminist statement which matched the practical feminism of Fay Taylour's life. The letter to John went on to say, 'I do not come because I take it on myself to speak for American women, who are well able to speak for themselves'.[36] In this, she recognised the strength and agency of other women in the USA. The letter has a speech-like quality to it, as if she was rehearsing her claim before the Contest Board, which it may well have been. The immediate concern of Taylour was that she, as a woman racing driver, should have the right to compete in the 1952 Pike's Peak Contest. This contest, now known as the Broadmoor Pike's Peak International Hill Climb, was similar to Alpine trials racing that Fay had taken part in pre-war. She believed that the Pike's Peak trial was just the sort of racing at which she excelled – 'there is no reason why women should not climb Pike's Peak against the stop watch if they desire. And there is every reason why I should do so'.[37] Taylour was determined to convince the Board, but she knew that it meant 'facing these conservative officials, who have so far refused to "recognise" me will be a severe test'.[38] Unfortunately, the one thing that Fay Taylour had not anticipated was the cowardice of the Contest Board. The meeting in Chicago was an 'open house' for all drivers. A number of male drivers were there when Taylour arrived. She felt that those drivers, 'the boys', were on her side, and she had prepared her case carefully. Her time to speak came, and the Board immediately adjourned the meeting. She objected but was told that the meeting was over and that she should send her request in writing. She had already done that and had visited the AAA in Washington. The Board meeting did reconvene that day, but in closed session. Unable to face Taylour, or her arguments based on her long history of racing, the Contest Board had simply hidden from her. Fay Taylour subsequently received a brief letter from the secretary, James H. Lamb, telling her it was because they had never licensed women to race, 'it is necessary to refuse your request (to participate in the Pike's Peak Hill Climb next Labor Day).'[39]

With two weeks before Christmas 1951, with the racing season over and her bank balance favourable for a change, Taylour decided that she would return to England to see her father, Dordy, who was now in failing health. Despite their political differences, and Fay's very long absences abroad, they had maintained a good relationship, and she was fond of him. However, his second wife, whom he had married in 1928, was unwelcoming not only of Fay, but of her two sisters as well. Fay Taylour returned to England by sea, although she could have flown. Perhaps surprisingly, it seems as if she was nervous of flying, noting, 'as always, I prefer surface to air travel, and sea is meat to my wanderlust. Air is too fast and too dangerous'.[40] A fellow passenger on the Cunard liner to England thought this strange from a woman who risked so much in dangerous motorsports, but her view was that if a tyre blew out on the track, or a nut worked loose, she could always react and fight it, but there was nothing she could do as a passenger in the air. The other aspect of sea travel that she enjoyed was meeting people. Almost to the end of her life, she revelled in the contacts and conversations on board ship. Nonetheless, her dislike of air travel might explain why despite racing everything from motorbikes to motorboats, she never attempted to learn to fly, much less try air racing, which had been one of the new popular sports of the inter-war period. After a very stormy Atlantic passage, including injuries suffered by crew and passengers, Taylour arrived in England and travelled on to her father's home near Lymington, Hampshire.

She found her father frail, having suffered two slight strokes in the preceding years. In her talks with Dordy, he reminisced about his old sporting life: riding to hounds, shooting, fishing, golf, then sailing and tennis. All that was gone, and, as Fay Taylour saw, 'he can barely manage a game of billiards now'.[41] It was a sad return for Fay. She and her father talked about her mother. He told her that her sister, Enid, in Africa, whose husband worked for the United Nations, and her other sister, Hilda, who lived 20 miles away, no longer kept in touch. Dordy also told Fay about a document box he had that contained family papers, including her mother's will and all her letters to her father, but he was too tired, and perhaps disinclined due to his age and sentiment, to go through the box with Fay. This would have some consequences for Fay after her father's death, as her mother's will contained a number of conditions that would impact on Fay's finances.

Taylour was back in the United States before the end of January 1952. She immediately returned to the task of maintaining her public profile, and appeared on several television shows, including 'TV Hour', 'Lunchtime at Sardi's', and 'Headline Clues from Broadway to Hollywood'. All of these appearances also filled time before the first racing of 1952. She was booked to race at the Speed

Week at the famous Daytona Beach, Florida, where, pre-war, Malcolm Campbell had broken five land speed records. The link with the famous Campbell added an extra excitement to Taylour's appearance. She was in her car, waiting for the mile dash 'at full throttle', only for the incoming tide to lead to the run being cancelled.[42]

From Daytona Beach, Taylour went to Miami and raced at the Medley Stadium. As usual, she enjoyed the pre-race promotion and marketing: 'a large crowd of sailors at the stadium give that funny whistle as I get into my car on the starting line. Wave to them, the promoter says, and then they whistle some more. But there the fun ends... at least after two laps. The engine bursts'.[43] After Miami, Taylour travelled to Kentucky. Although the full season had yet to start there, she raced at an indoor racetrack at the Armoury, Louisville. The wooden-floored track presented particular driving problems, but Taylour was able to have some practice laps before the race, which was to be run by cars that were 'smaller than the regular midgets'.[44] It was a short, fast oval track and the racing was tricky:

> In the first race I push to the front at once, and start increasing my lead. With each lap I get faster and faster. I'm enjoying myself, and I feel safe enough. No need to go so fast, the race is mine. At least everyone thinks so. But I'm taking no chances. The track's too short to look back. I enter the last turn on the last lap faster still, but safe as a rock. That's what I think.
>
> Suddenly I'm upside down ... unhurt ... and sliding alongside the fence, with the car on its side, towards the finishing line. I'm still in front ... so far ahead that maybe I can skid over that line first.
>
> The crowd roars. The floor is so slick that I'm now certain to make it. But no! A jagged board on the fence stops me ... 6 inches only from the line.[45]

Despite this dramatic defeat, Taylour had by this point begun to establish herself in US racing, particularly in midget car racing. There was a month to go before the racing season opened across the country, and Taylour took rooms in a residential hotel in New York City, filling her diary with race dates. Her intention in 1952 was to race her way back to California, just as the previous year she had raced her way to New York. She was successfully handling all her own promotion and publicity, as she had found the measure of the American race and entertainment scenes. She was looking forward to the year. 'I can hardly wait to get going, to be let loose on their tracks!'.[46] But at this point, fate intervened.

Chapter Fifteen

Banned from the USA

As Taylour was preparing for the 1952 season, a letter arrived from England telling her that her father was seriously ill. He was to undergo an operation, but the prognosis was not good. Taylour immediately sent a telegram to confirm that she would return to England and began to make preparations for the journey. This time she would fly. She booked a flight for two days later through American Express. She now had to ensure that she had the correct re-entry permit for her return to the US. At the Immigration Department she was told that it took ten days to issue one, but that there would be no problem if she obtained one from the American Consulate in London. Returning to her hotel she was finally able to contact England by long-distance telephone and was told that her father was going into hospital the next day, with his operation planned for five days hence. The manager of the hotel agreed to store all the 'clippings, clothes, racing gear [...] and other records' she had accumulated in the US until she returned.[1]

Wearing her 'What's My Line?' suit, and, as usual, carrying her racing helmet as a talisman, Fay sat next to a worried older woman who was on her first flight. Taylour tried to joke the woman out of her fears, and, probably, her own concern, by putting the helmet on. That she was worried is revealed by her later comment, 'I listen to each engine as the pilot races them on the ground. If you revved a car engine like that without load it'd burst.'[2] She arrived in England in time to see her father before his operation. She visited him at the hospital, and they talked about her mother, her father's first wife. He asked for a particular photograph of her, and Fay took it into him. Her father did not want the operation and she felt that, for the first time, he was afraid. He failed to regain consciousness after the operation, and died the next day, on 11 May 1952. The death of her father meant that Fay had no strong connections left in England. She had a very poor relationship with her mother-in-law, and she had no real contact with her sisters or her two cousins. She felt that her family took no interest in her career, while at the same time she took delight in the fact that she had flouted all the conventions they had lived by. That the two things were connected did, to some degree, impinge upon Taylour's understanding of the lack of sympathy she complained about: 'I could not expect sympathy from relatives who lead normal well-ordered lives, who never know what I may do next. Whose sense of humor does not list going to prison for fun ... or any of the other shocking things I did. Shocking to them'.[3]

The next two weeks were taken up with funeral arrangements and attempts by Taylour to ascertain what impact her father's death had on her finances. In letters to her family's solicitors Daley and Thompson, she acknowledged that her step-mother was the main beneficiary of her father's will. However, there was also a trust fund, set up by her mother's father. Her father had left this to the three daughters, to be shared equally between them. This, in Fay's mind, became a major issue. She claimed that her mother had wanted the larger part of the trust fund to go to any unmarried daughter, but this wish had not been incorporated into either her mother's or her father's will. Fay believed that this was because firstly her father had not wanted to bother his wife with legal details while she was dying, and then, in her father's last months, he had not wanted to open the box containing all the family documents. All of this, of course, had no legal standing as her father's will clearly left the fund to be divided equally between the three sisters. This subsequently became a source of friction between Fay and her younger sister, Enid. Ironically, while Fay contrasted the conventional lives her sisters lived with her own non-conformity and rebelliousness, that life also meant that she faced repeated financial challenges and had no home of her own. It was perhaps unsurprising that Enid refused to hand over her part of the trust fund to Fay, whom she considered to be reckless and financially inept.

So instead of the large portion of the trust fund that Fay had expected, she received a third share, plus a number of War Bonds. In addition, she asked the family solicitor to find out whether a £1,000 legacy promised to her in 1937 or 1938 by her godfather, Walter Lynden-Bell, still existed in her favour.[4] As that legacy depended on the death of Bell's second wife, it was perhaps unlikely that the money was available, and shows again how shaky her finances were, some-thing that she admitted in her letter to the solicitor, 'everything I managed to save out there [USA] has been used up in these two trips home (was back at Xmas too). Also I have lost many hundreds of pounds of racing contracts in coming back just now, when the American racing season was opening full swing'.[5] The solicitor, whom she called 'Brownie', had asked whether they could meet up, but she replied that she could not as she had to return to the USA as soon as possible.

While Taylour waited for the re-entry visa for the USA, she had a chance to race in England again. A promoter for the London Speedway had heard that she was back in London and asked if she would like to do some midget car racing at Walthamstow Stadium. This famous stadium was primarily a greyhound track, but from 1949–51 was also a venue for motorcycle speedway, along with some midget car racing. Taylour took up the opportunity, primarily because it would enable her to renew contacts with pre-war speedway friends. She also took the opportunity to renew her complicated friendship with Lionel Wills, phoning him to see if he would drive her to the track, which he did. At the track she competed against Alvin 'Spike' Rhiando, a well-known character on the circuit. In 1933 Rhiando had tried, unsuccessfully, to introduce midget car racing onto British speedway tracks. Post-war, he was among the first to adopt the new 500cc Coopers, being 'one of the first six customers for a Cooper Mk II [...] John Cooper stated that it was Spike who first suggested dropping a V twin into the Mk II'.[6] This was the first time that Taylour had driven a four-wheel drive midget racer, with her American experience being in rear-wheel drive cars. Later, she described the experience:

> How will four-wheel-drive handle after the rear-wheel-drive of American midgets? How will this dark-surfaced track feel? It looks less slick than the clay tracks of the States.
>
> The starter's flag goes down. I give the car full throttle. The drive on four wheels is lovely. I feel much safer than the drive on two. The rear end does not have the same tendency to over skid, yet one can powerslide the turns with the wheels all crossed up! The track holds beautifully too. One can get a grip, a 'bite' as we call it.
>
> I go into the lead and stay there, in spite of Spike's efforts to pass.
>
> Later, he tells me that his hair stood on end with surprise when I took him on the first turn. He did not believe that I'd go so well ... better than in my younger days![7]

To complete Fay's triumph, Lionel took her to dinner that evening and for the next few evenings. The race not only brought Taylour back on the track in England, but also advertised her presence more widely, something that would soon prove to be of importance. At that moment, however, she was keen to return to the USA, and only needed the re-entry permit.

Taylour went to the US Consulate in London, expecting to be able to obtain the necessary permit easily. She was told that she had to reapply for a visa, including providing fingerprints, TB test results and a blood test. However, as she had evidence of her racing contracts for 1952, the consul told her they would push the process through quickly and she would be able to collect the re-entry permit in about three weeks. On 4 June she returned to the consulate to collect the permit, but instead received a major shock:

> I was shown to a vice-consul's desk in the corner of a large room. My visa was on the desk. He handed me a form, telling me to read it carefully. He could not give me the visa unless I signed it. It was a dim carbon copy, and did not look important. The words at the top said: Mc. Carthy Mc. Carron [*sic*] Act, and I did not recognise the names for the importance they already had. The rest of the sheet was a first person statement starting: I swear ...[8]

Taylour was faced with the USA's Internal Security Act 1950, otherwise known as the Subversive Activities Control Act. Although the Act was intended primarily to be used against communists, it was couched in terms of combating the promotion of 'totalitarian dictatorship'. Part of its provisions also included tightening up on the entry of non-US citizens into the USA. Nonetheless, Taylour could have avoided its provisions had she been pedantically legalistic about the statement she was required to sign. She later remembered the statement required her to sign that 'I was not and had never been a member of any party connected with or affiliated to Communism, Nazism, Fascism, or the Falange'.[9] It would have been possible to claim that British Union, which she had joined in September

1939, was not 'connected or affiliated' in that it was a national organisation, with no formal links or ties with other parties or governments. Unlike the Communist Party of Great Britain, or the Communist Party USA, there was no Nazi or Fascist equivalent of the Moscow-based Comintern which directed, sponsored, and in the British case was primarily responsible for the existence of the Communist Party. Mosley's fascist movement did receive funds from Mussolini, but in 1952 few people knew about this, and Fay Taylour certainly did not. Further, the ideological core of Mosley's fascism was built around Italian fascism, with later additions borrowed from the Nazis. Had Taylour interpreted the statement she was required to sign in a literal sense, she could have done so. However, in her confusion at this surprise development, she 'burbled out something about having belonged to British Union'.[10] The vice-consul pulled the form from her and told her that she would have to wait before she heard more about a visa.

Taylour left the US Consulate feeling that 'the earth had dropped from under me'.[11] All that she could do was to wait to see what transpired. The Consulate contacted the British authorities for further information about Taylour. Security files in the UK National Archives show that this request came from the CIA and was passed to MI5. Their reply outlined Taylour's detention during the war, and brought her record up to date, noting, 'it is known that she maintained her Fascist and pro-Nazi associations from that date [October, 1943, on release from internment] until 1948. It is also known that she recently met a well-known member of Union Movement's staff.'[12] It is likely that the 'well-known member of Union Movement's staff' was Jeffrey Hamm, and that piece of information offset Taylour's claim to the Consul staff that 'I was no member of anything now'.[13] While that was true, the fact that she was still in touch with Mosley's post-war movement, Union Movement, would have been enough to convince the US authorities that she was still politically active, and was, to adopt the communist phrase, a 'fellow traveller' on the ultra-right. Although Union Movement was only a small group, with never more than about 1,500 active members and support of around 15,000 by the early 1960s,[14] it was particularly active in London and was associated with violent disorder, which would have been unlikely to convince the US authorities that there might not be a problem with Taylour's choice of politics.

Taylour finally received a letter from the US Consulate on, of all dates, 4 July. Her visa was enclosed but it was stamped 'cancelled'. This was a major blow to Taylour, as it effectively ended her new racing career in the USA. She was determined to fight the decision, but it would take three years. She reflected on the reasons, as she saw them, for why this had happened. Her analysis of the banning from the US had two elements. Firstly, she argued, somewhat disingenuously, that Mosley's pre-war fascism was simply 'conservatively right wing'.[15] In fact, Mosley's fascism envisaged a new system designed to minimise the role of Parliament and co-ordinate and direct key elements of the economy under state control in a proposed new order – the corporate state. It is difficult to see that as conservative in the British context. Interestingly, the vice-consul had suggested to

Taylour that 'Mosley's party and Communism were the same thing'.[16] That comment reflected a common view in the 1950s that, faced with Soviet power, the West, led by the USA, was continuing a struggle against totalitarianism, with Communism having replaced Nazism and fascism as the main manifestation of totalitarian politics. Needless to say, Taylour rejected that idea, and argued that the fascists had fought the communists and it should be seen as 'a recommendation now to have been a member of his [Mosley's] party. Wasn't Communism the big threat?'.[17] This was, at best, a rather naïve view, and she probably realised that it was a feeble response.

The second element of Taylour's analysis of her banning was that Mosley's fascism was 'a threat to Big Business'.[18] There was some truth in this, given Mosley's policy proposals both pre- and post-war, which put the state as the central controlling factor in the economy, rather than any version of the market. In the early 1950s he was clearly arguing that 'the position of the state is that of a leader and intiator', and that the future state would be a united Europe under the control of what he termed 'European Socialism'.[19] None of that would have sounded encouraging to the US authorities, even if Mosley had not carried the taint of his pre-war fascism. There was another aspect to Fay Taylour's understanding of Mosleyite opposition to 'big business' and to 'international finance' which had long been the *bête noire* of fascists and others on the ultra-right. Years later, in a letter to a former leader of British Union, R.R. 'Dick' Bellamy, Taylour reiterated her view that in the USA, the 'right wing' stood for '100% for International Finance, nothing less [...] They represent Vested Interests and are against socialism of any sort'.[20] For Taylour, and many other Mosley supporters, 'Vested Interests' was shorthand for international finance controlled by Jewish, later Zionist, influence, or 'Jewish conspiracy'. Taylour's reference to 'socialism of any sort' was a reference to what she had long seen as the socialism of Hitler, to which she later added Castro's Cuban Revolution, North Vietnam, Irish Republicanism, or any other cause that she felt was under attack from the US 'military industrial complex', or, in the case of Ireland, by Freemasonry in the form of the Orange Order. At the time of her banning from the US, she had yet to combine these apparently disparate ideas and enthusiasms. Later she blamed the ban on the nature of the 'American right-wing', saying that 'it was my very ignorance of what McCarthy/McCarron stood for, what the Right Wing in US stood for that caused what really did amount to persecution'.[21]

Taylour was stuck in London with rapidly diminishing funds. She moved to a cheaper hotel and began the difficult process of finding racing, and making it known that she was available to race. At this point she had a piece of luck, as one of the spectators at the Walthamstow race against Spike Rhiando was a man called Harrison who worked for the Frank Betts Literary Agency. He telephoned her and suggested a meeting to plan a series of articles about Taylour's racing that he could sell to a Sunday newspaper. She met Harrison at a restaurant in the Strand, and, still shocked by the refusal of her re-entry permit, she told him about it and why she had been refused. Harrison, however, did not seem to care about her wartime detention, or her politics, saying, 'that's finished, forgotten'.[22] Taylour agreed to write a series of articles focusing on her racing and experience of the USA, and Harrison sold the proposal to the *Sunday Chronicle*, which had a circulation of well over a million copies in the early 1950s. The day after meeting Harrison, Taylour received a telephone call from *The Daily Mail*. The newspaper was sponsoring a race at the Boreham Circuit, which was enjoying a brief period of fame with some soon-to-be famous drivers like Stirling Moss and Mike Hawthorn competing there. *The Daily Mail* wanted to boost the profile of the race and thought that having Taylour race would enable it to do that. The newspaper offered to find her a car and ensure she could race even though entries had closed. She agreed, and an Alta was found for her, the owner wanting to sell and believing that a good race would increase its value. Taylour described the car as being supercharged, so it is likely that the car was one of Alta's post-war GP cars, combining pre-war design with a new 1.5-litre engine. Taylour now had two new boosts to her finances, and the offer of a race. Before she could race on the GP circuit, however, she needed to renew her International Race Driver's Licence.

The licence was issued in Britain by the London Automobile Club, acting on behalf of the *Fédération Internationale de l'Automobile* (FIA), the international governing body for many motorsports events. Taylour already had a race licence, but it had to be renewed, as hers had lapsed. She now faced another battle with hostile male gatekeepers to her sport. Just as she had been unable to obtain a licence for road-circuit racing in the US, so it looked as if the same was going to happen in the UK. Her application was refused, with no explanation given. Taylour challenged this decision and was told that it was because she had raced midget cars in America. In part, her move to midget car racing in the US, for which no licence was needed, had been a result of being refused a licence for road racing. That refusal had been justified by saying that Taylour had raced as a professional and the road race licence she wanted in the US was only for amateurs. In London, she was told that her involvement in midget car racing was a problem. In answer to her questioning this, she was told, 'We don't recognise American speedway tracks, and we don't issue licenses to drivers who race on unlicensed tracks'.[23] The argument went back and forth, with Taylour being told that she should not have raced on dirt tracks if she intended to race on a road-type circuit. Explaining that racing was her livelihood made no difference. Taylour was outraged, seeing in the stubborn refusal of her licence the same anti-woman standpoint that she had faced in the US:

I'm suddenly reminded of a hotel board room in Chicago, and similar men refusing a similar licence. These men [...] have their prototype in America. They represent the Lord-High-Everything-Else of auto clubs, just as those men in America do. Ironically, the American officials refuse to recognise road racing, while these officials refuse to recognise the dirt tracks! But no, it's only ironic that they are so intolerant. I did not have to race on the dirt tracks, they suggest. My Irish fighting spirit is about to burst.[24]

The Daily Mail had already begun to advertise her appearance at Boreham, but unless she obtained a licence she would not be able to appear. The newspaper suggested that she use her Irish citizenship and obtain a licence from Dublin. This appeared to be the answer, as she was told that they would ask London to issue the licence on their behalf if she completed the medical tests. That gave her a day to get all the tests done. That evening she dined with two of her pre-war motorcycle speedway friends, George and 'Semmy'. These two were also involved in British midget car racing and appear to have been her closest supporters at this time. By some sleight of hand, George managed to fix Taylour's blood test result the next day without the usual three-day wait. Armed with the completed medical forms, Taylour obtained the licence and set off to the track with George and Semmy.

The Alta was ready for Taylour and she drove some practice laps: 'it's a beautiful track, with its fast curving bends [...] The car handles beautifully. The course is open and the grooves obvious. The circuit is approximately three miles round with right and left hand curves'.[25] However, in true Taylour form, there was a last-minute crisis. The car had been in storage for a year. During that time, the lining of the fuel tank had decayed, with metal flakes entering the fuel system and beginning to clog the filter. Taylour's two 'stalwart' friends worked through the night to get the car ready for the race in the 'Formula Libre' the next day, but the fuel tank and fuel feed problems turned out to be enough to end Taylour's race. There was a postscript, however, as she was called to see the stewards after the race and was accused of having nearly knocked down a flag official as she entered the track from the pits. Taylour denied this and believed that the stewards were colluding with the flag official, whom she described as being 'a youngish alien-looking man'[26] in order to create a case that could lead to her losing the licence she had just regained. The stewards questioned George and Semmy separately. Their accounts supported Taylour's and the issue was dropped. For Taylour and her two allies, this was another example of the anti-woman prejudice that she kept encountering, particularly from officials. Her comment that the complainant was 'alien-looking', which can be taken to mean that she thought he was Jewish, added an extra depth to her understanding of what happened. The reality of male hostility that she had always faced, and frequently beaten, was embellished by her anti-Semitism. The Boreham race experience was topped off for Taylour when she discovered that the owner of the Alta had, notwithstanding the fuel feed issues, sold the car and disappeared without paying her the agreed commission. She was left to pay George and Semmy their expenses out of her own pocket and was still faced with the problem of what to do next.

Taylour returned to the 'narrow room in the narrow high hotel in South Kensington'[27] and wrote the articles for the *Sunday Chronicle*, which were published in August 1952. She made another attempt that month to gain an entry permit for the US by travelling to Dublin and seeing the American consul, Mr Matthews. His only suggestion was that if she had influential friends in the

USA then they might be able to act on her behalf. But Taylour had no influential American friends, and she returned to London empty-handed.

Back in London, Fay was rescued from the narrow South Kensington hotel by Evelyn, a cousin of her mother. She was the wife of a retired senior civil servant in the Foreign Office, and the couple invited Fay to stay with them, and to remain even when they made their annual holiday to see relatives in France. Taylour was still hoping that her challenge to her father's will might be settled in her favour, but meanwhile her money was again running out. She was, in her own words, 'restless, I can't sit still',[28] and she turned again to her two loyal 'stalwarts' George and Semmy. Their advice was to buy a Formula 3 car so that instead of depending on other owners to be able to race, she could race on her own account and take advantage of the appearance money that was paid by most race circuits. This she did, buying a second-hand JAP-engined Cooper 500cc, and a jeep to tow a trailer for the car. She visited the now retired pre-war driver, Freddie Dixon. They had known each other well before the war, and it is likely that he had been sympathetic to her politics. Although no longer racing, Dixon was still a highly skilled engine-tuner and he gave Taylour advice on how to tune her Cooper.

The first race Fay entered was the Midland Automobile Club's Shelsey Walsh hill climb event, which has been held since 1905 and is regarded as the oldest such event.[29] She spent a day in practice runs, but they were cut short by problems with the fuel lines. These Taylour had attended to by a Cooper mechanic, and she made a last practice run to the top of the hill. There were a number of competitors' cars there, including a pre-war Bugatti. She admired the Bugatti and the owner recognised her. Chatting to him she told him that she had once raced a Bugatti like his at Brooklands, but that during the war it ended up being stored in a farm shed and was later sold for its scrap value. The owner told her that he was the buyer and the car in front of her was the same Bugatti. He invited her to race it the next day rather than using her own Cooper. Taylour was very tempted but decided to stick with her 'new baby', the Cooper. Reflecting on this, and probably on elements of her personal life, she thought, 'it's dangerous to play with an old lover. Even if no one gets hurt, it can be disturbing!'.[30] The next day she won the women's trophy in her Cooper, along with a £5 bet from a fellow driver who did not think she could win.

It was now late summer 1952, and even with her own car Taylour found it difficult to get races. She had sunk a good proportion of her remaining funds in the Cooper, and her hopes of it being a way of getting more races, and crucially some backing, appeared to have been misplaced. Sadly, she gave her Cooper a nickname, 'The Unhatched Chicken', reflecting the fact that she had, apparently, counted her chickens before they had hatched. However, 'The Unhatched Chicken' did prove its worth. Just as she was beginning to doubt her decision to buy, a letter arrived from Sweden, from the Stockholm Automobile Club. It would mark a new stage in her racing life.

Chapter Sixteen

'Tearing from Place to Place' – the 1952–53 Season

The letter Fay Taylour received in August 1952 was from the Stockholm Automobile Club, inviting her to race in Stockholm the following month. Sweden's biggest daily newspaper, *Dagens Nyheter*, was sponsoring the F3 500cc race, and was looking for a new angle to advertise the event. The 500cc races in Sweden were dominated by Sweden's own make of car, the Effyh, the product of the engineers Folke and Yngve Håkansson, who had been building the cars since 1947.[1] Racing in Sweden, as elsewhere, was also dominated by male drivers. According to Taylour, no woman had raced against men in a Swedish fixture.[2] *Dagens Nyheter* asked her to send photographs and publicity material about her racing, and the event organisers agreed 'good appearance money, and all expenses'.[3] Just over a week after receiving the letter, Taylour and her Cooper, 'The Unhatched Chicken', were on their way to Gothenburg, with Taylour travelling first class on the Swedish Lloyd line ship, MV *Saga*.

Arriving in Stockholm by train, Fay was first interviewed by the sports editor of *Dagens Nyheter*. He was concerned that, after the publicity he had given her, she might not be good enough, and asked her if she could really drive fast, saying that she didn't look like a racing driver. She reassured him and went to see the track, which was at an aerodrome in Stockholm. She was delighted by the track. It was about two miles long, with a half-mile straight, a sharp hairpin bend, and 'wide right and left hand curves that can be negotiated fast'.[4] She had a few days to practice and reassure the organisers and the sports editor that she could, indeed, drive fast. But the afternoon before the event, 'The Unhatched Chicken' blew its engine and, of course, Taylour had neither a mechanic nor a replacement JAP engine. A garage had been contracted to give her engineering support, but they had a backlog of cars to deal with and it did not look as if they would be able to get Taylour's car ready for the next morning. However, the manager of the garage stepped in, aided by the night watchman, and spent the night replacing the JAP with an Effyh engine provided by one of the Effyh brothers, Folke or Yngve Håkansson, who was at the track.

The race was run as a series of heats of five laps with eighteen cars per heat, with the first three going through to the final. Prior to the race, Taylour met the Håkansson brother who provided the replacement engine and thanked him. He joked that he hoped she would not beat any of the Effyhs. Most of the competitors came from Scandinavia and the Netherlands, with the Dutch champion there driving an Effyh. Also from England was the 23-year-old Rodney Nuckey, who was in his first season driving a Norton-engined Cooper. He was to race regularly in Finland, France, Germany, and Sweden over the next two years, winning at Falkenberg and Skarpnäck in Sweden, in both 1952 and 1953.[5]

Fay Taylour got off to a slow start in her heat because she missed the starting flag, which, unlike British practice, was flown from a high tower. However, she fought back, and later wrote a good account of her racing in the heat and the problems of racing:

> I give the car all it's got, powersliding all the bends except the hairpin at the end of the fast straightaway. This is a tricky turn, since one has to come almost to a full stop from full speed before attempting to take it. The gear box on these cars means changing down through each gear in turn. One cannot jump from top gear to bottom [...] It is necessary to use the accelerator on each of the three change-downs to make a fast smooth change. Otherwise I am meshing two gear wheels or sprockets so that the teeth lock with a jerk. Without accelerating while the gear lever goes through neutral, the toothed wheels will be revolving at incorrect speeds. This is the art of driving that cannot be ignored in racing. Many race drivers have not learnt, or sorted out for themselves, in these days of synchro-mesh and self-change, how to change down at speed. They race nevertheless, but abuse the transmission system, jerking and straining it. [...] But this is only one of the arts of race driving. The moment for making the gear change is another. The course you take on the turn another, and the use of your gas pedal as you turn still another. The least, if indeed it can be called an art, is holding your foot down on the straightaway. 'All out' at 100 can be easy. 'All out' at 140 can be easier. It depends on the car and the course.[6]

Despite her poor start, Taylour managed to claw her way back and crossed the line in third place. Through to the final, she tore on to the straight neck-and-neck with Dutch racer Pim Richardson driving a Beels-JAP.[7] But she fell victim to a field modification she had made to the accelerator. After the heat, she had readjusted the accelerator pedal to make it easier to control, but 'I brake hard for the turn. So does he [Richardson]. At the same time I rock my foot to tap the accelerator for the change down. The accelerator isn't there! My foot's under it ... it's caught ... I can't get it off the brake! I'll spin. I'm SPINNING!'.[8] Before the race officials could get her car back on to the track, the whole field had passed. Then she had, in her own words, 'the most wonderful chase',[9] during which she managed the fastest lap of the day. Although Taylour failed to be placed, her 'wonderful chase' and her fastest lap enabled the press to give her plenty of post-race coverage, with the evening newspaper headlining its sports pages with: '"FLICKA" [girl] IN COOPER FASTER THAN ALL MEN IN NERVE-RACKING FINAL". For a 48-year-old 'girl', it had proved to be a good outing for 'The Unhatched Chicken' and a sign that despite being banned from the USA, Fay still had a future in racing.

Before leaving Sweden, Taylour and one of the Håkansson brothers talked about the cars, comparing the merits of Coopers and Effyhs. She told Håkansson that she thought his racer would be perfect for the Australian dirt track midget racing circuit. Taylour knew Frank Arthur, a motorcycle speedway legend in the 1920s and 1930s, and, in the post-war period, an important Australian speedway promoter. Arthur 'combined riding skills with business acumen [and was] the last man in the world one would have thought to be a speedway rider'.[10] Taylour said much the same thing about Frank Arthur: 'that this quiet, unassuming, slim man could race as he did, was always a matter for wonder. In the hard international speedway contests before World War II, he was a consistent championship winner'.[11] Taylour had met Arthur in the late 1920s or early 1930s, either in England, where he won two British championships, or during her racing in Australia in 1929–30. She contacted him after Sweden. Although nothing came of the proposal for her to race Effyhs in Australia, Arthur did offer Taylour a contract to race for Empire Speedways. He cabled her with a proposal for her to race in five Australian cities, with a guaranteed £50 (Australian) per meeting appearance fee, 5% net of takings, transport in Australia and air fare paid, along with the provision of cars for her to race. The proviso was that she was needed in Australia as soon as possible.[12] That Arthur, who was recognised as both a leading rider and a successful motorsports businessmen, was so quick to take the chance to have Taylour race on four wheels in Australia, shows how highly her skills on the dirt track were still regarded.

Fay Taylour left London in October 1952, flying by British Overseas Airways Corporation (BOAC) Lockheed Constellation from Heathrow. The flight involved five stop-overs before arrival in Sydney, but the elegant Constellation was a luxurious airliner and the stop-overs included a night at the famous Raffles Hotel in Singapore. Arriving in Sydney on 22 October, Fay was met by a party from the speedway track with the car that would be hers to use while in the city. As usual it was decorated with her name and details of her appearances. It was over two decades since Taylour had been in Australia and she was pleased to be able to meet up with old motorcycle speedway colleagues. Frank Arthur took her to a bar where speedway men surrounded her to hide the fact that there was a woman in the men-only bar. Among the racers was the former Australian champion rider 'Cyclone' Billy Lamont, who had also raced successfully in England, as Taylour remembered him, 'the daring darling of all women fans when I first started racing'.[13] There were others there that remembered her from before the war, which did not entirely please Frank Arthur. His main concern as a promoter was to build the gate admission numbers to the races. As much of the midget car audience was too young to remember Taylour racing in 1930, he was stressing that she was a new figure on the speedway track. It was not only Fay Taylour who judiciously altered her age when necessary.

Publicity for Taylour's appearances had already begun at the start of October, with the *Daily Telegraph* of Sydney first mentioning her on 8 October, under the headline 'Woman to oppose men'. The piece noted that:

> She will be the first woman to drive against men in Australia. Miss Taylour was the world's best woman speedway motor cyclist before the war. She recently broke all Stockholm (Sweden) track records in open competition against men drivers. Miss Taylour has lapped the Brooklands track at more than 120 miles an hour.[14]

The following day, the press reported that Fay might have to race alone because 'she may have no-one to race against. There are no women speedway drivers in Australia, and Sports Ground manager Mr Bill Reynolds said last night that National Speedcar officials had refused to allow their members to drive against Miss Taylour'.[15] This was the first sign that Taylour might face opposition to her racing against men. The National Speedcar officials had previously said that their members could race against her, but subsequently changed their minds. It is not clear what brought about this change of heart, but it may have been related to money. Prior to the war, opposition to Taylour racing against men on the motor-cycle speedway came from riders who feared that a successful woman would lead promoters to reduce the fees paid for racing and for winnings. Concern about earnings did, in fact, exist among Australian racers and there would be a strike by them while Taylour was in Australia. The other explanation, of course, was that individual male drivers feared the loss of prestige in being beaten by a woman.

Whatever the origins of the threat to her racing against men, the story helped to generate more publicity for Fay, even while she was still in England. The question of individual drivers refusing to race against Taylour probably disappeared when one of the greatest midget car racers, Frank 'Satan' Brewer, said that he would race against her – 'I have seen her race in America and I know she is a capable driver'.[16] Coming from the New Zealander, Brewer, this was high praise. Brewer had raced in the US before the war, winning 'the 150 lap US Midget GP in 1940 and 1941 [as well as being] the 250 lap US National Midget Championship. He won over 30 races in the United States and became Western States Champion in 1946'.[17] He moved to Australia in 1948, where he, along with Ray Revell, became one of the most successful post-war drivers, eventually being three times New Zealand National Champion, and New Zealand's first professional racing driver. Taylour raced both Brewer and Revell once she arrived in Australia, and neither were disappointed in her ability. As well as the issue of her racing against men, the Australian press also found space to inform their readers of Fay's more feminine concerns, with a number of reporters running the usual story about her wearing 'pink satin pyjamas under my racing overalls ready for hospital'. The same piece noted that she had been injured 'in 25 serious track smashes'.[18] The story of the pyjamas under her overalls in case she had to be taken to hospital was one that Taylour repeatedly told the press. She was more than willing to provide the 'back stories' behind her racing that she knew appealed to a wide audience and would be eagerly picked up by the press. Frank Arthur and Empire Speedways publicised her appearances largely through advertising, but Taylour knew from experience that it was up to her to charm journalists and editors and generate the copy that would bring crowds in to see her race. She was just as good at this as she was at racing.

The day after arriving in Sydney, Taylour went to the garment factory that was booked to fit her out in racing overalls. A reporter, Sheila Patrick, and a press photographer were there to see her measured up by the owner, Robert Adcock. As usual, Taylour took advantage of the press and insisted that instead of her overalls being the standard white, hers had to be pale blue 'with a stitched blue belt to match'[19] and must, furthermore, be fitted to emphasise her figure. Adcock asked her why the overalls had to be blue, and she replied that it was 'romantic'. This response surprised the owner who said, 'But my factory only makes white overalls', adding, 'you call that ROMANTIC? Risking your neck on those tracks?'.[20] Taylour began to make a response, but realised that it would not be possible to explain to the tailor just how she felt about racing. Her later recollection was that, for her, racing was an intense, powerful experience:

> For a moment, as I wonder how I can make him understand, my mind goes to the race track. I'm in the pits, watching the race before mine. In a minute my car will be pushed to the starting line. The huge crowd in the stadium will watch me step into it, while they feel safe up there in the stands, but a little nervous for me. I won't be thinking of them. I'll be thinking of that mad dash into the loose-surfaced bend. Maybe this is the biggest race of my life. I'm going to drive as I've never driven before ... if I can keep the car from spinning out. I'm excited, a little afraid too, but I must pretend to myself I'm not. The challenge is worth everything... but how can I make Mr. Adcock see this is romantic? That I must be in my favorite color to work up a real do-or-die atmosphere inside me ... I don't try.[21]

In this passage resulting from the surprised query of the practical Mr Adcock, Fay Taylour managed to convey something of the force behind her relentless determination to race, whatever the obstacles. The report of the fitting that subsequently appeared in *The Australian Women's Weekly* under the headline, 'Racing driver dresses to suit her car' was more prosaic, but also showed how Taylour knew what worked for journalists and publicity. As usual, she provided just the right sort of copy for the journalist, giving Sheila Patrick a neat series of anecdotes about her lifelong love of racing, and a failed love affair that convinced her that only 'cars are faithful to me'. In return, Taylour was described as 'a fair-skinned, titian-haired Irishwoman of nearly 40 [who] has the proverbial charm of her race'.[22] In fact, Fay Taylour was forty-eight; clearly she understood Frank Arthur's approach to publicity. Media publicity was essential to ticket sales and Taylour was adept at maximising her appeal to the general, as well as the racing, public. Between 8 October 1952 and 11 January 1953, Australian newspapers carried at least 265 articles and mentions of Taylour, plus 129 advertisements for her racing, often headlining her, and twenty-two results columns in which she featured. This is an astonishing amount of press coverage for a sports star in what was a minor sport.[23]

After a few days of dealing with publicity, Taylour and Frank Arthur drove to a Sydney track for practice runs. On the way there, Arthur made some remarks that Taylour took to mean that she would, inevitably, have 'slowed down' compared to her racing two decades before. Of course, Fay Taylour took this as a challenge, which, perhaps, had been the promoter's intention. They stopped at the Sydney Showground where the races were to be held and where, on her last appearance there, she had crashed on what had been a 'heavy cinder track [that] was rough. Too rough for the size'.[24] That crash had sent her unconscious to hospital. It had been one of a number of crashes she had during the 1929–30 season in Australia. Since then, the track had been resurfaced with what Arthur described as 'beauti-ful smooth granite'. The practice track was close by, with Taylour's midget car waiting for her there. It was a Ford V8/60 in yellow and blue livery, emblazoned with a Union flag and a large green shamrock overwritten with 'Fay Taylour'. Photographs of Taylour sitting in the car subsequently appeared in the Sydney newspapers. Frank Arthur warned her not to go all out to save undue wear on the newly tuned engine, but after the conversation on the way to the practice that was probably a forlorn hope. Later, she described her practice runs:

> I forget everything except the nice shape of the curves ahead, and a midget racer under me [...] I put my foot full on the gas pedal, and leave it there. In one fast all-out power slide I take the first bend, and the second. Without easing up anywhere, I go into the second lap the same way, taking the curves wide, in a manner that's showy as well as fast. And how I'm enjoying it! But the fun is short-lived. Before I finish the second lap, flags are waved vigorously. I have to stop. The practice is over.'[25]

No doubt to her delight, Frank Arthur had stopped the run, shouting to his track officials, 'Stop her! Stop her! Save her for Friday!'[26]

That Saturday was Taylour's first midget car race in Australia. She raced against Bert Martin, Harold Barnes, and the 30-year-old Johnny Peers, New South Wales champion in 1947 (Peers would later be the last person to win at the Sydney Showground in a V8/60 engined car, in 1955). Meeting Peers in the pits before the race, Taylour described him as 'a serious and enthusiastic race driver [who] has a nice face and gentle manner'. She went on to remember that Peers said to her, smiling 'I'm going to put my best foot forward ... I can't afford to be beaten by a woman. I hear you're good.'[27] Arthur's advice to Fay was to take an immediate lead on the first bend and stay ahead. It was a rolling start and after one false start, it was on and Taylour took the first curve:

> The track is rough, but I'm used to rough tracks. I've driven much worse. The shape of these bends is better than most. I cut for a fraction of a second entering them. That's the fastest way. It halts too much sliding, and

consequent loss of driving grip. It makes spinning less of a hazard. The race is over four laps. That means eight skidding turns. I love them all, except the first. That first dash into the loose curve, alongside the other car is too tricky to be loved! But I think I love it, all the same.'[28]

Taylour won the race, but later discovered that Johnny Peers had been told that she would be slow into the first bend. It seems that Frank Arthur knew his promoter's trade in the smallest degree. She also won against Martin and Barnes. The next day the *Sunday Herald* announced, 'Woman Driver in Form', explaining that 'British woman speed-car driver, Fay Taylour, convincingly beat each of her three rivals in match races at the Showground Speedway meeting last night. About 12,000 people saw Miss Taylour in turn beat Bert Martin, Harold Barnes, and Johnny Peers'.[29] Not only did Fay beat these three drivers, she also 'registered the new world time with 21.35 seconds'.[30] It was an auspicious start for her in Australia, and probably gave many of the top male drivers something to think about. For the promoters, it meant that the gate of 12,000, at 2/- per ticket, had brought in £1,200 for the night (around £40,000 in 2022).

Taylour insisted that her car be retuned before her next appearance at the Sydney Showground. After agreeing, Arthur took a photograph of her with the mechanic, peering into the engine. The photograph subsequently appeared in the Sydney press, with Arthur feeding the journalist the message that Fay Taylour wanted 'more speed' for her next race. This publicity was followed by a cartoon, drawn by Brodie Mack, the sporting cartoonist, of Fay Taylour as 'The Lana Turner' of the track, a reference to the 'sweater girl' persona that she had established in the US. The cartoon had been suggested by Empire Speedways' finance director, Mr Sherwood, who had taken the sweater girl portraits of Taylour to Brodie Mack, who produced his cartoon with the text, 'The Lana Turner of the Speedways, takes the curves on the track, she will also take the built-in curves on her personal chassis'.[31] Other similar cartoons followed, with one in the *Sydney Sun*, by Emille Mercier, having two mechanics commenting, '... and furthermore, she's got a broadside that'll make you gasp!'.[32] The innuendo, and what would now be seen as outright sexism, merely made Taylour 'laugh till I have to put fresh mascara on my eyelashes'.[33] The biggest laugh, of course, was Taylour's continuing ability to beat the best male drivers on the track.

After Fay's first victories at the Sydney Showground, the talk was of matching her against Frank Brewer. He was also on Frank Arthur's books and had the fastest car in Australia, his 'Car no. 2'. As Taylour knew, 'what is under the hood of his V-8 60, no one but Frank himself knows'.[34] A young woman fan came to see Taylour at her hotel, asked for her autograph and wanted to know when she would be racing against Brewer, saying: 'You drive clean and smooth like Brewer, and you give the motor all its got ... that's why I'd like to see that! But it'd have to be on equal motors. You see, he gives his all it's got ... and it's got more than yours. It accelerates like a rocket.'[35] Taylour spoke to Frank Arthur, and the meeting was arranged.

As usual, Taylour arrived early in Brisbane, staying at Brisbane's top hotel, Lennon's, where the US General Macarthur and his staff had stayed during the early part of the war against Japan. She began the usual round of meeting the press, attending other sporting events and publicising the forthcoming race meet. She visited the track and made some practice runs. The track was new and offered specific challenges:

> This track is very different from the average oval speedway. Instead of two bends, it seems to have three. It means there are no long straightaways. One is in a broadside skid most of the way round … the sort of track you get lost on under floodlights if you haven't had a chance to see it first in daylight. I feel happier on the regular oval, but after practice I'm not exactly unhappy.[36]

Fay's first appearance was due the week before she was scheduled to race Brewer on Saturday 29 November, but her opponent called off. Reluctant to forego the takings, Frank Arthur announced that instead Taylour would race the clock in an exhibition drive. Prior to the event she ate dinner in the hotel dining room and was suddenly afflicted by doubts: 'suddenly I feel lonely, and a little frightened. It's the music. The sad and beautiful aria from *Madame Butterfly* is mingling into my thoughts. The dining room orchestra is playing 'One Fine Day', the prologue to Madame Butterfly killing herself'.[37] This is a rare admission in Taylour's various memoirs and writings that she was ever frightened of being killed. She had no need to worry, however: that evening she beat the track records. The Brisbane *Truth* reported, 'A 20,000 crowd at the Exhibition Speedway last night saw Miss Fay Taylour smash the women's lap record, AND BETTER, THE BEST FIGURES BY A MALE DRIVER, by 2.5 SECONDS'. Taylour reckoned that the gate takings were around £4,000, and that she could expect about £150. In fact, Frank Arthur deducted her hotel costs, and said that many of the spectators had passes, which reduced the takings. She was doubtful about this, but ruefully acknowledged that without a manager there was little she could do.

The stage was now set for her meeting with Frank Brewer. The press ran stories about the coming race, noting that it would be worth £100 to the winner:

> Fay Taylour will meet her toughest opposition this season against 'Satan' Brewer tomorrow night at the Exhibition Speedway. Brewer arrived in Brisbane last night [...] She has never met Ray Revell or Brewer [in midget cars], but has beaten the best of Australia's car drivers in Sydney in recent weeks [...] Miss Taylour also will race against Brewer, George Bonser, and Alan Taylor in the six laps scratch race. It will be the first time in Queensland that a woman has raced men speed drivers in an open event.'[38]

The contest between the two was the best of three heats, in addition to the scratch race. As Taylour was well aware, Brewer's car was very fast, and she was concerned that the car would give him the edge. She reflected that 'Brewer is a gentleman. And, by that, I mean a sport. If he were asked to use a car for this race more equal in speed to mine, he would do it. But he is not asked. And so he will drive his very fast "Special".[39] The issue for Taylour was that the racing fans would not be told about the difference in cars. In fact, *aficionados* of the sport would be well aware of the difference, even if the general public were not.

Brewer and Taylour tossed to see who would take the inside starting position for the first heat. Brewer won, but Taylour was happy with the outside position for the first heat as, 'it'll be easier to control the car from outside till I get the feel of the track at speed, less chance of spinning because one takes a wider curve'.[40] She was well aware that racing against Brewer was the biggest challenge yet in her midget car racing and that, 'I'll have to go harder than I've ever gone before'.[41] Brewer took the lead from the outset and crossed the line 30 yards ahead of Taylour.[42] For the second heat she took the inside position:

> The flag goes down, and so does my foot. I use every ounce of speed and skill I can muster. I'm in front! I'm holding the inside position! I haven't spun – and I'm going like stink! In his effort to catch me, Satan hits the fence. He bounces off, and keeps going. Another driver of his reputation might have stopped. Not Satan. He's too great – his sportsmanship is as great as his driving.[43]

Taylour narrowly won the second heat, leading Brewer by a length. It was crowd-pleasing racing, especially given Brewer's near mishap, and the heat emphasised how good both drivers were, as well as Taylour's value as an attraction. Brewer now had the right to take the inside position again for the final heat, but he offered it to Taylour. She refused and insisted on tossing for the position. She lost and took the outside. Brewer also won the deciding heat, leading Taylour across the finish line by 20 yards. Undoubtedly, Taylour would have dearly liked to have beaten Frank Brewer, but she had performed well and, as the press realised, there was truth in the fact that Brewer had the faster car:

> Fay Taylour, world's champion lady speedcar driver, was well beaten by American [*sic*] Frank Brewer in two out of three heats of a match race at the Exhibition Speedway last night [...] She certainly struck tough opposition in Brewer, and her driving ability was not nearly enough to combat Brewer's obvious extra speed.[44]

The meeting between the two drivers was the high point of Taylour's tour thus far, and for the promoters was another important event in both publicity and revenue terms. Fay Taylour's next high-profile race was, she came to believe, a staged event designed to maintain the publicity momentum.

Taylour's next fixtures were to be at the Sydney Sportsground Speedway, and to her surprise it was announced that she would be racing a woman driver, Edna Wells. Unknown to Taylour, this plan to race an Australian woman against Taylour had been in process for some time, at least as long as she had been in Brisbane. As Taylour put it, 'the new angle, kept a dark secret, is now sprung on me. I'm to race against a woman in my next Sydney appearance'.[45] Taylour's surprise was due to the fact that, up until being told about the forthcoming meeting, she had no idea that there were any women midget car drivers in Australia. Taylour was very probably right in seeing this as a 'new angle'. It is likely that Frank Arthur knew about the plans to, in effect, create an Australian female rival to Taylour. As events transpired, it seemed that there was a good deal more to the 'new angle' than merely finding a woman capable of racing Taylour on the midget car track. In her unpublished memoirs, Fay Taylour makes it clear that she was certain that the heats between her and Wells were rigged to some extent to enable the Australian woman to beat Taylour. This was the only time that Taylour complained that cheating against her took place, and it is clear from her account that this is what she believed happened in her race against Wells at the Sydney Sportsground Speedway on 5 December 1952. It is likely that Taylour was right in her assessment of events. The incentive for the promoters and the ground lay in the creation of the 'new angle'. If Taylour was more than a match for most of the male drivers, then a defeat at the hands of a home-grown woman racer added a new selling point.

In the run-up to the meeting, the press reported on the newly emergent woman challenger. Edna Wells, aged twenty-five, was described by the press as a 'diminutive, railway ticket collector [...] seeking a career as a speedcar driver'.[46] Prior to working on the railways, Wells had a varied career involving driving farm tractors, semi-trailer timber wagons, and had raced in club motorcycle events in her mid-teens. The *Sydney Morning Herald* gave an account of Wells's long infatuation with speed and driving, noting that, 'at 16, Miss Wells was issued a special driving licence to permit her to drive cars, trucks and semi-trailers; then she passed her test for a motor bike licence'.[47] Like Taylour over two decades earlier, Wells had been forced to resort to subterfuge to race against men, including using the same trick of hiding her hair beneath a helmet, just as Taylour had done in 1928. Wells certainly had extensive driving experience, but she had never raced midget cars before. However, she was being coached by Bill Reynolds, a former motorcycle and midget car champion. Further, as Wells explained, 'I will be driving Ray Revell's fast car, and if luck comes my way I hope to win'.[48] The stage was set for the match between 'world champion woman driver Fay Taylour' and the Australian newcomer, Edna Wells.[49]

The match between the two took place on Friday 5 December and was the usual best-of-three event, with each heat being of two laps. Taylour met the challenger before the race, and described her as 'short, neat, and good looking', noting that 'she's been doing men's jobs all her life, that's to say, for the approximate ten years since she left school'.[50] The starts were to be rolling starts, and Taylour said that the mechanics were told not to start her car until Wells had her car started. This was not particularly unusual, as 'starting is a tricky business because these cars have no clutch. Having no self-starter either, they have to be pushed off, and now two strong men are pushing her while I wait in my car and watch'.[51] Wells's car was into the first bend before the engine fired, Taylour's car was push started and she cruised round after Wells, waiting until both of them would come level with the starting line and take the starting flag together. But

Wells drove on as fast as she could and to Taylour's amazement, the first flag that showed was the chequered flag. Wells had won a race that Taylour was not even aware had begun:

> I pull into the infield, and stop. I hear the announcer say that Miss Edna Wells of Australia has won the first heat. Promoter Frank Arthur comes up to me looking puzzled.
>
> 'What are they doing?', I ask him. 'The race was never started. It wasn't a race.'
>
> Frank shakes his head in a mystified way. He just doesn't know. He leaves racing arrangements and control to the track manager and officials.[52]

A friend of Taylour's who had bet on her winning the meeting came across to express amazement that the 'race' had been allowed. Frank Arthur's advice was not to object because Taylour would easily win the next two heats.

Wells and Taylour's cars were in a corner of the pits while the next races took place. Taylour spoke to Wells, explaining how a rolling start was run, adding, 'I will be on the inside position for the next heat. That means she will have to keep level at the pace I set, as we roll round to take the starting flag'.[53] Wells agreed. The heat started and the rolling start worked exactly as intended. Taylour took the lead on the first bend and was ahead when her car's engine stopped. The usual practice if there was an engine failure on the first lap was that the race was re-started. But Wells continued to drive and was given the chequered flag after three laps. Taylour was angry and demanded to know why 'the race was not re-started, according to the A.C.U. (Auto Cycle Union) match race rules. The meet is run under these rules. I'm told that the cars are not bound by these rules – only motor cycles'.[54] Later she would be told that the meet *was* under the ACU rules, but by then it was of little use. Once again, Taylour felt the lack of a manager to fight her corner. That evening, cousins of Taylour who had watched her race took her to stay with them on their farm for the weekend. During the night Taylour received a telephone call from the mechanic looking after her car. His news was that 'the ignition coil on my car was burnt out, and half the leads from the distributor were loose. They jumped adrift with the swerve into the bend. No wonder the engine died!'[55]

The next day, press headlines ran 'Defeat for Taylour', and 'Shock Defeat of Champion'.[56] Nothing was said about the rolling start of the first heat, although the *Telegraph* noted that 'in the second heat Miss Taylour had a clear lead after one lap, but was forced to stop through engine trouble'.[57] Later reports identified the problem as being 'the high tension coil of her ignition burnt out'.[58] It was also announced that there would be a rematch between Wells and Taylour at Brisbane. For Taylour the fiasco at Sydney Showground had been annoying and frustrating. For the promoters and the race grounds, however, it had injected a 'new angle' into the Fay Taylour story with the success of a local Sydney woman against a 'world champion'.

Taylour and Wells flew together to Brisbane the next weekend, where they were to race two locally based cars of equal speed. At first, the atmosphere between them was strained, but their shared unease about flying led them both to put on their racing helmets, breaking the ice. At Brisbane Rowley Park speedway Taylour soon felt more confident that the officials there would ensure a fair race. She wondered whether they had heard about the events at the Sydney Showground. Before the race the track officials gave them 'a pep talk on the rules before we line up [...] "if one of you 'jumps the start', it'll be disqualified, and the race awarded to the other"'.[59] The rolling start went perfectly and Taylour, on the inside position, took the lead from the first bend, winning the heat easily. Taylour won the second heat as well, winning the rematch. After the race, Edna Wells invited Taylour to a party in her rooms at Lennon's Hotel where they were both staying. It went well, and Taylour later remembered that Wells was:

> Still in cover-alls, and is demonstrating her skill at Ju-Jitzu. Amazingly, she's able to floor men who are a foot taller, and maybe twice as heavy as herself. Her spirits have not been lowered by the defeat on the track. It means another race for her in Sydney. The officials reckon that the score is now level, and call for a decider.[60]

Whatever the difficulties on the track, it is clear that both women were, as Taylour would say, 'good sports'.

Interestingly, the same evening, a well-known male driver, Harry Neale, known as the 'Black Prince', had refused to race against Taylour at Rowley Park. His reasoning was that Taylour did not have sufficient practice on what he described as 'the most hazardous track in Australia'.[61] However, given that on another occasion Neale had scoffed at other male drivers 'if his fellow competitors couldn't drive like men they should take up knitting!',[62] it is more likely a simple case of sexism, and a fear of being beaten by a woman. Harry Neale subsequently withdrew his objection to meeting Taylour on the track. On 19 December Fay raced against him at Rowley Park. The next day the Adelaide *Advertiser* reported the 'biggest attraction at Rowley Park last night was again Fay Taylour. Her brilliant drive in a comparatively strange car earned her first place in the Speedcar Mixed Handicap Division. The driving was so keen that Australian champion Harry Neale was forced into second place and Rick Harvey's motor blew up'.[63] Neale may well have thought about taking up knitting.

For Taylour there was still the third rematch against Wells, which was initially scheduled for 30 December 1952 at Sydney, but was not in fact run until 9 January 1953. There was talk of Taylour being loaned a 1100cc Cooper for the race, although that did not happen. Before the rematch, Taylour raced at Tracy's Speedway, Maribyrnong, Victoria, where she 'easily beat Victorian Kev Young' before a crowd of 10,000.[64] She performed less well a week later at the same track when she spun her car, an event that was headlined in Melbourne press reports, showing the prominence of Taylour in midget car speedway.

The Taylour–Wells rematch took place at the Sydney Sports Ground on 9 January 1953, after heavy rain forced the match at the Showground to be cancelled the previous week. The general view was that Wells had a better chance at the Sports Ground which was a smaller track than the Showground, requiring tactics more than speed. If, after the Brisbane meet, Taylour thought the issues with Wells had been fixed, she was to be disappointed once again. On the Sydney track, she appeared again to face collusion between Wells and officials and a determined attempt to cheat Taylour of the race. Taylour's account of this meeting suggests very strongly that not only had Wells been coached on how to bend the rules to breaking point, but that the track officials also enabled her by not intervening when they should have done. The entire meeting left a bad taste in Taylour's mouth.

The first heat saw a rolling start in which Taylour was the pace leader in the preliminary lap designed to bring both cars level for the start. Instead, Wells continually hung back and, as Taylour slowed to let her come alongside, Wells dropped further back. The intention was explained by Taylour, 'the car hanging back can accelerate to full throttle BEFORE the car in front, catching the car in front exactly on the starting line as the flag starts the race'.[65] Race officials should have stepped in to warn the offender, and disqualified Wells if she persisted. The Sydney officials did nothing. Eventually Taylour opened up her car's engine a few feet from the starting line, with Wells shooting past her on the line, having opened up sooner. Taylour sped after Wells:

> I throw my car into a powerslide when still off the turn. Then, without cutting, I enter the wide sweep with my wheels 'crossed up' in a fast controlled skid. I pull down to the inside, leaving almost the full width of the track for her. She sees me coming. She's in the center. Oceans of room to pass. Suddenly she cuts clean across me. Maybe she's out of control. I spin infield to avoid hitting her – and there I am, stuck with a dead engine.[66]

Spectators objected to this foul by Wells. Someone trackside complained to the race officials. They declared a foul, and issued a reprimand to Wells, but still declared her the winner of the heat. The second heat went no better for Taylour. Wells was now on the inside and pace leader for the rolling start. Again, Wells failed to make a clean start, alternately racing ahead then slowing down. This cat and mouse approach led to Wells suddenly hemming Taylour in against the fence. Taylour backed away at the last second but still hit the fence, bouncing off to see Wells race away to start the heat. The race was very close but Wells again hemmed Taylour against the fence:

> At full throttle I hit the fence. It's too late. It's her or the fence! [...] My car climbs half way up, and keeps going. I ride along it for several yards. Then, in some miraculous way, regain the track without turning over. The same circumstances, at exactly the same spot, killed a driver just three weeks earlier.[67]

Wells won the heat, leaving a rueful and discontented Taylour to reflect, 'Edna risked a crash more than once. I could have hit her. She made a desperate bid. And she won. She beat me in guile. But it took courage'.[68]

The unsatisfactory Sydney meeting between Taylour and Wells was not the end of the rivalry. The next day they raced against each other at the Brisbane Exhibition Ground. As if to confirm Taylour's suspicions about the unfair partiality of Sydney race officials in favour of the local woman, the Exhibition Ground heats were run without problems. The next day, the Brisbane press announced Taylour's easy two-heat win against Wells:

> Although Sydney girl, speedcar driver Edna Wells, had beaten the Irish globe-trotter Fay Taylour twice on her home track, she was no match for Fay at the Exhibition Speedway last night, and was beaten in straight heats.
>
> They drove cars of equal power, but in the first heat Wells' car did not appear to run well and although she started from inside position Taylour drove around her, and was never in danger, to win by 30 yards. In the second, and deciding heat, they changed cars and starting positions. But Taylour simply drove away to win as she liked by 5 yards.[69]

The match was so easy for Taylour that press noted that she had won 'without dash'. Nevertheless, she had her revenge for the Sydney matches.

Taylour's schedule was hectic. She raced week after week, while publicity and socialising took up much of the rest of her time. Over Christmas 1952 she had taken time to reacquaint herself with an 'old flame' from her pre-war motorcycle speedway racing in Australia. This farmer and polo player, whom she called 'Charles', was married.[70] That, however, did not stop Fay from meeting up with him and spending a somewhat flirtatious night on the town, despite her sense that his wife and family disapproved. In the run-up to Christmas 1952, she raced at Adelaide, then at Melbourne on the Saturdays before and after Christmas. An initial invitation from Charles to spend Christmas Day with his family was withdrawn at the last moment in a letter delivered to Fay in Melbourne. She was certain in her mind that the cancellation was due to pressure from Charles's wife. Given that he had proposed marriage to her at Christmas 1929, this is perhaps unsurprising. Despite the letter, Charles appeared at the Melbourne track just before her race. Afterwards he took her, still in her pale blue racing overalls, to dinner, where he explained that it was general family disapproval of him meeting up with Taylour that had led to the abrupt cancellation of the invitation. That, in turn, had led Charles to fly down to meet her the next day at Melbourne. Dinner was followed by a night of talking, reminiscing, and dancing at nightclubs before Charles returned home the next morning by plane. The entire episode was described by Taylour in some detail in a version of her autobiography. The tone of the account is somewhat arch, and there is a sense of her delight in winning against Charles's family, including his wife. This was not the only time she appeared to have enjoyed this sort of 'victory' against another woman and suggests that her sense of being a risk-taker and someone who competed to win was not limited to the racetrack. In her defence, however, she bracketed the account of 'Charles' in Melbourne with an account of the downside of her peripatetic life: 'I've cut myself off too much from friends like this. Tearing from place to place, living in hotels, doesn't produce the social recreation I sometimes crave, contact with people and atmospheres familiar to my upbringing'.[71] As with long-term financial security, which Taylour never achieved, so too with a life spent among people of her own class, or a husband of her own – racing was not compatible with these things. Taylour knew this and revelled in the way in which she defied convention, while sometimes desiring the gains that would have come from not doing so.

Before the post-Christmas Melbourne race, Taylour spent some time with relatives on both sides of her family, including those named Fetherstonhaugh, Herring, and Chumley. These included one of Australia's foremost military men, General Sir Edmund Herring. His mother's maiden name was Fetherstonhaugh. 'Ned', as he was known to his family, was born in Maryborough, Victoria, in 1892. Educated at Melbourne Grammar, where he was captain of school, followed by Melbourne University, he then took a Rhodes Scholarship to Oxford where he joined the Officer Training Corps (OTC) in 1913. Herring was a formidable scholar and sportsman, and a fine soldier, winning an immediate Military Cross in the Macedonian campaign, followed by the Distinguished Service Order. By 1952, when Taylour met him, he had served with great distinction in the Western Desert, Greece, and in Australia's struggle against Japan in the Second World War. He was Chief Justice of the Supreme Court of Victoria, and Lieutenant Governor of the state. General Herring was a central figure in Victoria in many aspects of the state's life, not just law and politics. Taylour went to a tennis party held at the Herrings' and, perhaps surprisingly, told him about her difficulties getting back into the United States, and, furthermore, about the politics that led to the issue. He 'listens patiently and sympathetically, and advises me to keep trying. His attitude is encouraging'.[72] Sir Edmund's outstanding record in the Second World War notwithstanding, he had, in the interwar period, taken a political stance not that far removed from Taylour's. In the difficult decades between the wars, political and trade union unrest in Australia led many serving and ex-army officers to band together in a clandestine group known as the White Guard or League of National Security (LNS). Their aim was to forestall or fight any attempt at a communist revolution in Australia. Herring had been a member of this group, the White Guard. It was likely, therefore, that the sympathetic hearing Taylour reported was a result of her stressing the anti-communism of her politics.

As the new year began, Taylour continued her racing, appearing at Rowley Park, Adelaide, then Sydney. At Rowley Park, she raced Harry Neale again, and Rick Harvey. Neale was, in all probability, very keen to avenge the defeat he had suffered at Taylour's hands at Rowley Park on 19 December. In the rematch, Taylour first raced against Neale and Rick Harvey. Like Neale, Harvey was a noted competitor and a motorcycle police officer with the South Australian

Police. Tragically, he and two police colleagues were killed in a road traffic incident accident two years later. Harvey was only 27. The first heat saw Neale beaten into second place by Taylour, while Rick Harvey was forced out when his car's engine blew up. Neale was now faced with the prospect of being defeated again by Fay Taylour. As she later remembered, 'the men gang up on me to stop me':

> The fastest man driver isn't driving the fastest car. The fastest car isn't being driven by the fastest man. If the switch can be made, then the daring, dashing Harry Neale will start in the fastest car. Anything goes in this sportsmen's mecca. I do not say this with irony [...] because these boys are really sports. And the switch is permitted.[73]

Despite the car switch, Neale trailed Taylour until the final lap. On the penultimate turn Neale used his front bumper to 'edge me. I lose control, hit the fence, and lose the race. Harry takes the winner's flag'.[74] Afterwards, Taylour records that Neale apologised to her in a self-deprecating, humorous fashion, saying 'It was a dirty trick ... but I had to. I just couldn't let the boys down'.[75] Taylour laughed with him, saying, 'who could be cross, anyway, with such a good-looking rascal, who drives like he does? Hadn't I kept him at bay for seven laps? It was fun'.[76] This account encapsulates perhaps Taylour's association of speed, intense competition, and sex. For her, the three were often comingled. Neale, the 'Black Prince', appeared to be an embodiment of the three essentials. Sadly, he too was killed racing, at the Claremont Speedway, Perth, in 1959.[77]

Following the second Taylour–Neale meeting, Taylour had completed her contract with Frank Arthur. She had raced at four of the five big Australian tracks, with two or three appearances at each. That left only the Claremont Speedway, but the track said it could not afford Arthur's terms, as did a New Zealand track. This did not matter for Arthur, who wrote Taylour a cheque for her return air fare to England. However, she wanted more racing, and offered to reopen negotiations with both Perth and Auckland. This involved extended discussion with Frank Arthur about the terms of her contract and Taylour's unhappiness at what she saw as her limited profits once her expenses were taken into account. Finally, Arthur agreed that she could make her own terms with Claremont Speedway, and, in return, she would race again at Sydney. Taylour telephoned Perth and spoke to the Claremont manager, Mr Wyatt. He was less than enthusiastic, pleading small crowds and the difficulty of finding Taylour a car. But she wanted to return to Perth, where she had raced and beaten two of the greatest Australian motorcycle speedway racers, Frank Brown, and 'Super' Sig Schlam, in January 1929. Her victory over Schlam at Claremont was a major highlight of her motorcycle speedway career. Now, twenty-five years later, she wanted to replay those early victories, but on four wheels not two. Taylour drew on her long experience of publicity and sent Wyatt photographs, newspaper stories and figures of record crowds designed to convince him that her appearance would transform the 'take' from the gates. She also offered very generous terms: 'I told him I'd drive for a percentage of gate receipts above average [starting at 20% of first hundred, rising to 40% of third hundred above]. He needn't pay me if I don't draw'.[78] Wyatt agreed and telegrammed Taylour with the news that a car had been bought for her to race. On arriving at Perth, she was met by Wyatt, who greeted her by saying, 'you better pull a crowd, or I'm sunk'.[79] Fay was then taken by Wyatt's partner on the usual round of publicity visits to the media in preparation for the first racing, scheduled for 23 January 1953.

At the pits on race day, Taylour met the famous pre-war motorcycle speedway champion, Ron Johnson. Taylour had raced against him in England before she had been banned for being a woman rider. For example, in June 1928 they had raced at Crystal Palace Speedway, with Taylour 'having a tremendous tussle with Ron Johnson when she fell on the last lap. It was said that being a lady, her fall was "most graceful", though for a moment she was standing on her head'.[80] Johnson's racing in the 1930s was repeatedly interrupted by bad crashes, and in 1949 he suffered a fractured skull racing at Wimbledon. His attempts at a return to speedway the following year were not successful, and he retired to Australia. Only a few years apart in age, Taylour and Johnson talked about their early days racing, and her successes at Claremont a quarter of a century earlier. Johnson asked her, 'remember how you equalled a record last time you raced here? Can you do that again?'.[81] Naturally, Taylour took that as a challenge. The next day, *The West Australian* reported:

> Fay Taylour, the Irish woman driver, made an auspicious debut in car racing at the Claremont Speedway last night.
> The largest crowd of the season applauded her feats of superb driving skill and courage.
> In a series of spectacular drives, she equalled the one-lap rolling and two-lap standing start records for cars. She also won the second Speedcar Handicap event from 30 yards behind scratch. In this event, when nearing the pits bend in the second lap, Miss Taylour's car slid alarmingly almost to make a complete about turn. Quickly regaining control, she coolly continued in the race, made up her lost ground, and won.[82]

After that 'auspicious start', Taylour was to appear again at the Claremont Speedway the following week, to face the Western Australia champion, John Hamilton. Although 'Johnnie' had only begun his midget car career during the previous Australian season, he had already gained a formidable reputation, especially at Claremont. Sadly, in 1957 he would lose his life there in a multi-car accident.[83] Before meeting 'Johnnie', Fay took time to appear at 'the wheel of a high-powered craft' during the Australia Day Regatta at Crawley, generating more publicity.[84]

The match against Hamilton was expected to be a difficult one for Taylour, although the press also noted that 'if Miss Taylour beats Hamilton, it will be no great surprise. She has already mastered male opponents in Brisbane and Adelaide and only Sydney champions have been able to beat her on level terms'.[85]

Perhaps Taylour might well have disputed the 'level terms' that she faced in Sydney, but the acknowledgement of her racing prowess against men was true. Johnnie Hamilton was another driver who maintained and tuned his own car, and as Taylour knew, 'he knew how to tune'.[86] Ironically, Hamilton had also been tasked with preparing Fay Taylour's car for the racing at Claremont, which he did, with her car running well during the practice laps. For the first heat between Hamilton and Taylour, her car ran well and she led until the final lap when the engine began to overheat as a result of a blockage in the oil feed. Hamilton was behind but rapidly catching the now slowing Taylour. What happened next appeared to have been another unnecessary collision:

> He must realise I'm slowing, that he'll be able to pass. I pull right down to the inside. I keep moving, hoping against hope that some miracle may occur. But I'm slower ... and slower ... and now the car behind has caught up. I hear it's full-throttle roar ... then BANG! With sudden unexpected impact I'm hit. I'm spinning infield![87]

The result was that the 'mishap', as *The West Australian* reported it, left Taylour's car with a badly buckled rear wheel.[88] Taylour was stranded on the grass, and the pit attendants ran across to tell her the crowd was demanding a rerun of the heat. This was agreed. Efforts were made to fix the engine while a new rear wheel was provided. But Taylour's luck had run out, as the press reported the next day: 'although she drove hard and showed commendable grit in persevering with a faulty motor, Miss Taylour was unable to shake off her bad luck. Miss Taylour used a borrowed car in the re-run but was easily beaten'.[89] In her unpublished memoirs, Taylour records that mechanics at Claremont believed that Hamilton had deliberately rammed her car in the first heat: 'he hit you so that you couldn't go on showing your pace'.[90] There is a reasonable likelihood that was the case, but one of the attractions of midget car speedway to fans was the frequency of collisions, which was part of this very dangerous sport. As if to ameliorate the 'mishap', Hamilton offered his car to Taylour to allow her to make attempts on track records, which she duly did, equalling the record for a one-lap flying start.[91] Despite, or perhaps because of the drama of the night, the large crowd was informed that the two antagonists would race again the following Saturday, 6 February. That meeting went no better for Taylour as she was 'again dogged by engine trouble when making her final appearance at the Claremont Speedway [...] Starting three times in a match race series, Miss Taylour was forced to retire on each occasion'.[92] Taylour was frustrated and angry about what she saw as a concerted attempt to undermine her attempts to defeat Hamilton, the local hero. A letter to the press later raised the issue of Taylour's treatment at Claremont:

> In the three weeks that speed car driver Fay Taylour was at Claremont Speedway, I saw some questionable sportsmanship in the pits. The car she was given to drive was in anything but perfect order. It was said that children

interfered with it, yet children nor other spectators are not allowed in the pits before a meeting is over. When Fay Taylour one night appealed for pits assistance she did not get it, and I saw her drive out of the pits almost in tears.[93]

This allegation was subsequently rebutted by another letter which said that a great deal of work was done in the pits to repair Taylour's car.[94] Nonetheless, it is probably fair to say that, as at Sydney, Fay Taylour had met opposition off as well as on the track. She had, not for the first time, faced the brotherhood of the track.

After Claremont, Taylour travelled to New Zealand where she spent a month racing. She was the main feature in the *Speedway News* souvenir programme for the Taranaki Midget Car Racing Club event of 7 March 1953. A portrait photograph was on the programme cover, with photographs of her and her cars inside, along with a reprinted article entitled, 'Car Racing Her First Love', from *The Listener In*, December 1952. That night at the Stratford Speedway, Taylour attempted the three-lap record, and raced against 'Shock' Holmes, and in the 'Fay Taylour Handicap Race' against 'Shock' Holmes, George Amor, Johnny Callender, Peter Pellew and Theo Dodunski. She also raced at Auckland, where she defeated the New Zealand champion for 1951 and 1948, Snow Morris. It is not clear where else Taylour raced in her short time in New Zealand, as her various writings say little about the tour. By early April she was back in Australia, where she had a final race of the Australian season in Sydney. She was beaten by Ray Revell driving his Offenhauser, one of the fastest midget cars in Australia. That brought her tour to an end, and she left Australia on 6 April 1953 on the P&O liner SS *Stratheden*.

Fay Taylour's 1952–53 season tour of Australia and New Zealand was undoubtedly a success. Without a manager, she had created the opportunity to race there, using the opening of her racing in Sweden to convince Frank Arthur that she would be a good prospect for Australia. Once there, she was the first woman to race men in midget cars in Australia. She raced the leading midget car drivers, including Frank Brewer, Ray Revell, Johnny Peers, Harry Neale and John Hamilton, defeating Neale and Peers, while giving the others hard races. As usual, Taylour was responsible for almost all her own publicity, and cleverly exploited the fact that she was both a successful racer and a woman, giving stories to sports and 'women's interest' journalists. Taylour also had to contend with opposition from men unwilling to risk defeat on the track. At first, it had been unclear whether any men would race her, and even when that issue was decided, individuals like Harry Neale were reluctant to compete against her. Finally, Taylour was probably correct in her belief that Edna Wells was, in part, a creation of local Sydney racing patriotism and that her defeat at Wells's hands was far from fair, and, of course, was easily reversed by Taylour at Brisbane. The 1952–53 Australian and New Zealand season over, Fay Taylour had to return to England, still faced by an uncertain future and a renewed struggle to regain entry into the USA.

Chapter Seventeen

Intractable Problems

The SS *Stratheden* docked in London on 3 May 1953, and Fay Taylour was back in England to face two personal problems she had left behind during her tour of Australia and New Zealand. She was still hoping to obtain a visa to re-enter the US, and she also thought that she could convince the trustees that the larger share of her mother's trust fund should devolve to her now thar her father was dead. These two issues were to occupy a good deal of her time during the spring and summer of 1953. Nonetheless, she still did some racing in Ireland, as well as in Sweden once more, along with an appearance at Brands Hatch in October 1953.

Taylour does not appear to have stayed in London for long; instead she travelled back to Dublin. She had decided that she would have more chance of gaining a US visa from the consulate in Dublin than in London. It is not entirely clear why she thought this. Given that she had been barred from re-entering the US because of her political background, any such decision was likely to be referred to Washington. Indeed, the original decision to ban her under the McCarran Act had involved the US security services requesting information on her from their UK counterparts. Perhaps she hoped that the supposed pro-Irish sentiments of the US authorities would carry some weight if she applied as an Irish citizen from Dublin. However, her first visit to the Dublin consulate in 1953 was far from encouraging:

> I visited the American Consulate in Dublin. Eisenhower had just become President. Maybe new officials would take over. But the questioning depressed me. There, thirteen years after I'd been detained, I was being asked if I ever had any contact with those who had been detained with me, and if so, why?! I left in tears.[1]

It is not known what answer Taylour gave to that question, but she had certainly been in contact, both on a personal level and politically, with people that had been detained during the war. Unknown to her, MI5 had previously reported to their US colleagues that she had contacts with the reborn Mosleyite movement in the late 1940s. Further, if the consulate made enquiries of the Irish authorities, it is likely that they would have reported that she knew a variety of exiles from defeated Axis Europe in the immediate aftermath of the war. However, in her favour was the fact that more recently, with her racing in Sweden, Australia and New Zealand, her attention had been focused on her sport not her politics, which took a back seat for most of her post-1945 career.

Disappointed but not entirely discouraged, Taylour made another visit to the US Consulate in Dublin. This time she believed that she was 'trailed' afterwards. Her account of this event makes it seem plausible that the consulate did attempt to undertake some 'fact finding' on its own behalf regarding Taylour's current attitude to politics. After leaving the consulate, she took a bus home. Just as she was boarding the bus, a man dashed up and asked her, in a strong Dublin accent, whether the bus went to Nelson's Pillar. She thought this an odd question from a Dubliner given that the 134-foot-high Pillar was still a major landmark in the city. It was another thirteen years before the IRA blew it in half, fifty years after the Easter Rising. Taylour's suspicion that the question was merely an opening gambit by the man was confirmed, to her, when he sat next to her on the top deck of the bus and quickly began a conversation centred on politics:

> Before we reached the Pillar he had covered his ground [...] Money! Easy subject to get on to when searching for pennies to pay the fare. The Wages, Labor, Government, War, and Russia ... but not motor races. The world was in a mess, didn't I think so? He put the direct question since I'd ignored all his cues. 'Listen,' I said seriously but casually, as if offering an ignorant man some good advice: 'It doesn't pay to talk politics, take my advice and keep these views to yourself'.[2]

It is likely that Taylour was correct to assume that the man on the way to Nelson's Pillar was working for the US Consulate, making a simple and rather obvious check on her willingness to talk politics freely. It will be remembered that the UK authorities' decision to keep Taylour detained for longer than was usual for members of British Union centred on their fear of her talking freely about her politics among the general public. A few days after this second visit to the US Consulate, she received a letter from the consul inviting her to complete the forms necessary for a new application for a visa. This she did, but it would be nearly two years before she was given an answer.

The other matter that occupied Taylour in Dublin was the increasingly pressing need to ensure a more stable financial future. She was forty-nine that April, and even she must have realised that there was a limit to how long she could keep racing. Her problem was that racing was the main source of her income. Even if she had not been wholly committed to racing, she would still have *had* to race to earn money. She hoped to sell her racing story as a book or film and made further attempts to do so during her time in Dublin. But there were also, she thought, two other possible sources of income that would enable her to have a home, a base to which she could return between races and when her racing career was over. At this point, her ideal was 'to build a little home in Dublin now [...] and friends could live in it while I was travelling. It seemed likely I would never get back to the States'.[3] Her financial hopes lay with her mother's trust, and in the will of her late Aunt Mabel Webb of Dublin who had died in December 1949.

The question of her father's will and her mother's trust which, on her father's death, had passed to the three Taylour sisters, preoccupied Fay. Her belief was that her mother had meant the larger part of her trust to eventually pass to any unmarried daughter. This intention, Fay Taylour claimed, had been conveyed in a document signed by her father and her mother during the later stages of her mother's final illness in 1925. However, there were issues with the legality of that document. In reality, Taylour had few legal grounds on which to challenge the situation. Following her father's death and the reversion of the trust to the daughters, each daughter had received an equal share. Taylour herself explained:

> I had already handed my mother's statement to my father's trustee. It had been made as a will, but instead of being drawn up by a lawyer and witnessed, which my father had deemed quite unnecessary, he, himself, had written it out in his handwriting, with Mother's familiar signature at the bottom. The trustee said he would have to get permission from my sisters to hand me the fund because that statement was not a proper will, and my father's own will of recent date had indicated that the fund should be divided between the three daughters.[4]

Taylour was hoping, probably unreasonably, that her two sisters would defer to the wishes of their dying mother twenty-eight years previously, rather than their father's intention expressed a few years earlier. In the event, Taylour's sister Enid curtly refused the request in a telegram from South Africa where she now lived after a peripatetic African life with her doctor husband who worked for the United Nations. Fay Taylour then made a decision to visit Enid in South Africa at some point to persuade her of the justice of her case.

The other possible source of income that Taylour hoped to benefit from was Mabel Webb's will. She had died at the end of 1949, and left almost all her estate to her friend, Miss Carre. Taylour was, however, listed as a residual legatee, with the residue of the estate passing to her at once, and one-eighth of the remaining estate passing to Taylour on the death of Miss Carre. Taylour had enquired about the details of this in October 1950, but that seemed to have had no outcome. While Miss Carre lived, Taylour could expect nothing. In the event, she did receive £1,912 in August 1956 (around £53,000 in 2022), but in 1953 there was nothing available.[5]

Another constant was Taylour's attempt to sell her racing story either as a book or a film script. This had been a particular goal while she was in Hollywood, and the very nearly successful attempt to have her story made into a film continued to spur her on, as did the need for another source of income other than the track. At the beginning of June, she received an encouraging letter from her London literary agent, Frank C. Betts, addressed to her at Buswell's Hotel, Molesworth Street, Dublin. The agency told Taylour that, 'an Irish editor in the office from Dublin this morning was looking for a series. He has taken away your film version of the story based on your life. He wanted to know where you could be contacted'.[6] This was taken to be a good omen. Unfortunately for Taylour, the material was returned to the agents in October without an offer.

During the summer of 1953, Taylour must have been living off her earnings from her Australasian tour, as she appears to have done little racing. However, she kept in touch with the Irish press. *The Irish Times*, which had enthusiastically followed her pre-war career, published several mentions of Taylour that summer. On 22 May there was a long, gossip column piece about her under the by-line 'An Irishwoman's Diary'. This rehearsed many of the stories that Taylour liked to feed journalists, including the repeated 'she broke a lap record set up by the late Sir Malcolm Campbell at Brooklands', tales of her victory over men on the midget racetrack in the US, and the comment that 'this titian-haired woman [...] likes to describe her age as "the wrong side of 30"'.[7] Taylour's only racing in Ireland that summer appears to have been a few appearances at the Chapelizod track, where she just missed out on breaking the four-lap record at the Midget Racing Car Club's meeting on 2 September.[8]

Soon afterwards Taylour was back in Stockholm at the Skarpnäck track, racing an Effyh 500 Formula 3 car, and 'on the 11th [September] she lost a match race against the top Swedish driver Olle Nygren and the following day finished 7th in her heat and 12th in the final of an International F3 race'.[9] In October she raced at Brands Hatch in a Formula 3 race. In November, she travelled again to Australia, where she remained until April 1954, racing in speedcar dirt track meetings across the country.[10]

At the beginning of November, the Australian press announced that Fay Taylour was returning for the 1953–54 season and was expected in the country by early December.[11] This was to be Taylour's second and last tour of Australia as a midget car racer, twenty-four years after she had first raced there on two wheels. The previous 1952–53 Australian season had not been without its difficulties for Taylour, despite her victories and racing in all the Australian states, as well in New Zealand. Her second midget car season in Australia would prove as successful in terms of racing, but was also marked by more obvious opposition from male drivers, while Edna Wells, who had beaten Taylour under questionable circumstances the previous season, proved to be, if anything, more unsporting. There is a sense that Taylour was beginning to be less enthusiastic about touring around the world. Her second midget racing season in Australia receives little coverage in her various autobiographical writings, which may be a sign that she enjoyed the season less than she had before. Undoubtedly, the prolonged struggle to regain a visa to enter the United States was beginning to affect her mood. She felt that she had been unfairly shut out of a country where she felt at home. It must have seemed increasingly likely that she would never be able to return to the US. That left her with the question of where she could find a permanent home. She would be fifty in April 1954 and even with her characteristic single-mindedness she knew that she could not continue to earn a living from racing for much longer. Writing later about this period, she said, 'I felt lost wandering the world without any home, and never attaining the cash I'd hoped for by racing'.[12] Although she wrote that years later, her sense of being lost around the world was also reported by an Australian journalist who appeared to have interviewed Taylour in

Melbourne and wrote: 'Miss Taylour hopes to settle down after the present tour ends, and, being Irish born, she wants to make her home in Ireland, where she hopes to build and give up her "hobo existence"'.[13] That hope, of building a house in Ireland, depended entirely on Taylour's unfounded belief that she could convince her sister, Enid, to part with her inheritance from their mother's trust. Fay Taylour's desperate attempts to extract more than a third of the value of the trust meant that she intended to visit her sister Enid in South Africa after the 1953–54 Australian tour.

Taylour's tour began at Perth, where she had been engaged by Empire Speedways once more to race at two meetings at the Claremont Speedway. The *Daily News* ran a piece about her forthcoming appearances which recapped her previous year's Claremont racing and, interestingly, said that she had intended that season to mark the end of her racing career:

> Irish woman speedway driver Fay Taylour has arrived in Perth to appear at the Claremont Speedway. Since leaving Perth last year, after attracting three record crowds, Miss Taylour has driven in England, Ireland and Sweden. The globe-trotting Miss Taylour [. . .] had intended to retire after last year's Australian campaign. She changed her mind for two reasons – the first, she says, is personal; the second because her wander-lust is incurable. She is one of the few women racing drivers in the world, and probably the best-known. Far from being a novelty act, she handles a car with great skill, and is conceded to be stiff opposition by the best of male drivers. In fact, her ability to handle a car is her stock in trade, for she invariably competes in a strange car, on a track which she has had no chance of practicing on.[14]

The 'personal reasons' why Taylour had not retired were, of course, her financial problems. The comment about her 'wanderlust' is of interest. Although there were some signs that she was beginning to tire of 'racing from place to place', when she did finally retire, she still travelled, including a world cruise long after she had hung up her racing helmet. The final point in the *Daily News* about her 'invariably' competing on a 'track she has had no chance of practicing on' was not strictly true, as she often mentioned practice runs in her writing. It is true, however, that her opponents were usually far more acquainted with what, in Australia, were their local tracks. What seems to have enabled Fay Taylour to overcome this problem was a remarkable memory for the details of individual tracks.

Fay's first appearance at the Claremont Speedway was on Friday 11 December. She was due to race against 'men drivers tonight in various events'[15] on what was promised as a packed programme including supporting motorcycle events. In the event, Taylour only raced against Merv Dudley and Laurie Stevens, described as 'two of the States' best drivers'.[16] She beat both the drivers. But the night, far from being a packed programme, turned into a fiasco. Almost all the drivers, except Dudley and Stevens, called a last-minute strike. The drivers were members of the West Australia Speedcar Drivers Association (WASDA). They began the strike after the meet had started and the spectators were in the ground. The

WASDA spokesman, Mr J. Wyatt, told the press that, 'all the drivers want is a reasonable fee. Their overhead expenses are higher than those of solo and sidecar [motorcycle] riders and a request stating our demands was made to the management but was ignored'.[17] The management of Claremont Speedway responded that they had only received the 'demands' the day before and, as the chairman of directors was absent in eastern Australia, it was not possible to make a decision. The evening's racing was abandoned and large group of angry spectators demonstrated outside the pits, while 'the police stood by in case of emergency'.[18] Striking drivers heckled Dudley and Stevens for racing with Fay Taylour and there may possibly have been an element of the men not wanting to compete against Taylour for another Australian season. This was given as a reason for the strike by a report in the Victoria newspaper, the *Argus*, 'in Perth male drivers, faced with the prospect of having to compete against a woman [Taylour], went on strike'.[19] This was not the first time that Taylour was involved, however peripherally, in an earnings-related action by professional male riders and drivers. There had been a possible element of this when she and other women were banned from the motorcycle speedway track in the UK in 1930. The male riders feared that racing against women might reduce their earnings if promoters and tracks lowered rewards using the excuse of successful women riders. That fear certainly played a large part in the UK Riders' Association 1937 attempt to prevent foreign riders from competing in the country.

The row between the Claremont Speedway management and striking drivers continued, with the management subsequently refusing to recognise drivers who were members of WASDA. The management gave two reasons for this action. Firstly, it claimed to have met the initial claim by WASDA, but then the drivers' association refused a further compromise. This sounds like little more than an industrial dispute transferred to the speedway racetrack. The second reason, however, strongly suggests that many of the drivers really did not want to race against Taylour:

> The other reason for the ban [of WASDA by management] was that the speedcar association [WASDA] has taken over the responsibility of insuring all drivers against accident while competing but last Wednesday told the management that it would not be responsible for the insurance cover on Miss Fay Taylour, the visiting driver.[20]

It appears, then, that Taylour's successes during her 1952–53 tour of Australia had the effect of dampening the desire of many male drivers to compete against her on her return. The immediate outcome at the Claremont track was that its management withdrew recognition of WASDA and established a new drivers' association, the Speedway Racing Drivers' Association. These drivers then elected a former WASDA president, Harry Lewis, to the same post in the new association. This ended the strike, but the events were a foretaste for Fay Taylour of the difficulties she was to face in Australia that season.

Taylour's next stop was the Rowley Stadium, Adelaide, where she had beaten Harry Neale, 'The Black Prince', just over a year earlier. The Adelaide *Advertiser* announced her appearance at Rowley Park on New Year's Day, 1954, with the headline, 'Star Driver At Rowley Park Tonight. Miss Fay Taylour, "Ireland's Whirlwind", will race at Rowley Park Speedway tonight'.[21] This new sobriquet, 'Ireland's Whirlwind', could be added to the long list of nicknames Fay Taylour acquired during her career, which included 'World's Wonder Girl', 'Flying Fay Taylour', 'Lady Leadfoot', and the 'Lana Turner of the Track'. The previous season, Harry Neale had at first refused to race against Taylour, saying she was too 'inexperienced', a laughable claim which, when he did put it to the test, saw him beaten by Taylour. In the later rematch Taylour led until the final lap when Neale deliberately bumped her car from the track. While taking that in good part, Taylour was in no doubt that the Rowley Park men had 'ganged up' on her. She was to find that nothing had changed in the intervening year, and the next day, the motorsports columnist for the *Advertiser*, 'Camshaft', covered the night's events under the headline, 'Effort To Stop Fay Taylour':

> An all-out effort by the men prevented international woman driver from winning the third of her three starts at Rowley Park Speedway last night. The effort was so strong that Harry Neale, noted for his aggressiveness, took the wheel of Len Golding's powerful car. He succeeded in catching Miss Taylour, but only after many laps, and pushed her out on a corner into the fence, to take first place himself. However, Miss Taylour proved that she can really drive. The clean handling of her car secured long leads and wins in both the Speedcar Handicap heat and final. Desperate attempts were made by Rick Harvey, Ron Riley and Kym (Bullo) Bonython to take the lead but Miss Taylour gave them no chances.[22]

'The Black Prince' was no more able to beat Taylour fairly in 1954 than he had been in the previous season. The account of Taylour's handling of her car, and her defeat of the other drivers, is a good example of her outstanding skill on the midget car speedway track, which matched anything she had achieved in motor-cycle speedway a quarter of a century earlier. Further, these achievements were in the face of determined male opposition to her beating them on the track.

With Perth and Adelaide behind her, Taylour next raced at the Baxter Speedway, Brisbane, where she was scheduled to race on 17 January. After her earlier appearances, there was some speculation concerning the Brisbane drivers' attitude to facing her on the track, although a few days before the meet one newspaper noted, 'up to now they haven't murmured one word of disapproval'.[23] The Baxter Speedway track was a new venue which had only opened in November 1953,[24] so the track was new to Taylour, as was the experience of midget car racing in day-light rather than under floodlights. She won the heat of her first race at Baxter, but on the last lap of the final, when she led the field, a rear tyre on her car had a blow-out and the race was won by Alf Baker. That seems to have been the total of her racing at the Baxter Speedway that afternoon, and the bad luck of the blow-out in a way symbolised the difficulties of the tour. She raced there again on 24 January before heading back to Sydney. Talking to a journalist after the first Baxter meeting, she said that she would be racing in New Zealand, before visiting Canada to race.[25] In the event, she never raced in Canada, and the New Zealand appearances appear to have been few. It was in the same interview that Taylour said that she wanted to 'settle down' to end her 'hobo existence'.[26]

Two days before Taylour's appearance at the Sydney Showground, where she was to drive Johnny Peers's fast V8-60, it was announced that Taylour's woman rival, Edna Wells, wanted to race Taylour again.[27] A new female opponent was also being touted as a challenger. This was Enid Nunn, a speedboat racer, who was best known for 'racing the boat "Do" in January 1950 in an attempt to break the world water speed record'.[28] Before meeting Wells again, Taylour used Peers's car to take two speed records at the Showground on 7 February.[29] She then raced at the Exhibition Speedway on 13 February, where there were signs that the difficulties and opposition she had faced were beginning to tell. For the first time, Fay Taylour lost her temper with track officials. Her appearance was cut short – much to the annoyance of the crowd:

> Ace woman speedway driver Fay Taylour clashed with officials at the Exhibition speedway last night. At one stage she angrily threw her helmet to the ground. Some sections of the crowd demonstrated with hoots, cries, catcalls and whistles when Miss Taylour's appearance was finally cancelled. Miss Taylour spoke over a microphone at 8.30 and said she believed she had been loaned 'a very fine car,' and felt confident that she would at last get close to the local lap record of 19 sec. However, when she got in this car and drove hard for two laps, it was announced her fastest time had been 25 sec. She returned the car to the pits, and it was announced that mechanics found defects in the car [...] Then it was announced that local driver Scotty Russell had agreed to lend his car for her programmed match race with Alan Belcher. There was considerable delay [... and] a nonscheduled race [was run] to fill the time. While this race was on Miss Taylour was seen to dash across the track to the centre of the ground, and try to speak to officials who appeared to ignore her.[30]

Matters escalated and it was announced that the meet was over. It was at this point that Taylour threw her racing helmet before taking the microphone to denounce the organisation of the meet to the crowd, saying that the officials 'seemed to put obstacles in my way right from the start'.[31] It was another disappointment for Taylour.

Fay met Edna Wells again at the Sports Ground on 19 February. Their rivalry during the previous season was marked by what certainly looked like collusion by track officials to favour Wells, as well as Wells's willingness to indulge in dangerous foul play. Yet when Taylour had met Wells at Brisbane back in January 1953, in a match that was run fairly, she had beaten Wells in straight heats.[32] Their 1954 meetings were a replay of the previous season's. The Sydney meeting on the

19th revealed that Wells was no more sporting than she had been the previous season. Wells defeated Taylour at the Sports Ground, but only by driving Taylour off the track, much to the crowd's disgust:

> Australian woman speed-car driver Edna Wells last night defeated Irish woman Fay Taylour in straight heats, two-lap, rolling start. Spectators heckled Miss Wells after she had completed the second heat, during which Miss Taylour's car crashed into a safety fence. Miss Wells' car locked with Miss Taylour's car when they entered the first bend, and continued locked together for 100 yards.[33]

Taylour's car suffered a buckled wheel, ending her racing that evening. However, their next meeting, at the Sports Ground on 5 March, ended differently. Prior to the rematch, it was announced that Taylour and Wells would compete in both race and time trials. Taylour was loaned George Bonser's car, which was 'one of the fastest on Queensland tracks',[34] while Wells drove Harold Barnes's vehicle. The outcome, as in their rematch the previous season, was wins for Taylour in both the race and the time trial. Taylour had her revenge. It is difficult not to conclude that the unsporting, and dangerous, tactics of Wells in the first meet had something to do with the Sydney ground managers' desire to create a spectacle to draw in bigger crowds. Interestingly, the rematch was heavily advertised in the press, with an advertisement headed, 'The Ladies Are At It Again!', and the text, 'Ladies! Bring your menfolk to see how these dare-devil females handle their racing cars'.[35] Speedway was a way of life for Fay Taylour and other drivers, but it was also a business.

After her victories over Edna Wells, Taylour had just over a month left in Australia. Her final races were at the Baxter Speedway, and the Exhibition Speedway, where she rounded off her season in 'a knockout' style: 'she broke two track records and equalled another. She then beat Reg West, one of Australia's best [...] and finished off the evening by winning the A grade handicap by 100 yards'.[36] This highlights the extraordinary skill and success of Taylour, a woman of nearly fifty who regularly beat male speedway drivers who were often half her age. By the time that report appeared in the *Sporting Globe*, Taylour had left Australia and was on her way to South Africa by sea. Her intention was threefold: to race, to challenge her sister, Enid, about the trust fund, and to pursue the USA visa again.

Taylour had last visited South Africa in 1939 when she had raced in the fifth South African Grand Prix, before taking part in midget car races when she beat Dennis Woodhead, Gus Collares and Betty Trew. That visit had lasted six months. Her second visit to South Africa lasted more than a year, and she raced several times at the Wembley Stadium, Johannesburg. She was, for example, star billing for the meeting at Wembley on 14 August 1954. Posters and flyers advertised her appearances, announcing, 'Hey! Don't Miss Fay at Wembley Speedway!' and that she was to race Stan Johnson.[37] Johnson was the 1954 South African midget car champion. The fact that the special match race was between Taylour and Johnson shows how high Fay Taylour's standing was. A special

Wembley Speedway souvenir programme was printed to mark her appearances, with a full cover of Taylour with her helmet and race goggles. The programme carried advertisements by Tyresoles tyres and Saker's car dealership, endorsed by Taylour. The editorial focused on her, noting that the male drivers were to be 'sharing their very exclusive field with a woman ... a woman who has frequently shown up men drivers (contrary to the supposed role of the woman driver!) ... and that must require sportsmanship of the very first order'.[38] There was also a special greeting to Taylour from 'one of the boys', Ken Robinson, saying that 'the boys' had all been discussing her racing especially after seeing her practice, adding, 'there is a rumour that we are going to do away with goggles at the meeting and wear field glasses [binoculars] instead. That's so we can see which way you went'.[39] In addition, there was a reprinted piece on Taylour taken from *Motoring Life*, and three pages by Taylour extolling the virtues of the South African male drivers. As for the racing itself, a photograph of Taylour taken in Johannesburg has a note by her reading, 'Raced at the Wembley track with a speedway car and broke the Lap Record. Also won 4 out of 5 races and defeated the Transvaal champion in a match race'.[40] The 'Transvaal champion' was probably Stan Johnson. In addition to midget car speedway, Taylour also took part in road racing, competing, for example, at the Grand Central Circuit later in August, and at Queenshaven, Johannesburg.

At some point, Taylour met with her sister, Dr Enid Evans, to raise the question of the trust fund. During 1954, Enid and her husband, also a medical doctor, moved from South Africa to Lusaka, Northern Rhodesia (now Zambia), so Fay must have met her prior to Enid's move, or perhaps Enid visited Fay in South Africa. They had been out of touch for a number of years, except for the terse communications about the trust. Unsurprisingly, Enid saw no reason why she, or their older sister, Hilda, should give up their equal shares of the trust fund to benefit Fay. Enid disapproved of Fay's racing, thought (correctly) that Fay was reckless and spendthrift with the money she did earn, and saw no reason to acquiesce to her sister's fantasy of building a house in Ireland with all the trust fund money. The meeting did not go well. Eventually, the two sisters were reconciled, but that was in the future, and after Fay had retired from the track.

Following the failure to extract money from her sister, Fay Taylour was left with the issue of the visa for the United States. Early in the new year, she visited the US Consulate in Johannesburg, and explained that she had applied for the visa in Dublin but would like it to be handled by the consul in Johannesburg. That was possible, with the consulate telling Taylour to contact Dublin directly and give permission for the paperwork to be sent to South Africa. The documents took several weeks to arrive, and then she was asked to arrange medical tests and obtain new passport photographs. She still thought it unlikely that she would be successful, and 'I settled down for another long wait, still without the certainty or even hope that I'd get the darned thing'.[41] The next day was Friday 13 May 1955, and Taylour received a telephone call from the US Consulate asking her to call in to collect her new entry visa into the United States.

Chapter Eighteen

Return to the USA

Fay Taylour arrived back in New York City on 30 June 1955, aged fifty-one, more than four years after she left the US to visit her ailing father. The enforced absence had brought an abrupt end to her American racing career. Her successful coast-to-coast midget car racing tour of 1950–51 was a distant memory. Had the McCarran Internal Security Act of 1950 not prevented Taylour's return, it is likely that she would have been able to build upon the 1950–51 tour. None-theless, landing back in the US, she was reinvigorated with what would soon prove to be a false optimism: 'I was happy to be back in the Land of Opportunity. Knowing I had much to offer a suitable firm. I would head back to my old stamp-ing ground in the West – Hollywood – when the race tour ended'.[1] Taylour believed that she had already secured a good contract to race and would be able to reinvigorate her racing career. But the next year and half would prove to be the most difficult period of her life, including the three years spent in detention during the Second World War.

The contract that Taylour thought she had was for 100 races, to start soon after her arrival. However, she quickly realised that the contract was not what it seemed:

> The contract, promising a hundred racing appearances, disintegrates after three or four races. Appearances, not racing performances, is all that matters to the promoters of this particular racing organisation. They control numer-ous speedways, and my role is to appear here and there in match racing, with a race car provided by the organisers.[2]

Taylour had been hired as a 'novelty act', to help draw crowds when necessary. The promoter was not interested in her racing ability and competitiveness. At one race meet she was given a car that had been throttled down, while at another her 'race' was put on after the entire meet had closed. This led to comment in the local press, which appears to have quoted Taylour being critical of the event. The result of that bad publicity for the promoter was that he 'turns up at another race track, and threatens to hit me in public'.[3] Worse still, the next car Taylour was given to race was dangerous to drive, with serious steering problems. After this, and a refusal to pay her, Taylour returned to New York, where the 'control-ling organisation' behind the promoter continued to refuse payment and told her that the contract was not legally signed in any case. At this point, Taylour decided to cut her links with the promoter. This left her in New York with no immediate prospect of racing. She knew from past experience that she needed an agent to represent her in America, not just for racing contracts, but also to help her racing story to be taken up and to get back on television.

One problem that Taylour faced was that few New York agents had racing drivers on their books. Entertainment, literary and media people formed most of their clientele. At first, Taylour thought that she had found a good agent who was interested in her history and appeared enthusiastic. However, he came up with nothing, but it was some time before Taylour realised that he was wasting her time. She fell back on trying to promote herself, something that she had been very successful at in the past. She also thought of new 'angles' to make money from her racing and driving expertise, including proposing to a lecture bureau that she could give a series of safe-driving lectures. She expanded this idea into a series of short films that she hoped a car manufacturer might take up. Finally, Taylour managed to find a woman agent who took her on. At the same time, Taylour was engaged to drive 'a single-seater Indianapolis type racing car' in an exhibition drive at a New Jersey State Fair towards the end of the summer.[4] Her appearance at that 1955 state fair led to her being contracted to undertake a mid-west tour of state and county fairs in the autumn of 1956. Taylour thought that the contract would also enable her agent to arrange more contracts to boost the value of the tour through appearances and sponsorship, but the agent achieved nothing. Taylour was still in New York, living in the 'cheaper hotels on 49th Street'. She took a job, which proved short-lived, as a theatre usher.[5] Towards the end of August, she had one appearance at the Florida State Fair in Tampa. She was to drive in three race meets in exhibition driving but found that the track was 'dangerously slick', and she spun into a concrete wall, hitting it hard, although she was not injured.[6] That was her final appearance on the track in 1955. It was not until March 1956 that Taylour's luck improved, when an Irish American couple whom she met on St Patrick's Day asked her to 'house sit' for them, while the husband went on an extended tour of Ireland and his wife spent the summer in their holiday home in New Jersey.

The first year back in the US had been a difficult one, and it was made worse for Taylour by her increasing belief that her banning from the US, her detention during the war in the UK, and her political background were all working against her. It does appear, perhaps unsurprisingly, that checks were made on her, and it may have been that some of the obstructions she faced in terms of being published were the result of a blacklist. Her ban, under the McCarron Act, was part of the general McCarthyite atmosphere, which, although fading, had such an impact on publishing and media. The only difference was that Taylour was a fascist, while almost all the others affected were communists or were seen as communist sympathisers. Taylour also saw more than just US government interference in the repeated failures to find sponsors, media companies, or publishers that would feature her or her work. She linked this blocking to her detention by the UK government during the war, and her refusal to retract her views:

> It is impossible to enumerate, or even remember all the other attempts that were made to tie me up with suitable firms. I had already proved myself as a

speaker, and, to quote a critic, 'good entertainment' on radio and TV. American [press] clippings proved I could get easy sponsorship for any sponsor. First approaches to firms brought immediate interest. [...] Such firms as the Ford Motor Co. were approached. But uncannily there was always a final 'no'. [...] It was to take quite a time yet before I would be forced desperately to remember the Camp Commandant's [of the detention camp on the Isle of Man] words: 'you will always be an outcast', because I wouldn't sign a retraction.[7]

Whatever the truth of the matter, blacklists did exist, the UK and US security services did exchange information about Taylour's detention and politics, and she had been banned from the US under the Internal Security Act. For Taylour, an even more obvious sign of interest in her on the part of the FBI came in the form of the 'pick-up'. Taylour used the term 'pick-up' in two senses. Firstly, the common sense of a pick-up for sexual reasons. She was more than familiar with that. In her racing across the mid-West in 1956 she would experience it more than ever before. The second sense in which she used the term was in reference to men and women who would engage her in conversation, which then took on a political aspect. Taylour provided a number of examples of this type of security services' 'pick-up'. One occurred very soon after she landed in New York and was staying at the McAlpin Hotel:

This ham called my room with the excuse that he had seen me from his window on the opposite wing (which would not give him my number). I guess he was tired of waiting for me to come out of my room. I was suspicious at once, and agreed to meet him downstairs. He forgot his interest in me, broached the usual political topics and questioned me as to what I was doing and where I was going. [...] Then, quite soon, having fired all his leads and questions, he said: 'I haven't the money for second drinks,' got up and left.[8]

Taylour was due to leave New York on 2 August 1956 to begin the race tour of the state and county fairs. In preparation, she packed all her belongings into thirteen cases and came to an agreement with the manager of the apartment building she was living in that the cases would be stored until she sent for them. She did this not without some misgivings, as on her return to the city, she had discovered that all the belongings she had assumed were safely stored while she was visiting her dying father were gone. They had been in storage at her old hotel until after she returned to New York, but in the two weeks it took her to go to collect them, they had been sold, without permission, by a hotel porter, and 'the clipping books, photographs, and other papers had been burnt'.[9] This would be only the first loss of stored belongings, and the second would involve a much greater loss. It seemed, in some ways, that Taylour had to keep on starting afresh.

Before leaving New York, Fay wrote to John Barclay in Tujunga, California. Barclay was helping her to write up another version of her life story, entitled 'Lady Leadfoot, or Despite the Devil', which was billed as the 'story of the world's greatest woman race driver'. Barclay appears to have been a ghost writer. The fact that Taylour had found one in a suburb of Los Angeles was another sign of how she saw her future in California, connected with Hollywood. The letter to Barclay is interesting in that, in addition to matters relating to his work, and her explaining that she would be heading back to the state as soon as her last race in Shreveport, Louisiana, was over on 29 October, it also gives an insight into her mood. After the long wait to return to the US, Taylour had a difficult first year back, reflected in the letter to Barclay when she wrote:

> The enclosed copy of letter to friend of my English literary agent will keep you up with my developments... which are nothing to report. Just the usual effort, and no real result. Tomorrow I may meet Frank Scott as one more prospective agent, but he will be lazy I'm sure, and not want a new type of person [i.e. a woman racing driver] to exploit. The letter may sound defeatest [*sic*], but it is written in that mood purposely. And, also, it would be odd if my optimism hadn't dropped.[10]

It was no surprise that Taylour's optimism 'had dropped' but, true to form, she was looking forward to the tour, 'twenty-five race meets in a row. The idea is delicious! The tour will take three months'.[11]

Taylour had been engaged to race by National Speedways of Chicago. The tour started on 5 August at Faribault, near St Paul, Minnesota. The Faribault County Fair was, and is, typical of such fairs throughout the US. They are important fixtures for local communities and feature a range of events, including music, rodeos, tractor events, and motorsports. They were not dedicated race meets. Even more than the other racing Taylour had taken part in, the emphasis was on entertainment. The standard car for the tour was the Offenhauser single-seater, which dominated Indianapolis-style racing from the 1930s–70s. Various engines were fitted to the 'Offys' and the car was built in midget car and larger car forms. These were the cars Taylour raced during the state and county fair tour. 'The cars are typed as "Big Cars". They are larger than the "Offenhauser" Midget, and the tracks are larger than the ¼-mile midget oval. We will race on ½-mile circuits mostly, occasionally a mile one'.[12] The drivers came from across the US. In effect, they formed a travelling circus of racers. Typically, the driver would travel from fair to fair in their own truck, towing their car. Wives and girlfriends often accompanied them, along with mechanics, and they lived an itinerant life throughout the summer. As Taylour noted, 'for the boys, this annual "Fair Circuit", as the tour is called, comprises the last half of their season's program'.[13] For Taylour, however, this would be her only racing in 1956. Further, she was without a car of her own, and travelled by train or long-distance coach. She soon discovered that the between-races socialising that she usually enjoyed was absent on the tour. Instead, drivers turned up at the last moment and left soon after the racing was over. She found this difficult and it is clear that it had a depressing effect.

There was no opportunity at the fairs for practice laps as the races were usually held on the same grounds that horse events were staged, with one following the other in succession. Drivers used the qualifying heats to develop a sense of each track, but Taylour's contract was for exhibition driving as well as races. When she was allotted exhibition driving only, she had no chance to get a feel for the track. The combination of the powerful Offenhauser cars and track unfamiliarity was dangerous, and Taylour said that during the tour two drivers were 'lost'. Given that she mentions other drivers injured and hospitalised, 'lost' seems to mean killed.[14] The drivers taking part in the tour were experienced and well known, and included Bobby Grim, Jud Larson, Hershel Wagner and Johnny Poulsen. Taylour faced a long, difficult tour, spending much time between meets on her own. Her unpublished writing about the tour differs from her other accounts of tours and races in that she focused more on the technical and race challenges she faced, rather than the people she met.

Taylour explained the need for a driver to be able to *feel* what the car was doing and how it was responding to the track. Male drivers were physically much bigger than Taylour and they fitted the small open cockpits of their cars much more snugly. She knew that the men were able to feel the car's responses through their backs, whereas being smaller she had to build that sense through her legs against the cockpit sides. Even that required her to make temporary modifications to the cars she was loaned:

> I come to every race track with a peculiar tool kit of my own. A kit that might be compared to a jockey's saddle. Like a jockey, I ride other people's racers, and even if I had my own race car with me, it could break down and necessitate my driving a substitute. And so my kit consists of what I call 'distance pieces', an assortment of special cushions and pieces of sorbo rubber. Also wire, string, and insulation tape for keeping the distance pieces in place. Pliers and scissors complete the outfit. The distance pieces amount to padding. When I hit the turns in what looks, and in fact is, a mad slide, I have to feel contact with the side of the car from my thigh to the knee. That's to say, on the right side. We are turning to the left, so the thrust is to the right. In this way, I seem to be able to hold the car, and FEEL every movement of it. If my right leg cannot lean firmly against the side of the cockpit I'm straining muscles near the thigh and get a pain in my leg after one lap. This support for my leg leaves the right foot able to work the gas pedal more lightly. It also means that I do not have to use the steering wheel to keep myself in place. The tracks become very rough as racing progresses, and the safety belt is not rigid.[15]

Taylour also referenced what her old friend, Freddie Dixon, the well-known racer and famous engine tuner, had told her many years before, 'You can't drive unless you feel everything fits you'.[16] What is also revealed by Taylour's account of her field modifications to cars is the heavily physical nature of the racing. Writing about racing on another track during the tour, she said, 'the strain to keep the heavy powerful car from spinning on the too tight curves was heavy on the arms. It was a fight all the way'.[17] Yet, just as in the days of her motorcycle speedway racing, she was able to cope and win. As she said, it was 'no fun if it was easy'.[18]

For her first appearance of the tour, Taylour was booked to drive exhibition races against the clock, as the regulations only allowed her to compete in this way at Faribault, presumably because she was a woman. The event immediately before saw Bobby Grim crash, turning over his car. He was fortunate enough to escape with a badly bruised leg, but the fact that as good a driver as Grim had crashed indicated how dangerous the track had become. Taylour was pushed out onto the track as the announcer ran through some of her past victories. It was 'just' an exhibition, but she knew the way to make the most of it:

> I have been a showman since Johnny Hoskins, the greatest speedway promoter of all times, took me in hand for my first appearances in England. I must do a lap as if I were just a woman driver! Sliding a little on the bends, but rather nervously. Then, when the spectators are not expecting too much, open out like a man.[19]

After her first, deliberately cautious lap, Taylour signalled for the starter and 'for five laps I enjoy myself'.[20] It was a good beginning to the tour. But, with so little socialising associated with it, she felt that the tour was strangely impersonal, 'like a robot, my job is to present myself at the various Fairs in time for racing. Be at the track – that's all I have to do'.[21] The socialising, publicity and promotions that had taken up the time between appearances in the past had gone, and Taylour found it disorientating. Unusually for her, racing did not now involve relationships with motorsports drivers or officials:

> I do not hitch up with a companion for the tour. I want more than just a bed partner. Bed partners are everywhere. I want someone who thinks and speaks a dialogue I understand and respect. Such a person doesn't appear. And so I wander round alone, laughing off the insinuous [*sic*] query; what are you doing with yourself tonight? I look on this recurring invitation with appreciation more than disgust. The questioner, after all, is sincere. The query is natural to him. Probably he thinks I'm un-natural. Anyway, it deserves a laugh rather than a brush.[22]

On the tour, Taylour stayed at the best hotels she could afford, like the Fort Des Moines at Des Moines and the Jayhawk at Lincoln, as she believed that it was only at the best hotels that she was likely to meet interesting people, perhaps people who could help her with publicity or contacts. The promoter had done little in the way of exploiting Taylour's presence on the tour, so she saw it as important that she make up the difference. But the nature of the tour, the last-minute arrival of the drivers at the fairs, and the fact that the overall publicity was run by National Speedways from Chicago, meant that Taylour was unable to make any real difference to what she saw as limited publicity for her.

At Sedalia, despite Taylour's unhappiness at the paucity of good publicity, she had top billing on the posters for the 'Auto Races. Missouri State Fair' on 18, 19 and 25 August. The posters featured a large photograph of Taylour in a race car, with the legend, 'See in Person. FAY TAYLOUR. World's Champion Woman Driver'. Not even such a recommendation was enough for her, however, as her archive contains a photograph of the poster which she has amended, crossing out 'in Person', replacing it with 'in Action!'. After the Missouri State Fair, it was necessary to travel quickly to Wausau, Wisconsin, a road trip of nearly 700 miles, in less than 24 hours. There was no public transport that could get her to Wausau in time, so Taylour had to take a lift in the back of a converted truck owned by another driver. It was a less than pleasant experience:

> I'm packed into the converted back of a truck. The conversion is a low roof covering two stretchers, an emergency sleeping arrangement. Clearance does not permit sitting up. There is no window anyway. I lie like a parcel of mail while we eat up the miles at terrific speed, towing a heavy race car on a trailer. It's quite frightening, unable to move or see, and wondering if it isn't time for the driver to fall asleep at the wheel. Weird noises out of nowhere hit the ears with a roar now and then, and I discover later that we've been passing trailers snorting along a narrow road at a speed as fast as ourselves. We are travelling, as I also discover later, somewhere between 70 and 80 m.p.h.[23]

The driver, and fellow racer, for this claustrophobic trip was Joe Gemsa from El Monte, California. Gemsa was as famous for his brilliance with engines as he was for his racing. One of his most well-known cars was 'Poison Lil', the car he was towing between Sedalia and Wausau.

The final week of August 1956 saw the travelling racers in Des Moines for the Iowa State Fair, for the last of fifteen races in the month. The tour then began to slow, with seven races scheduled for September, and only four for the final month of October. After Iowa, Taylour raced in Lincoln at the Nebraska State Fair on 5, 6 and 7 September; Topeka, Kansas; Nashville, Tennessee; then Birmingham, Alabama. The time between races lengthened, with, for example, a ten days' wait before racing in Nashville, and a twelve days' wait before appearing at Birmingham. Taylour thought that all this time was wasted because, unlike her previous racing experience, no attempt was made to arrange events where she could boost her own publicity and that of the forthcoming racing. Instead, 'there was nothing to do while waiting to race'.[24] A meeting with 'Bill', one of National Speedways' publicity men, in a hotel lounge in Birmingham, led to Taylour complaining about the enforced idleness and the lack of publicity that she could have been involved with. He had, however, arranged a newspaper interview for her on the following day, and he thought that she should be 'having a good time'. Taylour's response was, 'dates offered in hotel coffee shops don't appeal [...] They're like cheap commercials. Same words, same theme ...'.[25] The 'commercial' was 'Staying here? Alone? What's your room number? ... '.[26] Yet Taylour seems to have liked Bill, 'we seem to make each other laugh. He's human in this machine-like promotion. In his company, I feel less like a robot'.[27] She later had an affair with Bill and, after she had finished racing, she lived for a short while in a property he owned.

The last races of the tour were in Shreveport at the Louisiana State Fair during the final week of October. *The Shreveport Journal* ran a feature article on Taylour entitled, 'Fastest Woman on Wheels Here'. The article consisted of the usual stories about her personal and racing life that Taylour routinely gave to journalists, but also noted that, 'future plans for the fastest woman on wheels are both "definite and indefinite" [she ...] intends to put her driving experience to "good use" by lecturing on driving techniques in aid of road safety'.[28] As the tour drew to its end, Taylour was forced to think about her next steps, and it is probable that she knew that she had finished with racing. In preparation for the end of the tour she had bought a second-hand car before she left Birmingham for Shreveport. She called it a jalopy, but it was a 1949 Plymouth De Luxe sedan, and it was in good condition. The car salesman, perhaps not unexpectedly, assured her that it had only one previous owner. In fact, Taylour thought that was probably true, as the engine was in very good condition, as 'are the brakes, clutch and steering. There's a little slack in the transmission, but nothing to worry about'.[29] She bought it for $350 cash, and named her new car 'Nostalgia'.

Fay Taylour appeared twice at the Louisiana State Fair, racing on Saturday 27 and Sunday 28 October. In her penultimate race on the 27th, Taylour won in a 'comfortable car',[30] and she expected to use the same car the next day. But:

> In the very first race this car is smashed up, and I'm left wondering what number will be allotted to me. The track's rough and tricky. Hershel Wagner, one of the top four, goes over the fence when he is out alone in his qualifying round. [...] the track gets more and more slick, more and more bumpy.[31]

Eventually, Fay was given an indifferent car, number 42, to race against Eddie Loetscher. This was her last-ever race. Although she did not acknowledge that fact in her unpublished autobiography, Fay devoted ten pages to a description of the race. It is the most detailed account by Taylour of her racing a midget car, of the struggle between her and the competitor, and the challenge of mastering the car on a difficult speedway track:

> I fight the car fiercely as I go into the next turn on the inside. Eddie's right behind, slightly to my right. I have to drive in close again, whether I like it or not, and, once more, he's much too close for comfort. My car starts the usual 'side-stepping', and this time I slide right out across his pat. I can't help it. Somehow he avoids a crash. I feel a bump on a back wheel. He must have de-throttled and half spun. Now he's genuinely behind.
>
> [...]

I'm in a perfect power slide again. Never really came out of it... just a little waltzing. My front wheels, steering in their broadside angle, point towards the curving fence on my right. I'm turning to the left. My wheels steer right to 'correct' and hold the sliding rear wheels. The low nose of the car points to the fence, but straight ahead. I'm nearing the apex of my sweep, the half way mark.[32]

Taylour's description of her drive, of her battling against the odds of track and car, ends triumphantly with her winning, and being saluted by Eddie Loetscher. That was the final race for Fay Taylour, over thirty years after she had first entered a motorcycle race.

The next day, 'with the 25-race contract over, and New York behind me at last, I pointed my car towards California'.[33]

Chapter Nineteen

Life After Racing

When Taylour drove out of Shreveport heading for Hollywood, she had a road journey of over 1,600 miles in front of her, through Texas, New Mexico, and Arizona before she would reach California. It would take her a year. Just a few hours into the journey, she stopped 'Nostalgia', her Plymouth sedan, at the Grande Lodge Motel in downtown Dallas. There she took cottage number 39. She intended it to be an overnight stop, but she stayed for the weekend, then for a further nine months. Those nine months marked the sea change in her life brought by the end of racing. She made a few more efforts to gain new racing contracts, but there is a sense from her writing that they were at best half-hearted attempts. She soon realised that no new contracts would come. In her unpublished writing she wondered why, after longing to return to California, she now delayed for so long. A few years later, in 1962, she wrote, 'one might call it a re-actionary break-down though I was not broken down. I must have been fed up with race promoters, and battling on my own against male prejudice, which was my penalty or due for invading a man's world!'[1] Her final tours, both the state and county fairs tour, and the second Australian tour, had certainly been replete with examples of 'male prejudice' and irritating promoters. The final tour had been 'a tour that seemed to promise so much, and produced so little'.[2] However, the nine-month stay at the Grande Lodge Motel was something more than a reaction to the difficulties of touring and racing against men. Her time in Dallas was a period of decompression from the life at speed, under stress, that she had lived for over thirty years. It was also a period when Taylour had to adjust to a new future. It was a watershed that came with the end of motor racing.

Her motel cottage was a small, whitewashed adobe-style bungalow with a low-pitched pantile roof. There were eighty-five cottages arranged in small streets, backed by woodland. Each cottage had bushes and flowers in pots and small flower beds. The complex itself had an open-air swimming pool and shops. It was a pleasant temporary retreat for Taylour, the 'little cottage, in the pretty motel "street" calls me to stay. It's peaceful and countrified. It's a contrast. To have a kitchen again is a novelty. The smell of fresh vegetables cooking, and porridge oats, is a nostalgic tonic'.[3] Taylour left two albums of photographs she took of this time in Texas, 'all photographs by my 25-year-old Camera bought, used, for $6!'.[4] The first album covers her life in the cottage, while the second has photographs she took of the damage caused by a tornado in Dallas, along with her drive west after she left Dallas. The cottage was small, but smartly furnished, with a 'fully equipped kitchen', and she described it in a caption to a photograph of the interior as, 'so homely after hotels'.[5] She had bought a tape recorder sometime towards the end of the state and county fairs tour and had used it to interview some of the other drivers. In the photograph album she describes it as 'my new toy, the Pieveie [Peavey] Tape Recorder'.[6] It is not clear why she bought the recorder, but it may have been to record her own memories as a stage in the writing of her autobiography, which would soon become a constant element in her life. However, she was soon using it to record dramatic sketches, writing scripts and 'arranging, editing, acting, splicing' the tapes into shows for her own amusement.[7]

At this point, Taylour had not started to write a definitive version of her life. She had previously written different versions of her racing life, in a lightly fictionalised form, with the intention of obtaining a book or, more welcome, a film contract. In addition, she had written newspaper and magazine pieces about herself and racing, although the main purpose of those had been to heighten her profile in relation to forthcoming racing appearances. In the motel cottage she was not yet ready to write her autobiography. It may well have been that she was still too close to the racing that had finished for good just weeks earlier. Instead, she began a novelette, *Wanting You*, along with short stories, one of which was entitled 'A Package of Unevenness'. She had always been an enthusiastic letter-writer, and had periods when she wrote doggerel verse, produced articles for the press, synopses and fully worked-out scripts and fictionalised versions of periods of her life. Now that she had retired from racing, she wrote more, and tried different forms. Later she reflected on the apparent paradox of someone who had spent much of her life in physically challenging motorsports also being someone who felt compelled to write:

> Maybe, as an occupation, writing isn't so far removed from auto racing after all. Off the track, my desire is to control words, to arrange them myself. I like writing better than reading. On the track, the desire is to control wildly skidding cars. I like to drive better than watch. It boils down to a challenge, the challenge to one's ego. The desire to take the wheel. To do the creating oneself.[8]

Taylour had far less success with her writing than she did with her racing, but she never gave up. The novelette *Wanting You*, for example, was returned to her by a literary agency, A.L. Fierst of New York, in August 1957, with a negative response in relation to the plot, although the agent conceded, 'the writing style is better than the story – which is encouraging. It is crisp and clear'.[9] Interestingly, Taylour seems to have begun to use a pseudonym for her writing as the letter is addressed to 'Miss Haugh'. In all likelihood, this was Taylour trying to avoid the effects of what she believed was blacklisting.

Most of the other residents of the motel cottages were salesmen and their wives, and Taylour was only able to make passing friendships. More permanent company was provided by two stray cats she found living in a hole next to a heater vent near her cottage. With food, she enticed them out and into the cottage.

But the gregarious Taylour, even in this quiet period of her life, wanted more company. In particular, 'I could do with a man, but what chance has a woman alone to meet a nice man? Where can a woman go without an escort? It is a vicious circle'.[10] That problem was highlighted when she was in Dallas shopping. She went into a cocktail lounge at one of the big hotels, only to be ordered out because she was taken for a call-girl.

During this time, Taylour made sporadic attempts to find car-related employment. She heard from a friend in California that the biggest race promoter there had no interest in taking her on in the future. In addition, she wrote to the Ford Motor company, which had a new model about to be released, the ill-starred Edsel. Taylour wrote to the Ford Dallas representative offering to work to promote and sell the new car. Perhaps fortunately for her the offer was not taken up, as the Edsel had a very short production life of less than two years after its introduction in 1958. However, at the time, these rejections fed into Taylour's sense of uncertainty about her future. She was aware that 'time is passing, even if the spirit has not yet moved me to leave Dallas'.[11] April arrived, and with it a tornado that ripped through areas of Dallas near to the motel. Afterwards, Taylour photographed the tremendous damage that had been done, with entire streets destroyed, the wooden buildings turned to matchwood. She photographed survivors, including a dog which refused to leave the wreckage of what had been a house. Later she photographed the owner, who returned to pick up his dog and salvage his Bible and other books.

Taylour remained in Dallas for a further six months. She began, for the first time, to worry that there was something wrong with her. Unusually for her, she had a sleepless night, and in the dark, decided that there must be something wrong with her, 'otherwise I'd have reached California long ago ... I wouldn't be playing with cats, and the tape recorder, and writing stories for no reason'.[12] She went to see a doctor and told him that she was suffering from 'frustration'. He took this to mean sexual frustration, much to Taylour's amusement. She explained that she thought it was 'frustration in my work, and I'm afraid it's softening my brain'.[13] The doctor gave her an introduction to an oil entrepreneur who sponsored race cars, a contact that proved to be of no use. Instead, she went 'back to the novelette, and the two stray cats. The strays, so much nicer, I'd decided, than auto racing promoters, are also nicer than oil men'.[14] It is difficult to know why Taylour went to the doctor and what exactly the 'frustration' was. It is tempting to see it as a form of depression, but perhaps it was more a product of the profound change in her life and the realisation that she had to forge a new future after racing. Finally, Taylour began to make preparations to continue her journey west. She collected together all her manuscripts, the press clippings from her last tour, and checked that the 'majority of my belongings from New York are safely stored at a transport company's office in Los Angeles'.[15] These belongings included trophies, press clippings from tours outside the USA, notable fan mail, and photographs, all of which she must have brought with her from South Africa. Sadly, it would turn out that they were not 'safely stored'. The last thing to deal with was the two cats. Taylour was not able to find a home for them, so, after giving them sleeping tablets, she took them to a vet's to be put down; 'I WANT to leave Dallas now. I'm ready to move on'.[16] It was the second week in September 1957.

However, Taylour was still in no hurry to get to California. She drove her overloaded Plymouth, containing a chaise-longue among other things, out onto the road to El Paso, after which she intended to head to Tucson and Phoenix, Arizona, a distance by road of over 1,000 miles. She took photographs as she went, particularly of desert landscapes and plants.[17] She was now clear that she would not race again, certainly not in California, where in 1951 she had been cold-shouldered and banned by 'the sports car boys'. Instead, she hoped to find an agent who 'can market me as a sports personality, linking my background to some promotion of other'.[18] Stopping in Tucson for petrol, she asked about racing in the city and was told that until not long before a speedway had been run by Dudley Froy. Taylour had probably last met Froy at Carrell Speedway, but had known him since before the war, probably as early as 1928.[19] Froy was the same age as Taylour and he too had recently retired from motorsports after a notable career in England and the US. Taylour telephoned him and had dinner with Froy, his wife and two children. The next morning, she drove on to Phoenix. Gripped by a sudden nostalgia for the sport she had finished with, she stopped outside Phoenix to look at a speedway track. Only the caretaker and a stray kitten were there. After chatting to the caretaker she left with the kitten, berating herself for being 'soft'. The kitten was 'the color of Whiskey. He went to my head, so I call him Whiskey'.[20] The next day, Taylour and Whiskey crossed the state line into California. She stopped her car at the top of a hill, looking back at 'the clean, green, hilly landscape'.[21] Descending, the outskirts of the city began, and after the hundreds of miles of open landscape, desert, and sparsely populated areas, she was back in Los Angeles. Compared with her time there in 1951, the city seemed far busier and noticeably more polluted: 'was there ever a Paradise so smelly and crowded?'.[22] But she was back. She checked into a motel on Cahuenga, 'half way between Hollywood and North Hollywood'.[23]

The next eighteen months would be the most difficult period of Taylour's life. She was alone, aged fifty-four, rapidly running out of money, had only the slightest chance of finding an agent to market her as a sports personality, and few transferable skills to enable her to find work easily. Life after racing would prove to be very tough, and the next eight years would see Taylour having to make repeated fresh starts until she finally managed to achieve some stability. To her credit, she picked herself up after some serious blows, and climbed out of what, for a while, looked like depression and the spectre of suicide.

It was not very long before Taylour moved out of the motel, then into a cheap hotel. By late summer 1958 her home was a semi-derelict shack. Taylour took numerous photographs of 'The Shack', often with the two cats, 'Whiskey' and 'Soda', that she had acquired. Her new home was a clapboard bungalow with a small veranda, surrounded by an overgrown garden and a low picket fence.

Externally it looked in good condition; internally it was spartan. It had no stove or fridge or bed, but Taylour used the chaise-longue from Texas for a very narrow substitute. There was a gas-fired hot water boiler and she bought a two-burner gas plate and a gas fire from Woolworths for $9. Although it seemed as if it were in the countryside, with orange, peach and eucalyptus growing around, the shack was on a plot located 'between Chandler and Magnolia Boulevards, not far from Whitsett Avenue', North Hollywood.[24] As Taylour soon found out, its location meant that the plot was due for development, the shack and other buildings for demolition. She was renting it from another tenant who was illegally subletting. The constant threat of being evicted to make way for the bulldozers hung over Taylour for the year she lived there, adding to the stresses that eventually brought her to a point where suicide seemed a logical response to the position she found herself in.

Her immediate concern was financial. She had a few hundred dollars in the bank in Hollywood. In her London bank, she appears to have had a small amount of money, and some War Bonds, but she saw these as an insurance.[25] She knew that she needed a source of income soon. Thinking that she might be able to find a place in a sports shop, she advertised in the local press for a job as 'a lady with an international sports background'.[26] The only replies she received were from 'male models' who asked if she was 'interested in Nudism'.[27] She was still hoping to find an agent who would be able to help her turn her sporting life story into a money-spinning venture, either as a book or film, or as background for car-linked lecturing or sales. Finally, and for Taylour surprisingly, she did find an agent who gave her practical advice on how to present herself. In a meeting, he went through the manuscripts, the photographs and cuttings she had sent him, and 'erased all my ideas that are surplus or untimely. He pointed to the only target, and he'll help me shoot for it. His prescription, I realise, is the only solution. It will finally open the way to all my other aims, that now must be shelved'.[28] Taylour returned to the shack and her typewriter with a fresh enthusiasm. But this was a state of mind that was short-lived.

The next day, Taylour received a summons for a minor road-traffic accident, in which she had clipped a car in front of her at a crossroads. The owner's insurers had not been able to recover the cost of repairs, as it transpired that Taylour's own insurance was with a fraudulent company that had recently gone bankrupt in Texas, the managing director fleeing to Mexico. Taylour was being pursued for $180-worth of repairs. This was the start of a protracted legal wrangle that was not settled until November 1958.[29] The episode involved Taylour disputing the amount, obtaining other garage quotations for repairs, seeking *pro bono* advice from lawyers, attending two different minor courts, and issuing a counterclaim. The wrangling began to take over a good part of her life. It is difficult not to see it as a type of displacement activity that she used to keep herself from working on the tasks the agent had set her. Worse, when she decided to recover the belongings that she had brought from England, then sent to California from New York, she found that they had been sold at auction, with all her papers burnt. These papers she had intended to use to write her story in the way suggested by the agent. Eventually, she came to see this misfortune as the result of a plot against her by the security services. However, in her account of the loss of her belongings, she gives the more likely explanation. Instead of employing a haulage and storage company to move her belongings from New York, she had only hired a haulage company which, as was its usual practice, only held on to goods for a year. The company had written to her, but the letters had not caught up with her as she raced in the state and county fairs tour. Nonetheless, this was the second time she had lost stored belongings. It was a sad, upsetting blow:

> I try to forget it, telling myself I've only lost THINGS, not people. Others lose everything in fires, plane crashes, tornados; even their lives. It's ridiculous to be so depressed. But these things DO represent people. They are the only link with 'Dordy', my beloved father. With mother too, and my dearest friends in far parts of the world [...] They mean people, places, my life [...] And my racing credits ... they meant so much too. The photographs, press clippings, silver trophies, special fan mail ... everything that was so treasured, gone![30]

This second, and greater, loss of her belongings, and the drawn-out insurance claim against her, impacted upon her ability to focus on what she thought were the valuable suggestions of the agent.

Instead of completing the writing tasks set by the agent, Taylour began to write her autobiography at length, entitled *I Laughed at Security*. This grew to a multi-part manuscript that occupied almost all of her time in the shack and which she continued to write and rewrite until late in 1960. As well as this, she returned to her lifelong habit of writing long letters to friends around the world. She had written these letters from an early age and would continue to write them throughout her life. At the shack she wrote letters that she described as 'letters of resignation, not hope'.[31] There may have been an element of her looking for help from friends in these letters. She wrote in that vein to her sister Enid in Africa, whom she blamed for not receiving all, rather than a third, of their mother's trust fund. Unsurprisingly, that letter did not result in any positive response from Enid. Taylour's descriptions of writing her autobiography in the shack, and the letter-writing, seem at times to have been almost manic in intensity. It was as if, in the silence after years of racing and travelling, she was reassuring herself that she existed, that all her efforts had been real, and amounted to something significant. She convinced herself, or tried to convince herself, that if only she could finish her life story then all would be well. It would be taken and her money troubles would be over. Yet all her previous experience in that direction should have told her that this was a very long shot, with little hope of a good outcome. However, she continued, 'I sit in the porch writing, day after day, the shack and the writing become my life'.[32] The writing was only broken by occasional unwanted visits from her landlady bringing repeatedly deferred deadlines for eviction. The insurance case, too, dragged on. And all the while Taylour's funds diminished. Warned that the court might seize her bank account on behalf of the insurance company, she withdrew her last $150. She began to cut back on her food, reducing many meals to one or two eggs and toast, buying unwanted cuts of meat, and imperfect food sold cheaply. In July, the gas boiler broke down, leaving her with cold water only. Two possible agents appeared, but nothing came of their initial interest. Taylour began to have trouble sleeping and was often awake until three or four o'clock in the morning. Increasingly, she needed sleeping pills to get a night's sleep, taking up to three at a time. The depressive effect of these barbiturates was probably not the best thing for her. She had begun to turn night into day, 'I go to bed with a head full of frustrating questions. Questions to which there is no answer'.[33]

Taylour made occasional trips into Hollywood to buy food and postage stamps, collect letters and pay bills, all with the knowledge that money was running out. By late summer she was down to her last $50. On these trips into town, men often tried to pick her up, but, as she was always clear, 'sure I like men. But I also like to choose'.[34] Taylour also continued to think that some of these attempted 'pick-ups' were merely the FBI trying to check on her. By this point, it was unlikely that this was the case, but her justifiable concerns about the security services were inflated by her sense of isolation, which she called her 'hermit existence'. None-theless, Taylour did, occasionally, choose a man. Thinking back to her time in Dallas she wrote about one man she picked up, in a hotel lounge while she was having tea:

> There are some men you fall for at once, though. My mind goes back ten months. To that day when my answer WAS different [...] A man at a nearby table seemed to be waiting too. We waited separately, then together. My cup of tea changed to a drink. The drink changed to an aperitif. The aperitif became dinner ... and the evening was followed by a memory. Next day he was thousands of miles away. The plane he'd been waiting for in that hotel lounge had changed into the plane next morning.[35]

Although Taylour talked of marriage proposals turned down, and sometimes partly regretted, she knew that she would never have been able to settle with one man, and that her preference was for 'choosing' men. There were drawbacks, especially when she wondered about 'security', but also in other respects. One of her casual one-night stands in this part of her life also gave her a sexually trans-mitted disease (STD). She passed off initial symptoms as being part of the menopause, and the STD went undiagnosed for many years, eventually affecting her feet and legs.

At the beginning of September 1958, Taylour finally received notice to quit her shack. She was given a weekend to leave. By then she was down to her last $27. All she had were a few belongings, clothes, her typewriter, a long typescript of her autobiography, the two cats and her car 'Nostalgia'. She had intended to use sleeping pills and carbon monoxide from her car's exhaust to kill the cats before she left, and now she wondered if she should do the same for herself:

> The vacuum inside me is no longer intolerable. It seems to have pushed out fear and self-pity. I can view the future calmly and dispassionately. I weigh the pros and cons of taking that last journey tonight with the cats. It's a good idea all right! We can all go to sleep in Nostalgia. Nobody will disturb us [...] But I'll wait till the world's asleep.[36]

Taylour used piping to create a leak-free connection from the car's exhaust into the car, then returned to the shack to put her papers in order, with a letter leaving them to a friend, Matt. She then telephoned him saying that she was leaving America that night, by the 5am plane from Burbank, and asked him to look after her papers and leave her clothes with the Church Army. But she was still not entirely sure, and decided to toss a coin, 'aloud I say: "Heads I go, Tails I don't"'. The coin flicks. Over and over it turns, then comes down tails. Tails! I don't go'.[37] She then decided she would try the 'best of three', and with the cats watching the coin spin in the air, it fell, bounced, and disappeared under the sink, inaccessible. Taylour took this as a sign of fate. The next morning, she packed her car, put the cats on the back seat, and drove away from the shack.

The time spent in the Dallas Grande Lodge Motel, then in the shack in North Hollywood, represented Fay Taylour's difficult transition from a life built around racing. After a life at speed, often the focus of attention, struggling against obstacles to racing placed in her way by some male racers, promoters, and officials, she was suddenly becalmed. Unlike the three years she spent in detention during the Second World War, or the period immediately afterward in Dublin, she was not surrounded by people with a similar outlook, in the same position. Instead, she was on her own trying to make sense of what she had achieved and what she could attempt next. Taylour had characterised her time in the shack as living a hermit's life. After leaving, her life became, as she put it, that of 'a vagabond'.[38] Between September 1958 and September 1965, still in California, Taylour had eleven different jobs and moved between temporary homes nearly as many times. Although she did a variety of jobs, she usually took casual work that came with accommodation. Her first job after leaving the shack was a year working as a gardener and 'handy woman' for a widow in North Hollywood. That job came with a cottage in the garden of her employer's house. That was followed by child-minding in return for accommodation in a 'garden flat'. During this time, she was still trying to create an opportunity from writing about racing and driving. However, she put the autobiography away after rejection from a publisher who had seen a few pages of it. Nonetheless, Taylour still wrote letters and, interestingly, some political writing. During this second period in the US, she developed her political outlook, adding new heroes into her pantheon of political leaders of note. She was a supporter of President John F. Kennedy and would come to believe that his subsequent assassination was because he intended to rein in the power of finance and large corporations. In the aftermath of the failed CIA-backed invasion of Cuba in April 1961 by Cuban exiles, the famous Bay of Pigs debacle, Taylour wrote a long poem, in her typical doggerel style, entitled, 'Castro! Why Not?'. The poem attacked US interests, 'Uncle Sam's poor sugar men', and celebrated Castro's popularity in Cuba. In addition to attacking US business interests in Cuba, she also took a sideswipe at the UK Prime Minister Harold Macmillan's support for US policy.[39] Ironically, although the Bay of Pigs invasion had been prepared under President Eisenhower, it was Kennedy who gave the final authorisation for the invasion, albeit with restrictions that guaranteed its failure. In addition to Fidel Castro, Taylour would come to support an eclectic mix of political figures and movements, being particularly supportive of 'armed struggle' Irish Republicanism after the onset of the 'Troubles' in Northern Ireland.

Although Taylour already felt that her racing was forgotten, and that she was as 'vintage as the Bugatti' she once drove, it was not entirely true. Not only did her friends from her racing years remember her and sometimes kept in touch, but she also still received letters from racing fans. In 1961, she was contacted by a much younger woman motorcycle rider and journalist from West Germany, Anke-Eve Goldmann, who was building a notable sporting journalism career while riding and racing motorcycles herself. In addition, Goldmann was important in establishing the Women's International Motorcyclist Association (WIMA) in Europe and corresponded with women riders around the world.[40] Taylour and Goldmann wrote to each other during 1961, exchanging photographs of themselves riding and racing motorcycles. Goldmann was particularly fulsome in her praise of a photograph of Taylour broadsiding on a Douglas:

> That simply breathtaking motorcycle photograph you had enclosed in your last writing. You remember, it shows you on the dirt track Douglas in full action, sweeping the bike through a bend, in a grand broadside slide, all clad in your racing leathers, and wearing your black leather face, all in all: a very thrilling, marvellous sight! I am sure that it is one of the most exciting photographs I ever saw, and when I look at it I remember what is being said of you: that you were the only girl capable of beating male racers on a dirt track motorcycle![41]

Taylour had asked Goldmann about other pre-war women motorcyclists, and Goldmann told her what she knew of the post-racing lives of women like Eva Askwith, Theresa Wallach, Jessie Hole, and Betty Shilling (one of only three women at the time who had lapped Brooklands on a motorcycle at over 100mph).[42]

Taylour moved on from the garden flat when it and her employer's house were to be demolished to make way for property development. After two short caretaking posts she moved out of Los Angeles to a farm where she cut the grass and weeded. There is also a sense in her writing about this period of being 'a vagabond' that this was now her life, and that there were compensations, but Taylour still felt that she was marking time:

> I was alone most of the time, enjoying the country surroundings and peaceful atmosphere, with 'Whiskey' and 'Soda' still keeping me company. Cows grazed in the irrigated fields below the house, and the San Jacinto Mountains ringed the background. But my mind wasn't at peace. There was a nagging awareness that my racing exploits were slipping further and further into the background while I was existing in an entirely unrelated manner, cut off from any chance of making useful contacts. I had not even dug out the script which I'd intended to work at, and which had been my reason for coming to the farm.[43]

Taylour never gave up on the idea that she would be able to capitalise on her racing career, even as it slipped ever 'further into the background'. By the time she left the farm it was May 1962. From there she went to live in a three-room trailer on a fruit ranch in the San Fernando valley. In return for some pay and the trailer, she was responsible for watering the orange trees. This, too, lasted a year before the local authorities intervened, the trailer being illegally situated on the farmland. Taylour moved, this time into a friend's house in another part of the valley in exchange for gardening and child-minding. She was beginning to tire of the constant moves and her inability either to find the time or the real motivation to return to her writing projects. For the last few years, she had been offered a place in the east, in Maine, by a long-time friend, Bill, whom she had last seen in Birmingham, Alabama during her state and county fairs tour. He had been a motorsports promoter, working across the USA. He lived in a large, new-build house in Bangor, Maine. After his employer died, Bill, or Billy, continued to run the firm for his employer's widow. A much older woman, she had finally retired to Maine, and Bill had gone with her. In his letters to Taylour, he assured her that there was a cottage attached to the house, and that both he and his employer's widow, Edith, were keen to have her stay with them. The offer had been open for a number of years. It is clear that Taylour suspected it might not be a good prospect, something that at least one of her good Californian friends strongly agreed with. But by December 1964, Taylour thought that the offer might enable her to get back to her writing.

She left Los Angeles on a cargo ship bound for New York via the Panama Canal, arriving in the city early in January 1965. She took a train to Boston where she was met by Billy, who drove her the 240 miles to Bangor. Very soon, Taylour realised that, just as she had feared, the arrangement was a disaster. There was no cottage for her. She had to live in the house with Billy and Edith, who clearly did not want Taylour there. Edith took to her bed and issued draconian rules about living in her house. Taylour recalled, 'the beautiful picture [painted in Billy's letters] turned out to be a nightmarish caricature, and the peaceful homey atmosphere a daub of clashing personalities and domestic regimentation'.[44] After a month or two of the 'nightmarish caricature', Taylour bought a second-hand

Buick and was back on the road again, with $180 in her purse. She had seen an advertisement in a Bangor newspaper for 'dormitory directors' at Endicott Junior College (now Endicott College, a higher education institution) in Beverly, a shore-side suburb of Boston. She drove back to Boston and to the college, where she applied for the post. Then she drove on to an old friend who lived in Norwalk, Connecticut, 180 miles away. The friend put Taylour up and from there she renewed her search for casual jobs involving accommodation, which proved to be elusive. However, Endicott College contacted her to offer a post as a dormitory director to start in September 1965.

The job at Endicott proved to be challenging, but it also brought a degree of stability that Taylour had not had before. Before she set out to take up the post, she realised she felt 'apprehensive'. She was aware that the role of dormitory director meant that she would be at the college almost all of the time, at least during term time. Perhaps that had echoes of her detention during the war. More so, she was concerned about how a 'vagabond [could] fit into such an austere and orderly life?'.[45] She comforted herself with the thought that 'at least it didn't have to be "security"'. The contract could be terminated on two weeks' notice'.[46] Once she was at Endicott College, Fay discovered that, as she had suspected, the hours on duty at the dormitory were long, with one day off a week. There was little privacy for the dormitory directors, known by the young women students as 'House Mothers'. Mostly, the dormitory directors were widowed middle-aged women, one of whom said to Taylour, 'we're just a bunch of old women whose lives have already been lived'.[47] On her day off, Taylour had to vacate her small bedroom and bathroom to allow the on-duty dormitory director to take over. She usually spent that free time in snack bars, but one day she went to the beach. It was then that she decided that she had to have a purpose for being at the college other than it just being a job. That purpose would be that she would spend the summer vacation back in Ireland. In May 1966, the college offered her another year's contract for the 1966–67 academic year. Not having saved enough money to return to Ireland, she borrowed money from her sister Enid in South Africa to make the trip.

Taylour left New York on 19 June 1966 aboard the freighter *American Importer*, arriving in Liverpool eight days later. From there she visited an elderly cousin in London, Evelyn Caillard, and went to Hampshire to visit her sister, Hilda, and her niece, Sheelagh. Unlike Enid and Fay, their sister Hilda had remained in Hampshire, living not far from her late father who had settled in Lymington after Irish independence. Fay had not seen Hilda since their father's funeral in 1952. She described her sister as having not remarried 'after divorcing David in the late 'thirties [...] unlike me she never travels, for she possesses neither wanderlust nor ambition'.[48] From there, Taylour travelled to Belfast where she was met by her old school friend, Norah, with whom she had taken part in the 1933 Monte Carlo rally. Unlike Taylour's return to Ireland following release from wartime detention in Britain, this time, two decades later, she sought out old personal and family friends, as opposed to mixing with political associates. She waxed lyrical about Ireland and the Irish, as an Irish American might:

> I was home again amongst my old friends, and I found that all the poetical compliments about Ireland and her people, too familiar to recognize when you live there, were after all no exaggeration. I found myself stepping outside the doors just to sniff the air. It was unbelievable that trees and grass and just plain earth could smell so beautiful, let alone the flowers. Or that the sea along the beaches could be so clean. And everywhere I was greeted with a smile and words that had the sweetness of flowers.[49]

Taylour spent the summer in Ireland, driving down to Dublin in Norah's car to meet family friends, and one of her old political contacts from 1943–47. This was Pascal Barre, a French designer who may well have been an exiled supporter of the Vichy regime. This time, however, Taylour's interest in him was more personal than political.

She arrived back at Endicott College in time for the start of the September 1966 term, planning to repeat her summer's visit to Ireland in 1967. By now, Taylour had settled into the job at Endicott. While the living conditions were still below the standard she wanted, she was much happier with the work. Her attitude was now that the work was bearable because it gave her the freedom to spend the vacations, including the long American summer vacation, travelling and meeting up with old friends. As usual, she spent a good deal of her free time writing letters. She still received fan letters, some of which have survived. For example, she received letters from young children, including three that she kept. One was from a small American girl called Karen, thanking Taylour for her letters, while another was from an English girl called Kathie who asked, 'will you send me all the stories in magazines about you?'.[50] Adults also wrote to Taylour about her racing career, including a particular fan from Canterbury, England, called Tom Partington. He had seen Taylour in her first motorcycle speedway race at Crystal Palace in 1928. Taylour and Partington became long-term correspondents and met when she returned to England in the 1970s. Partington was an avid Taylour supporter, as shown by his letter to *Motorcycle* magazine in January 1975, correcting a magazine piece and saying, 'the honour of being the first female expert [in motorcycle speedway] must, without any shadow of doubt, be accorded to Miss Fay Taylour who, between 1928 and 1930, was recognised throughout the world as the queen of speedway'.[51] Taylour also kept in touch with old political friends from the 1940s. During the Christmas holiday of 1966, Taylour wrote a long letter to Joyce Pope, who prior to the war had lived in Gstaad, Switzerland, and whose innocent but intercepted letter to Taylour in early 1940 had caused Taylour trouble with MI5. In her 1966 letter to Pope, Taylour spent several pages attacking the US's war in Vietnam. In Taylour's view, the real motives for US intervention were both economic and political. She argued that US corporations made such 'enormous profits [...] that they go to war to capture markets for their surplus capital in far away lands – lands like

Vietnam'.[52] That Vietnam was not in the US's 'sphere of influence' meant that confrontation with communism was inevitable, and that the US itself had a very sensitive notion of its own sphere of influence, and here Taylour cited Cuba. The political aspects identified by Taylour were both domestic and external. Firstly, the excuse of fighting communism (which she thought had to be approached through co-existence) helped keep American workers docile. Secondly, Taylour correctly identified the US's wartime policy of dismantling the British and French empires and replacing their direct colonial rule with indirect control and the expansion of US capital at the expense of British and French interests. Taylour's fundamental target in this letter to Joyce Pope was international corporations and finance, allied to the 'greed' of an ascendant US. Interestingly, in the same letter she linked the Vietnam war with the American Civil Rights movement, writing:

> It's no wonder that the negroes in this country started pushing for 1st class citizenship with more vigour than ever before. They are good enough to fight alongside the white man on the battlefield, but not good enough to sit alongside him in a restaurant or even in a cheap snack bar![53]

Taylour was just as politically engaged as she had been before, although now it was only at the level of letter-writing and conversation with friends whom she knew shared her views.

For the summer vacation of 1967, Taylour repeated her previous summer's visit to Ireland and England, returning to the US on the Greek mixed passenger and cargo ship, the *Eurybates*. She then returned to Endicott College, working there during term time, and living in the flat in Norwalk, Connecticut, during the short vacations. She had not given up on finding a publisher for her auto-biography, intending to rewrite it once she had enough free time. At some point in 1968, Taylour decided that she should take a sea cruise in order to tackle the rewriting of her book. In early 1969 she agreed with the college that she could take a year out of her job and return at the beginning of the 1970–71 academic year. At first, Taylour planned a passage on a mixed passenger and freight vessel from New York to Cape Town. These ships had become her favourite form of transport: they carried a small number of passengers and docked at ports often not typically used by liners. The destination of Cape Town suggests that she intended to visit her sister Enid again, probably hoping for a more sisterly visit than she had managed in her last, brief meeting. The passage on a Hellenic Lines ship, the *Hellenic Leader*, would cost $355, and Taylour booked it in April 1969. The ship was scheduled to sail in late June or early July, calling at Cape Town, Port Elisabeth, Durba, Lourenço Marques in Portuguese Mozambique, Jeddah, Aqaba, Port Suda and Djibouti, before returning to New York. All of this, Taylour intended, would enable her to avoid distractions and finish a redraft of her autobiography. However, soon afterwards she was informed of the death of her cousin, Evelyn Caillard, whom she had visited in London in 1966. Caillard left Taylour a legacy, and that changed Taylour's cruise plans. Instead of the New

York to Cape Town passage, she rebooked with Hellenic Lines a much longer passage from New York, stopping in South Africa, Saudi Arabia, Kuwait, Abu Dhabi, Iran, Pakistan, and India. Taylour booked this voyage in first class on the *Hellenic Hero* for $1,440 (nearly $12,000 in 2022). It was typical of Taylour that despite her long-term financial worries, she chose not to save part of her Caillard inheritance, but to spend it on a sea voyage, with all the incidental expenses that implied as well as the cost of the voyage.

The *Hellenic Hero* left New York on 17 July 1969 with Fay Taylour aboard, equipped with her typewriter and reams of paper. She planned at that point to return to the USA in December. Interestingly, in two letters written very early in the voyage, Taylour asked friends in the US to forward copies of two left-liberal magazines, *The Nation* and *The Progressive*.[54] The likely attraction of these magazines was that they both covered international affairs and US foreign policy (frequently from a hostile standpoint). *The Progressive* had been banned during the McCarthyite years. Taylour was critical of US policy abroad, which she saw as another example of the operation of corporate capital and the expansionism that she felt provoked conflict. It is a reminder that, although she had a history of being on the ultra-right, the international outlook of that right-wing politics exhibited a pronounced anti-Americanism in some quarters. Taylour herself was also increasingly eclectic in her world view.

Taylour reached Cape Town by the beginning of August 1969. She was met by her niece and daughter before meeting Enid. The visit would mark a rapprochement with her sister. In an amusing account of the meeting, Taylour told an American friend that, 'Enid [...] lectured me in her bossy authoritative way about having wasted my life [and having] no idea of money or jobs'.[55] Ironically, on the same day that Taylour wrote that letter she also wrote to her friend who was looking after her cat in Norwalk bemoaning, 'my story [autobiography] is progressing though slowly. Please God that it may turn out a success and make me rich! Then the ever-lasting worries about money [...] may at least abate!'.[56] Perhaps the truth of her sister's comments about money had hit home. In any case, Taylour wisely decided not to post the letter. It is worth remembering that Enid was a doctor, as was her husband, Tom. He had recently retired from his World Health Organization work in the Congo, but he and Enid were still working, Enid at a home for children with learning difficulties. Despite Enid's 'bossy' lecture, the visit went well, and once Taylour's voyage continued, the two exchanged pleasant letters, with Enid noting:

> I think you are much nicer than you were 14 years ago. It seemed to me then that you only wanted to get money from me that Daddy had left me and that you were not interested in me one way or another. Of course there was wrong on my side too as I had not written to you for a very long time.[57]

Enid was, of course, correct in her estimation of Fay's previous visit.

The voyage continued up the coast of east Africa to the port of Aqaba in Jordan, the approach to which was still being heavily patrolled by the Israeli navy following the Six-Day-War in 1967. Taylour was enjoying her voyage, occasionally working on the rewrite of her autobiography, but more often writing long letters to friends around the world. Her other main occupation was socialising with the other passengers, who tended to change at each port, and included missionaries, nuns, and expatriate Europeans returning to overseas jobs. By December 1969, having visited Pakistan, India, and Ceylon, Taylour was back in South Africa, disembarking from the *Hellenic Hero* in Durban on 30 November. She had chosen to break her journey and now did not plan to return to the US until the late summer of 1970. Instead, she went to stay at her sister's cottage in Hermanus, Cape Province, a small seaside town. Enid and her husband spent most of their time in Cape Town, about 70 miles away, working, so for most of the six months Taylour was in Hermanus she was on her own, and free to write. By now, however, the rewriting of her autobiography had lapsed. She was increasingly troubled by a sore throat she did not seem to be able to lose, a rash that she had had two years before, and problems with her feet and legs. The latter she put down to age, saying that 'like a car, I am now secondhand and needing repairs'.[58] It would later transpire that all these were symptoms of her undiagnosed STD. In August 1970, she rejoined the *Hellenic Hero* at Durban for the voyage back to New York.

Taylour did not return to her job at Endicott College, choosing to retire instead. She moved back to her flat in Norwalk, Connecticut, before moving again to Darien, just a few miles away. This was her last home in the United States. Even while on the *Hellenic Hero* she had been writing to friends asking if they knew of anywhere in Ireland or England where she might move to. As she had since leaving the shack in California and before working at Endicott College, she hoped to find someone who would accept gardening, house-minding, child-minding or something similar in part rent. She also advertised in newspapers in England. On 8 January 1971 she left the USA behind, sailing on the SS *Eurybates* for England. The voyage across the Atlantic took three weeks in very heavy weather. Part of the cargo shifted, and the ship took on a list, while Taylour's car, which typically, if oddly, she had not sold but had taken with her, was damaged. Finally she arrived in England, where she spent several weeks visiting old friends in London before moving to Cranswick in East Yorkshire. She remained there until July 1973 when she moved to a low-rent cottage in Godstone, Surrey. In January 1974, Taylour was hospitalised with what turned out to be the long undiagnosed STD. Her legs were both infected, and she was in hospital for at least a week. In a letter to her oldest school friend, 'Dormouse', she admitted that it was 'quite a shock' to discover the cause of her illness. Taylour also referred to her pre-war stay in the Bayswater nursing home when she had had an abortion. She contrasted her treatment then, for what was an illegal operation, with the treatment for the STD: 'I had to suffer alone as on the previous occasion when I had that awful sixteen days in the Bayswater nursing home with the bullying night nurse. But on this occasion I was made to feel that it was quite normal by the doctors'. She concluded her letter by writing that she would never marry anyone without them first having been 'vetted by a doctor'.[59]

Soon after Taylour left hospital, she made a last voyage to South Africa to visit Enid who was by then ill. Taylour's older sister, Hilda, had died in December 1970, while Fay was still living in Connecticut. Not long after Fay arrived in South Africa, Enid died. For a while, Taylour harboured the unreasonable belief that her sisters' two children would allow her to live in Enid's home. That, of course, did not happen, and she returned to England, leaving Cape Town on 5 May 1975 on the cargo ship SS *Kaapland*. Two months later, she moved yet again to a cottage, 'Dairy House', in Winterborne Tomson, Dorset. It was to be her final move and her last home.

Taylour spent the next eight years writing letters, rewriting her autobiography, and keeping in touch with old friends. She also maintained her interest in politics, creating an eclectic personal ideology that fused her ultra-right views with elements from other ideologies. She wrote other long letters to friends such as her oldest school friend, 'Dormouse'; former racing driver and fascist, Enid Riddell, from whom she learned the details of Anna Wolkoff's death in Spain; her fellow ex-detainee Hildegard Gooch; and an ex-IRA man from the Irish War of Independence, Liam Grant. Taylour's political letter-writing notwithstanding, and unknown to her, the British security services, MI5, finally closed their file on Fay Taylour on 19 March 1976. Taylour was just short of her seventy-second birthday and had been 'of interest' to MI5 for nearly thirty-seven years.

In July 1982, Taylour was a guest, along with the ill-fated motorcycle stunt rider, Eddie Kidd, on a BBC Radio 4 programme hosted by Ned Sherrin. Taylour came across as lively and bright, and sounded younger than her seventy-eight years. Prompted by Sherrin, she rehearsed some of the familiar episodes from her racing life, particularly from her early years on the motorcycle speedway track. She was asked about her motivation, and revealingly said that if someone said to her, 'you can't do that', then she would make every effort to prove them wrong. If there was a single motivating factor to her life, in sport, politics and her personal life, that was probably an accurate self-assessment. Finally, Sherrin asked her which moments from her life she was particularly pleased with. Taylour responded by citing her pre-war Brooklands performance, when she beat Malcolm Campbell's time,[60] with her second moment being when she 'beat' Dorothy Kilgallen's questioning on 'What's My Line?'. Fay Taylour's appearance on Ned Sherrin's radio show was her last time on radio. Shortly afterwards, she had the first of a series of strokes. She was treated in Weymouth General Hospital in the last year of her life. A friend of Taylour's kept coming in to see her, bringing with her suitcases 'full of photographs, often bundles in brown paper, with perished elastic bands'. Sometimes Taylour 'would give her visitor photographs and papers to take away, sometimes she would bring more back'.[61] Right to the last, it seems, Fay Taylour was attempting to finalise her autobiography. But it was too late, and she died, following a stroke, on 2 August 1983, the final rewrite of the manuscript unfinished.

Notes

Abbreviations:
FT   Fay Taylour
FTA   Fay Taylour Archive
TNA   The National Archives (UK)
TS   Typescript
SB   Special Branch
MI5   British Security Service, responsible for national security

Prologue

1. *The Irish Times*, 27 August 1929.
2. Ibid., 2 September 1929.
3. Ibid., 2 September 1953.
4. Ibid., 27 August 1929.

Chapter 1. Early Years and the Beginnings of a Racing Life

1. Details taken from a copy of Fay Taylour's birth certificate, dated 13 January 1969, and FT's own note on a photograph of the house where she was born; in the FTA. Various other dates have been given for her birth, and at times even the UK authorities were unsure. For example, in a letter from Police Inspector Ayres to MI5, February 1941, her date of birth was given as 12 December 1902; TNA, KV 2 1 2143 3846216.
2. Details of Herbert Taylour's RIC service taken from undated (probably 1922) letter from 'RIC Office. Dublin Castle'; FTA, document DE 11.
3. Jim Herlihy, *The Royal Irish Constabulary* (Four Courts Press, Dublin, 1997), pp. 60–61.
4. Ibid., p. 84.
5. Ibid.
6. FT in her written appeal against detention, dated 16 July 1940, TNA, KV 2 1 243 286 216.
7. FTA, FT, TS, 'I Laughed at Security', Chapter 2, Part 1, p. 38.
8. Ibid.
9. Ibid., p. 44.
10. Declan Warde, March 2020. College of Anaesthetists of Ireland, Dr Ella Webb (1877–1946) – The College of Anaesthesiologists of Ireland (anaesthesia.ie), accessed 20 October 2022.
11. Ibid.
12. FTA, FT, TS, 'I Laughed at Security', Chapter 2, Part 1, p. 44.
13. Ibid.
14. FTA. DE3, letter, dated 23 January 1933, from A. Wilfrid Adams, MS, FRCS.
15. FTA, FT, TS, 'I Laughed at Security', Chapter 2, Part 1, p. 37.
16. FTA, document DE 11, letter from 'RIC Office. Dublin Castle'.
17. FTA, FT, TS, 'I Laughed at Security', Chapter 2, Part 1, pp. 41–42.
18. Ibid., p. 51.
19. TNA, Report of the Advisory Committee, following Fay Taylour's appeal against detention, 28 August 1940. KV 2 1 243 286 216.
20. TNA, KV 2 1 243 286 216, Fay Taylour, appeal against detention, 16 April 1942.
21. Fay Taylour's written appeal against detention, 16 July 1940. TNA, KV 2 1 243 286 216.

22. FTA, FT, TS, 'I Laughed at Security', Chapter 2, Part 1, pp. 45–46.
23. Ibid., p. 46.
24. Ibid., p. 49.
25. Ibid., p. 53.
26. Ibid., p. 54.
27. Jim Herlihy, *The Royal Irish Constabulary*, p. 152.
28. FTA, FT, TS, 'I Laughed at Security', Chapter 2, Part 1, p. 58.
29. Ibid., p. 59.
30. Ibid.
31. Ibid., p. 60.
32. Ibid., p. 61.
33. Ibid., p. 63.
34. Deirdre Beddoe, *Back to Home and Duty: Women Between the Wars 1918–1939* (Pandora, London, 1989), pp. 51–53.
35. FTA, FT, TS, 'I Laughed at Security', Chapter 2, Part 1, p. 63.
36. Ibid., p. 66.
37. Ibid., p. 67.
38. These figures were for Britain and its Empire. Very sadly, the same newspaper cutting gave the figures of France's casualties as 1,071,300 dead, at least 3,000,000 wounded, and 314,000 'missing'.
39. Virginia Nicholson, *Singled Out* (Viking, London, 2007).
40. FTA, FT, TS, 'I Laughed at Security', Chapter 2, Part 1, p. 67.
41. Ibid., p. 68.
42. Ibid., pp. 70–71.
43. Ibid., p. 74.
44. FTA. Letter from Pensions Commutation Board, London EC2, to Herbert Taylour, dated 4 May 1925. It informs Taylour that he had been awarded a £250 lump sum (around £17,000 in 2022), thereby reducing his annual pension by £26:6:0 a year.
45. FTA, FT, TS, 'I Laughed at Security', Chapter 2, Part 1, p. 77.
46. Ibid., p. 78.
47. Ibid.
48. Ibid.
49. Jeff Clew, *Vintage Motorcycles* (Shire Publications, Princes Risborough, 1995), p. 9.
50. FTA, FT, TS, 'I Laughed at Security', Chapter 2, Part 1, p. 79.
51. Ibid.
52. Ibid., p. 79.
53. Ibid., pp. 79–80.
54. FTA. FT, TS, 'I Laughed at Security', Part 1, Chapter 1, p. 3.
55. Ibid., p. 4.
56. Description of Cottle's memorabilia which was sold by Bonham's Auctioneers in 2010. 'Bonhams : The Marjorie Cottle Collection' accessed, 24 October 2022.
57. FTA, FT, TS, 'I Laughed at Security', Part 1, Chapter 1, p. 5.
58. Ibid.
59. Brian Belton, *Fay Taylour Queen of Speedway* (Panther Publishing, High Wycombe, 2006), p. 27.

Chapter 2. Speedway Queen, Summer 1928

1. From FT's written appeal against detention, 16 July 1940. TNA, KV 21 243 386 216.
2. FTA, FT, TS, 'I Laughed at Security', Part 1, p. 104.
3. From Taylour's written appeal against detention, 16 July 1940.
4. A.P. Herbert, *Punch* magazine, 3 October 1928; quoted in Jack Williams, '"A Wild Orgy of Speed": responses to speedway in Britain before the Second World War', *Sport in History*, 1999, Vol. 19 (1), p. 1.

5. Brian Belton, *Fay Taylour: Queen of Speedway* (Panther Publishing, High Wycombe, 2006), pp. 29–30.

6. Ibid., p. 30.

7. Williams, 'A Wild Orgy of Speed' (1999), pp. 2 & 14; the upper figure is given in Mike Huggins & Jack Williams, *Sport and the English* (Routledge, London, 2006), p. 66.

8. Ross McKibbin, *Classes and Cultures: England 1918–1951* (Oxford University Press, Oxford, 1998), p. 364.

9. Ibid., p. 364.

10. Figures for tracks and attendance are taken from Huggins & Williams (2006), p. 66.

11. Sprouts Elder (1930), *The Romance of Speedway*, London, Warne, p. 14; quoted in Huggins & Williams (2006), p. 19.

12. Huggins & Williams (2006), p. 142. The records of the Auto-Cycle Union are held at the Modern Records Centre, the University of Warwick, England. They are in rather poor condition, having suffered water damage.

13. Huggins & Williams (2006), p. 142.

14. FTA, FT, TS, 'I Laughed at Security', Part 1, Chapter 1, p. 3.

15. Ibid., p. 7.

16. Robert Bamford, Dave Stallworthy, *Speedway: The Pre-War Years* (Tempus, Stroud, 2003), p. 185.

17. FTA, FT, TS, 'I Laughed at Security', Part 1, Chapter 1, pp. 7–8.

18. Taylour used the phrase 'The Love that Lasted' for various iterations of her life story, including film scripts and versions of her unpublished autobiography.

19. FTA, FT, TS, 'I Laughed at Security', Part 1, Chapter 1, p. 9.

20. Ibid., p. 9.

21. Ibid.

22. Wills Lionel (speedwaymuseumonline.co.uk), accessed 11 September 2022.

23. FTA, FT, TS, 'I Laughed at Security', Part 1, Chapter 1, p. 9.

24. Norman Jacobs, *Crystal Palace Speedway: A History of the Glaziers* (Fonthill, Stroud, 2012), p. 9. For Lionel Wills' role in introducing speedway to Britain see also, Bamford and Stallworthy, *Speedway: The Pre-War Years*, pp. 16–17.

25. FTA, FT, TS, 'I Laughed at Security', Part 1, Chapter 1, p. 10.

26. Ibid., p. 10.

27. Ibid., p. 11.

28. Ibid.

29. FTA, FT, TS, 'I Laughed at Security', Part I, Chapter 5, p. 102.

30. Ibid., Part 1, Chapter 1, p. 16.

31. This was the reminiscence of Theresa Jenkins-Teague, who nursed Fay Taylour towards the end of her life. In conversation with the author, 17 April 2013.

32. FTA, FT, TS, 'I Laughed at Security', Part 1, Chapter 1, pp. 11–12.

33. Ibid., p. 12.

34. Ibid., Part 1, Chapter 1, p. 13.

35. Ibid.

36. Quoted in Belton (2006), p. 67.

37. It is not entirely clear how her surname was spelt, with 'Asquith' and 'Askwith' being used.

38. David Mason, *Freddie Dixon; the man with the heart of a lion* (Haynes Publishing, Yeovil, 2008).

39. Ibid., pp. 90–91.

40. Ibid., p. 231.

41. TNA, KV21243 386216, from Taylour's smuggled letter to Freddie Dixon, in a report dated 9 January 1941 from Police Inspector Edward Ayres, Reigate Borough Police, to MI5.

42. TNA, KV21243 386216, report by 'M/3' of 24 April 1940.

43. TNA, KV21243 386216, Inspector Ayres to MI5, 9 January 1941.

44. Ibid.

45. FTA, FT, TS: 'I Laughed at Security', Part I, p.100.
46. Ibid., p.103.
47. Ibid.

Chapter 3. Australia and New Zealand:
Tour 1, with a Wembley Interlude

1. FTA, FT, TS, 'I Laughed at Security', Part I, Chapter 1, p.18.
2. Ibid.
3. Ibid.
4. Ibid., p.20.
5. *The Daily News* (Perth), 3 January 1929.
6. Ibid., 7 January 1929.
7. Ibid., 3 January 1929.
8. *The Register News-Pictorial*, 7 February 1930.
9. Ross McKibbin, *Classes and Cultures; England 1918–1951* (OUP, Oxford 1998), p.365.
10. FTA, FT, TS: 'I Laughed at Security', Part I, Chapter 1, p.1.
11. *The Cairns Post* (Queensland), 7 March 1929, reported, for example, that Taylour's appearance at the speedway track in Melbourne was responsible for the 12,000 crowd.
12. FTA, FT, TS: 'I Laughed A Security', Part I, Chapter 1, p.21.
13. Ibid., p.20.
14. Ibid.
15. Ibid., p.22.
16. Ibid., p.23–24.
17. Ibid., p.24.
18. *Hoskins Weekly*, 2 February 1929, quoted in ibid., p.25.
19. *The West Australian*, 28 January 1929.
20. FTA, FT, TS: 'I Laughed A Security', Part I, Chapter 1, p.26.
21. Ibid., p.28.
22. Ibid.
23. Ibid., p.29.
24. Ibid.
25. Ibid., p.30.
26. Ibid., p.32.
27. Ibid.
28. Ibid., p.34.
29. Ibid., pp.34–34a.
30. Ibid., p.34a.
31. *Sporting Globe* (Melbourne), 24 April 1929, quoted in ibid., p.34a.
32. Richard Armstrong, 'Fay On Four Wheels', unpublished TS, 2013, p1.
33. FTA, FT, TS, 'I Laughed at Security', Part I, Chapter 4, p.92.
34. *The West Australian*, 3 June 1929.
35. FTA, FT, TS, 'I Laughed at Security', Part I, Chapter 4, p.93.
36. Ibid., p.93.
37. Ibid., pp.93–94.
38. Ibid., p.93.
39. Ibid., p.96.
40. *The Motor Cycle*, 13 June 1929; quoted in ibid., p.97.
41. Brian Belton, *Fay Taylour: Queen of Speedway* (Panther Publishing, High Wycombe, 2006), p.75.
42. FTA, FT, TS, 'I Laughed at Security', Part I, Chapter 7, p.120.
43. Ibid.
44. Belton, *Fay Taylour: Queen of Speedway* (2006), p.76.
45. FTA, FT, TS, 'I Laughed at Security', Part I, Chapter 7, p.120.

46. Taylour and Askquith did race against each other again, in a special match race at Southampton in July 1930; after women had been banned from competing against men in the UK. Taylour beat Askquith 2–0 in that match.
47. Jessie Hole, on the Vintage Speedway web site: http://www.motorcycle-uk.com/vsm/jessie.html, accessed 28 February 2010.

Chapter 4. Australia and New Zealand:
Tour 2, Success on the Track and in the Press

1. *The West Australian*, 13 November 1929.
2. *The Daily News* (Perth), 13 November 1929.
3. FTA, FT, TS, 'I Laughed at Security', Part I, Chapter 6, p. 107.
4. Ibid., p. 108.
5. *News* (Adelaide), 27 November 1929.
6. *The Advertiser* (Adelaide), 29 November 1929.
7. Ibid., 5 December 1929.
8. FTA, FT, TS, 'I Laughed at Security', Part I, Chapter 6, p. 113.
9. For an account of Schlam's fatal accident see, SIG SCHLAM (speedwaypast.com), accessed 4 October 2022.
10. *Sunday Mail* (Brisbane), 15 December 1929; *The Register News Pictorial* (Adelaide), 30 December 1929; and *The Sydney Morning Herald*, 21 April 1930.
11. FTA, FT, TS, 'I Laughed at Security', Part I, Chapter 6, p. 114.
12. Ibid., p. 115.
13. Ibid., p. 116.
14. Ibid.
15. Headlines and photographs in the *Auckland Star*, 11 and 25 February 1930.
16. Ibid., 24 February 1930.
17. *The Register News-Pictorial* (Adelaide), 9 December 1929.
18. Armstrong, 'Fay on Four Wheels'. The SS *Orama* was later to be a victim of the German heavy cruiser, *Admiral Hipper*, on 8 June 1940, sunk in the same action that saw the sinking of the aircraft carrier HMS *Glorious*..

Chapter 5. Banned from the Speedway Track, and on to Four Wheels

1. Jessie Hole gave an account of the incident on the online 'Vintage Speedway' site, http://www.motorcycle-uk.com/vsm/jessie.html (accessed 28 February 2010).
2. Prior to this, the position with regard to women taking part in speedway in the UK was to some extent fluid. Women did not compete in the speedway leagues, but, like Jessie Hole, Eva Askquith, and Fay Taylour, as individual competitors. Huggins and Williams (2006), *Sport and the English*, p. 142.
3. FT, quoted on the website, 'Diamonds MCC' – 'Profiles on women riders', http://www.diamondsmcc.org.uk/profilesoffroad.html, accessed 20 November 2013.
4. Williams (1999), 'A Wild Orgy of Speed', p. 6.
5. Ibid., p. 5.
6. FT, quoted on the website, 'Diamonds MCC' – 'Profiles on women riders'.
7. FTA, FT, TS, 'I Laughed at Security', Chapter 7, p. 124.
8. *Southampton Echo*, 24 July 1930; quoted in FT, Ibid., p. 125.
9. John Hyam, 'Famous Names: Fay Taylour', Midget Car Panorama, posted 27 March 2009: http://www.midgetcarpanorama.proboards.com/thread/16/famous-names-fay-taylour (accessed 7 October 2022); first published as 'Queen of the Speedways', *Short Circuit* magazine, February 2002.
10. Belton, *Fay Taylour: Queen of Speedway* (2006), p. 194.
11. FTA. Letter L77, from Rudolf Grossmann, Munich, to FT, dated 19 September 1930.
12. *New Zealand Truth*, interview with FT, 6 March 1930.

13. FTA, FT, TS, 'I Laughed at Security', Chapter 4 (Part 2), pp. 171–172.
14. Ibid., p. 172.
15. Richard Armstrong, Unpublished TS, 'Fay on Four Wheels' (2013)).
16. FTA, FT, TS, 'I Laughed at Security', Chapter 8, Part 1, p. 134.
17. Ibid., p. 137.
18. Ibid., pp. 144–145.
19. Ibid., p. 147.
20. *The Straits Times*, 9 June 1931, cited by Armstrong (2013).
21. FTA, FT, TS, 'I Laughed at Security', Part 2, Chapter 1, p. 152.
22. Ibid. p. 153.
23. Ibid., p. 154.
24. Ibid., p. 156.
25. Ibid.
26. Armstrong (2013), p. 5.
27. Jean Williams (2013), 'Wisdom, Elsie Mary [Bill] (1904–1972), *Oxford Dictionary of National Biography*, Oxford University Press (accessed 29 December 2013).
28. Rachel 'H-G', 'Speedqueens', http://speedqueens.blogsport.co.uk/2011/109/paddie-eirane-naismith.html (accessed 29 December 2013).
29. Jean-François Bouzanquet, *Fast Ladies: Female Racing Drivers, 1888–1970* (Veloce, Dorchester, 2009), pp. 81–82.
30. Universal Aunts – Established 1921, accessed 10 October 2022.
31. FTA, FT, TS, 'I Laughed at Security', Part 2, Chapter 1, p. 159.
32. Ibid., pp. 161–162.
33. Ibid., p. 163.
34. In 2022, a one-bed house in Lucerne Mews was worth in the region of £1,500,000.
35. FTA, FT, TS, 'I Laughed at Security', Part 2, Chapter 1, p. 164.
36. Ibid., Chapter 4, Part 2, p. 172 and p. 173.
37. Ibid., Part 2, Chapter 1, p. 167.
38. Ibid., p. 168.
39. Ibid., Chapter 4, Part 2, p. 174.
40. Ibid.
41. Alvin 'Spike' Rhiando – 500race.org, accessed 10 October 2022.
42. FTA, FT, TS, 'I Laughed at Security', Chapter 4, Part 2, p. 175.
43. Ibid.
44. Ibid., p. 178.
45. Armstrong (2013), p. 5.
46. FTA, FT, TS, 'I Laughed at Security', Chapter 4, Part 2, p. 18.
47. Ibid., p. 182.
48. Ibid., p. 187.
49. Ibid., p. 188.
50. Ibid., p. 189.
51. Ibid., p. 192.
52. For a list of drivers and cars in the 1934 Monte Carlo Rallye, see: Final results Rallye Automobile de Monte-Carlo 1934 (ewrc-results.com), accessed 11 October 2022.
53. FTA, FT, TS, 'I Laughed at Security', Chapter 4, Part 2, p. 193.
54. Ibid.
55. *The Irish Times*, 26 May 1934.
56. Ibid.
57. Ibid., 2 June 1934.
58. Ibid., 4 June 1934.
59. FTA, FT, TS, 'I Laughed at Security', Chapter 4, Part 2, p. 202.
60. Derek Bridgett, *Midget Car Racing: Belle Vue Speedway 1934–39* (Fonthill, Stroud, 2013), p. 11.

61. FTA, FT, TS, 'Abbreviated version of first part' of 'I Laughed at Security', p. 48.
62. FTA. Letter, L202, dated 25 January 1934.
63. Derek Bridgett, *Midget Car Racing*, p18.
64. Ibid.
65. FTA, FT, TS, 'Abbreviated version of first part' of 'I Laughed at Security', p. 49.
66. Derek Bridgett, *Midget Car Racing*, p18.
67. John Hyam (2009), 'Crystal Palace Motorsport' website, MIDGETS ARRIVE 1934 | CRYSTAL PALACE MOTORSPORT (proboards.com), accessed 12 October 2022.
68. Armstrong (2013), p. 7.
69. Hyam (2009).
70. FTA. Enclosure with Reville's letter to Taylour, L202. This mentions that 'Palmer Reville & Co' were to offer the 'Palmer Special' midget car racer for 'approximately £150'; around £12,000 in 2022.
71. FTA, FT, TS, 'I Laughed at Security', Chapter 4, Part 2, p. 202.
72. Ibid., p. 202.
73. Ibid., p. 203.
74. *The Irish Times*, 3 October 1934.

Chapter 6. Problems, a Change of Gear, and Last Years of Peace, 1935–39

1. TNA, KV 2 1 2143, 386216.
2. *Evening Post*, 10 August 1935.
3. TNA, KV 2 1 2144 386216, Fay Taylour in evidence given at her appeal against detention, 1 April 1942.
4. Armstrong (2013), p. 8.
5. *The Irish Times*, 4 July 1935.
6. Ibid., 15 July 1935.
7. Ibid., 19 July 1935.
8. Armstrong (2013), p. 9.
9. Ibid., p. 11.
10. FTA, FT, TS, 'Summary of Autobiography', dated 1979, p. 7.
11. Ibid.
12. FTA, FT, TS, 'I Laughed at Security', Part 2, p. 168.
13. FTA, FT, TS, 'Summary of Autobiography', p. 7.
14. Ibid.
15. Ibid., p. 8.
16. Ibid.
17. FTA. Letter L169 dated 15 June 1937.
18. FTA. Letter L172 from FT to solicitors, Davey & Thompson, Bedford Row, London, dated 26 May 1952.
19. Armstrong (2013), p. 11.
20. Ibid.
21. Ibid., p. 13.
22. FTA, FT, TS, 'Abbreviated Version' of 'I Laughed at Security', p. 58.
23. *The Irish Times*, 3 January 1939.
24. FTA, FT, TS, 'Summary' of 'I Laughed at Security', p. 5.
25. FT, in evidence given in her appeal against detention, 28 August 1940: TNA, KV 2 1 243 386 216.
26. John Hyam, 'Famous Names: Fay Taylour', Midget Car Panorama, posted 27 March 2009. http://www.midgetcarpanorama.probboards.com/thread/16/famous-names-fay-taylour, accessed 23 September 2013.
27. FTA, FT, TS: 'Abbreviated Version' of 'I Laughed at Security', p. 60.

28. FT, in her written appeal against detention, 16 July 1940. TNA, KV 2 1 243 386 216.
29. Ibid.
30. Ibid.
31. Ibid., 28 August 1940.
32. Ibid.
33. Ibid.
34. Ibid.
35. Ibid., 16 July 1940.
36. *Action*, no.1912, 26 October 1939.

Chapter 7. Joining the 'Peace Campaign'

1. Special Branch (SB) report of 28 October 1939, TNA, KV 2 1 243 386 216.
2. FTA, FT, TS 'The Political Experience. In Detail', May-October 1962, p.5.
3. Ibid., p.5.
4. Stephen M. Cullen, 'The Fasces and the Saltire: The Failure of the British Union of Fascists in Scotland, 1932–1940', *The Scottish Historical Review*, Vol. 87 (2), 2008, pp. 314–317.
5. Thomas P. Linehan, *East London for Mosley: The British Union of Fascists in east London and south-west Kent, 1933–1940* (Frank Cass, London, 1996), pp. 74 & 184.
6. Tim Tate, *Hitler's British Traitors: The Secret History of Spies, Saboteurs and Fifth Columnists* (Icon Books, London, 2019), pp. 1, 5–12.
7. Ibid., p.87.
8. Ibid., p.132.
9. Ibid., p.137.
10. FT in a letter dated 2 February 1940 to H.T (Bertie) Mills, a British Union activist; TNA, KV 2 1 243 386 216.
11. FTA, FT, TS, Political Experience, p.5.
12. From the transcript of FT's appeal against detention, 28 August 1940: TNA, KV 2 2143 386 216. The map was from *The Daily Telegraph* of 21 February 1938.
13. SB report dated 28 October 1939: TNA, KV 2 1 2143 386216.
14. FT in her appeal of 28 August 1940; TNA, KV 2 1 2143 386216.
15. Ibid.
16. FTA, FT, TS. 'Abbreviated Version of I laughed at Security', p.63.
17. FT in her appeal of 28 August 1940; TNA, KV 2 1 2143 386216.
18. *Action*, no:1912, 26 October 1939.
19. Stephen M. Cullen, 'The Development of the Ideas and Policy of the British Union of Fascists, 1932–40', *Journal of Contemporary History*, Vol.22 (1987), pp.129–131.
20. Tate, *Hitler's British Traitors*, p99.
21. John Broom, *Opposition to the Second World War: Conscience, Resistance & Service in Britain 1933–45* (Pen & Sword, Barnsley), p.57.
22. Richard Thurlow, Fascism in Britain: From Oswald Mosley's Blackshirts to the National Front (I.B.Tauris, London, 1998), pp.154–6.
23. Tate, p.157, quotation taken from, The National Archives, HO 45/23775.
24. FT in her appeal of 28 August 1940.
25. This is the last date stamp on Taylour's MI5 file, under which is stamped 'File Closed'. She was nearly 71 years old at that point. TNA, KV 2 1 2143 386216.
26. From the 'Statement of Case Against Frances Helen Taylour', August 1940. TNA, KV 2 1 2143 386216.
27. Charlie Watts' personal details courtesy of his daughter; in letters and e-mails to the author, March 2012.
28. From the 'Original statement of the case against Charles Frederick Watts', dated 28 June 1940; TNA, HO 283/74 C496259.

29. Transcript of the 'Advisory Committee to consider appeals against orders of internment', 19 September 1941, Charles Frederick Watts; TNA, HO 283/74 C496259. Figures given by committee deputy chairman, Archibald Cockburn KC, confirmed by Watts.
30. Report on Watts to the Under Secretary of State at the Home Office, 31 July 1940; TNA, HO 283/74 C496259.
31. Martin Ceadel, 'The First Communist "Peace Society"; the British Anti-War Movement, 1932–1935', *Twentieth Century British History*, Vol. 1 (1), 1990, pp. 58 and 70.
32. Special Branch report on FT, February 1940; TNA, KV 2 1 2143 386216.
33. FT in her appeal against detention, 28 August 1940.
34. The Report of the Advisory Committee on internments, following FT's appeal on 28 August 1940; TNA, KV 2 1 2143 386216.
35. Allegation put to FT at her appeal against detention, 28 August 1940.
36. FT in her appeal against detention 28 August 1940.
37. Report of 21 May 1946; KV 2 1 2143 386216.
38. Two of the first German Heinkel 111s to be shot down over the UK were brought down on 7 December 1939 during a reconnaissance mission over the River Forth and the bridge.
39. From FT's appeal against detention 28 August 1940.
40. Stephen M. Cullen, *In Search of the Real Dad's Army: The Home Guard and the Defence of the United Kingdom, 1940–1944* (Pen & Sword, Barnsley, 2011), pp. 32–33.
41. FT's appeal against detention, 28 August 1940.
42. FT's appeal against detention, 16 April 1942; TNA, KV 2 1 2143 386216.

Chapter 8. Going Underground – Covert Anti-War Activity

1. By the summer of 1939, membership of The Link was around 4,300 in total, with about 40 members in the inner London branch: Stephen M. Cullen, 'Strange Journey; the life of Dorothy Eckersley', *The Historian*, no: 119, 2013, p. 21.
2. From 'Original Statement of the Case Against Charles Frederick Watts', dated 28 June 1940; TNA, HO 283/74 C496259.
3. Lushington, quoted by M.A. Doherty, *Nazi Wireless Propaganda; Lord Haw Haw and British Public Opinion in the Second World War* (Edinburgh University Press, Edinburgh, 2000), p. 20.
4. Roger Tidy, *Hitler's Radio War* (Robert Hale, London, 2011), p. 49.
5. A.J. West, *Truth Betrayed* (Duckworth, London, 1987), pp. 208–209.
6. Watts kept to this line throughout his detention, see, for example, his evidence to the Advisory Committee hearing of 9 July 1940: TNA, HO 283/74 C496259. But it is clear that the security services were sure that Watts was behind the HDM.
7. Copy of letter from Watts to the Home Office, 24 May 1940; TNA, HO 283/74 C496259.
8. The Advisory Committee to consider appeals against orders of internment had 'no hesitation in recommending the release from detention of C.F. Watts', after hearing of his volunteering for heavy duty clearance work after the Liverpool Blitz (he had been held in the Huyton camp) and his desire to join the Pioneer Corps; report of 22 September 1941, TNA, HO 283/74 C496259.
9. Mr A.T. Miller KC, question to FT during her appeal against detention, 28 August 1940; TNA, KV 2 1 2143 386216.
10. The view of Norman Birkett KC, Chairman of the Advisory Committee to consider appeals against orders of internment, at Watts' appeal hearing of 9 July 1940; TNA, HO 283/74 C496259.
11. FT in her appeal against detention, 28 August 1940.
12. Ibid.
13. FTA, 1940.
14. Henry Hemming, *M: Maxwell Knight, MI5's Greatest Spymaster* (Preface Publishing, London, 2017); Richard Davenport-Hines, *Enemies Within: Communists, the Cambridge Spies and the Making of Modern Britain* (William Collins, London, 2018); Tim Tate, *Hitler's British Traitors* (Icon, London, 2019).

15. Taken from the Special Branch report on FT, late February 1940.
16. Richard Thurlow, Fascism in Modern Britain (Sutton Publishing, Stroud, 2000), p. 55.
17. Numbers given by Mr Justice Atkinson summing up at the libel case brought by the detained Cpt Ramsay against the *New York Times* and its London distributor in July 1941. Bryan Clough, *State Secrets; the Kent-Wolkoff Affair* (Hideaway Publications, Hove, 2005), p. 43.
18. FT, written appeal against detention, 16 July 1940; TNA, KV 2 1 2143 386216.
19. FT, written appeal, 16 July 1940; TNA, KV 2 1 2143 386216.
20. FT, 'Your Attention is Arrested Under Defence Regulation 18-B' (privately published, no date, but probably mid 1970s.
21. FT, appeal against detention, 28 August 1940; TNA, KV 2 1 2143 386216.
22. Richard Thurlow, *Fascism in Britain: From Oswald Mosley's Blackshirts to the National Front* (I.B. Tauris, London, 1998), p. 52.
23. FT, appeal against detention, 28 August 1940.
24. A.W. Brian Simpson, *In the Highest Degree Odious: Detention without trial in wartime Britain* (Clarendon Press, Oxford, 1992), p. 141.
25. Christopher Andrew, *The Defence of the Realm; the Authorized History of MI5* (Allen Lane, London, 2009), p. 224. Subsequently, A.W. Brian Simpson criticised strongly Andrew's work, and raised issues concerning the academic worth of an authorised history of the security services. Simpson made particularly harsh comments concerning Andrew's handling of MI5's contribution to the interning of 30,000 'enemy aliens' and 1,700 British citizens. A.W. Brian Simpson, 'Snooping', *London Review of Books*, 3 December 2009'.
26. Clough, in *State Secrets*, has demolished Joan Miller's various accounts of her role in MI5's use of the Right Club and its handling of the Kent-Wolkoff affair; see, in particular, pp. 23–26.
27. Maurice Manning, *The Blueshirts* (Gill & Macmillan, Dublin, 1970); Mike Cronin, *The Blueshirts and Irish Politics* (Four Courts Press, Dublin, 1997); Fearghal McGarry, *Eoin O'Duffy; A Self-Made Hero* (Oxford University Press, Oxford, 2007.
28. R.M. Douglas, 'The Pro-Axis Underground in Ireland', *The Historical Journal*, Vol. 49 (4), 2006, pp. 1155–1183; and R.M. Douglas, *Architects of the Resurrection; Altir• na hAiséirghe and the fascist 'new order' in Ireland* (Manchester University Press, Manchester, 2009), in particular, pp. 92–142.
29. Special Branch report of 4 February 1940.
30. Friends of Oswald Mosley, The Defence Regulation 18b British Union Detainees List (November 2008), 18b Detainees List (oswaldmosley.com), accessed 8 November 2022.
31. A.W. Brian Simpson, *In the Highest Degree Odious* (1992), pp. 175–176.
32. Intercepted letter from FT dated 2 February 1940.
33. Ibid.
34. Douglas, *Architects of the Resurrection*, p. 125.
35. Stephen M. Cullen, *Long Road to Berlin: Socialism, Stalinism and Nazism; Dorothy Eckersley's journey to German wartime radio* (Allotment Hut, Warwick, 2021).
36. James Barnes & Patience Barnes, 'Oswald Mosley as Entrepreneur', *History Today*, March 1990, p. 13.
37. Ibid., pp. 13–16.
38. West, *Truth Betrayed*, 1987, pp. 15–21.
39. Ibid., p. 91.
40. Stephen M. Cullen, 'The British Union of Fascists, the international dimension', *The Historian*, 80, 2003, p. 35.
41. West, *Truth Betrayed* (1987); Doherty, *Nazi Wireless Propaganda* (2000); & Tidy, *Hitler's Radio War* (2011).
42. Cullen, *Long Road to Berlin* (2021), p. 63.
43. FT's appeal against detention, 28 August 1940; TNA, KV 2 1 2143 386216.
44. From the statement of the case against Frances Helen Taylour, August 1940; TNA, KV 2 1 2143 586216.
45. FT in her appeal against detention, 28 August 1940; TNA, Ibid.

46. Ibid.
47. Ibid.
48. FTA, FT, TS, 'The Political Experience. In Detail', 1962, p. 5.
49. FTA, MS copy of letter to her sister Enid, dated 9 February 1974.
50. Ibid.
51. Ibid.
52. Ibid.
53. FT in her appeal against detention, 28 August 1940.
54. Ibid.
55. R.M. Douglas, *Architects of the Resurrection* (2009), p. 36.
56. From a briefing report, dated 16 October 1943, sent to the Irish Defence Ministry (ref., PF 48693/B.1H); TNA, KV 2 1 2144 386216.
57. FT to R.R. 'Dick' Bellamy, letter of 4 March 1974 (held by author).
58. It is true that in Warsaw in 1882, both Polish Catholics and Russian Jews had been disproportionately involved in the first attempt to establish a revolutionary party, 'Proletariat'. But the context for this disproportionality was the Tsarist national policies regarding Poland and Jews; Leonard Schapiro, *The Communist Party of the Soviet Union* (Eye & Spottiswoode, London, 1960), p. 23; see also pp. 66, 96, 171, 475, 537 & 542–544, University Paperback edition 1964. See also, Matthew B. Hoffman & Henry F. Srebrnik, *A Vanished Ideology: Essays on the Jewish Communist Movement in the English-Speaking World in the Twentieth Century* (State University of New York Press, Albany, 2016).

Chapter 9. Last Days of Freedom – Arrest and Detention

1. Richard Thurlow, 'The evolution of the mythical British Fifth Column, 1939–46', *Twentieth Century British History*, Vol. 10 (4), 1999, p. 478.
2. Tate, *Hitler's British Traitors* (2019), p. 141; reference to TNA, CAB 65/2.
3. Hemming, *M: Maxwell Knight, MI5's Greatest Spymaster*, p. 258.
4. FT, *Your Attention is Arrested*, p. 11.
5. Ibid.
6. From a Metropolitan Police Special Branch report, dated 27 May 1940; TNA, KV 2 1 2143 386216.
7. FTA, FT, TS, 'The Political Experience, In detail' (1962), pp. 6–7.
8. Jeremy Lewis, *Shades of Greene: One Generation of an English Family* (Vintage Books, London, 2011), pp. 281–282. Simpson, *In the Highest Degree Odious* (1992), pp. 98, 137–139, 252, 295, 306/07, 329.
9. Hemming, *M. Maxwell Knight* (2017), pp. 306–307.
10. Lewis, *Shades of Greene* (2011), p. 297.
11. Anthony Masters, *The Man Who Was M; the life of Maxwell Knight* (Basil Blackwell, Oxford, 1984), p. 97.
12. Simpson, *In the Highest Degree Odious* (1992), p. 162.
13. Marjorie 'Amor' appears to have been Marjorie Mackie. It is unclear what name she actually went by as an MI5 agent, as both Hennessey and Thomas, *Spooks* (2009), p. 322, and Masters, *The Man Who Was M* (1984), pp. 80 & 85 refer to her as 'Amos', while Clough, *State Secrets* (2005), p. 7ff, refers to her as 'Amor'. Fay Taylour also knew her as Amor, and I have followed that here.
14. Bryan Clough, *State Secrets: The Kent-Wolkoff Affair* (Hideaway Publications, Hove, 205), p. 23.
15. Masters, *The Man Who Was M* (1984), p. 84.
16. Richard Thurlow, *Fascism in Modern Britain* (Sutton Publishing, Stroud, 2000), p. 104.
17. FTA, FT, TS, 'The Political Experience', p. 14.
18. TNA; KV 2 1 2143 386216.
19. Copy of detention order, dated 20 September 1940; TNA, Ibid.
20. Ibid.

Chapter 10. Women Detained

1. Anon., *Persecuted Women in Britain To-Day* (18B Publicity Council, London, no date, probably 1944), p. 1.
2. Ibid., p. 5.
3. FT at her second appeal against detention, 16 April 1942; TNA, KV2 1 2143 386216.
4. FTA, FT, TS 'The Political Experience', p. 15.
5. Ibid., p. 8.
6. FT, 'Your Attention Is Arrested', p. 6.
7. FTA, FT, TS 'The Political Experience', p. 10.
8. FTA.
9. These women were named as fellow detainees Taylour wanted meet up with again in a letter to R.R. 'Dick' Bellamy, dated 1 February 1974 (in author's possession).
10. FT in a letter to R.R. 'Dick' Bellamy, dated 4 March 1974 (in author's possession).
11. Watts's marriage broke down, and following the war he went to live in Cornwall where he later became active in the Cornish nationalist group, *Mebyon Kernow* (Sons of Cornwall); Charlie Watts' details courtesy of his daughter, Eileen Mackrory, in letters and e-mails to the author, March 2012.
12. Thurlow, *Fascism in Modern Britain* (2000), p. 107.
13. Joan Miller, *One Girl's War* (Brandon, Dingle, County Kerry, 1986).
14. FT in a letter to Dick Bellamy, 4 March 1974 (in author's possession).
15. Ibid.
16. FT, *Your Attention Is Arrested*, p. 21.
17. Ibid., and in letter to Bellamy, 4 March 1974.
18. Ibid.
19. FT in letter to Bellamy, 4 March 1974.
20. Tate's description, *Hitler's British Traitors*, p. 167.
21. FT, *Your Attention Is Arrested*, pp. 21–22.
22. FTA.
23. Letter from FT to Aunt Evelyn, 10 December 1940; TNA, KV 2 1 243 386 216.
24. FT in a letter to Freddie Dixon, postmarked 14 December 1940; TNA, KV 2 1 243 386 216.
25. Ibid.
26. Report dated 19 May 1942; TNA, KV 2 1 243 386 216.
27. Ibid.
28. Report of the Governor of Holloway to the Home Office, dated 20 March 1942; TNA, KV 2 1 243 386 216.
29. FTA, FT, TS, 'The Political Experience', p. 19.
30. Ibid.
31. Ibid., p. 18.
32. Ibid, p. 19.
33. Ibid.
34. Ibid, p. 20.
35. Ibid.
36. Ibid.
37. Ibid.
38. The National Archives files on FT are grouped in two volumes. The second volume is dated between 21 December 1955 and 19 March 1976, and the covering minute sheet shows that in December 1957, and at various times up to 1959, files were destroyed, particularly those relating to FT's detention, especially on the Isle of Man.
39. Report dated 15 June 1943; TNA, KV 2 1 243 386 216.
40. FT in her appeal against detention, 16 April 1942; TNA, ibid.).

Chapter 11. Released from Detention, and a Refuge in Dublin

1. FT at her appeal against detention, 16 April 1942; TNA, KV 2 1 2144 386 216.
2. FTA, HO Letter, 6 July 1943.
3. FTA, FT, TS, 'The Political Experience', p. 21.
4. Ibid.
5. Ibid.
6. Ibid., p. 22.
7. Ibid.
8. Ibid., p. 23.
9. Ibid.
10. Ibid., p. 24.
11. Ibid.
12. R.M.Douglas, *Architects of the Resurrection* (2009), p. 215. For the riots, see pp. 213–217.
13. FTA, FT, TS, 'The Political Experience', p. 25.
14. Ibid., p. 24.
15. Ibid., p. 25.
16. Ibid.
17. Ibid., p. 25.
18. Ibid.
19. Ibid.
20. Ibid., p. 26.
21. For example, a letter was sent to the Defence Ministry in Dublin on 16 October 1943, warning the Irish authorities of Taylour's forthcoming arrival, and outlining her background. The letter also noted that Dr Webb 'does not sympathise with her niece's politics', and that MI5 was intercepting all Taylour's correspondence. TNA, KV 2 1 2144 388216.
22. FTA, FT, TS, 'The Political Experience', p. 26.
23. Letter from the Governor of Holloway re Taylour, dated 21 January 1941, noting that Dickson had been 'recently released from detention under Regulation 18.B'; TNA, ibid.
24. British intelligence report of 28 May 1946; TNA, ibid.
25. Report on FT's activities in Dublin, dated 21 May 1946; TNA, KV 2 1 243 386 216.
26. MI5 intelligence file, dated 21 May 1946; TNA, KV 2 1 243 386 216.
27. Daniel Leach, *Fugitive Ireland; European Minority Nationalists and Irish Political Asylum, 1937–2008* (Four Courts Press, Dublin, 2009), especially pp. 81–104 and 104–133.
28. British intelligence report of 28 May, 1946; TNA, KV 2 1 243 386 216.
29. Ibid.
30. British intelligence report of 21 May 1946; TNA, ibid.
31. Brian Simpson, *In the Highest Degree Odious* (1992), pp. 175–176.
32. FTA, FT, TS, 'The Political Experience', pp. 26–27.
33. FTA, letter from FT to her father, dated 29 October 1947.
34. Ibid.
35. Ibid.
36. Ibid.
37. Richard Thurlow, *Fascism in Modern Britain* (2000), p. 108.
38. Graham Macklin, *Very Deeply Dyed in Black: Sir Oswald Mosley and the Resurrection of British Fascism after 1945* (I.B. Tauris, London, 2007), p. 30.
39. Ibid., p. 31.
40. FTA. TS, 'What of England's Pre-War Fascists?', by 'S.D.', May 1946.
41. FTA, FT, TS, 'The Political Experience', p. 28.
42. FTA, FT's Pocket Diary for 1948.
43. Stephen Dorril identifies these groups as 'the Big Four' that went to make up Mosley's post-war Union Movement; Dorril, *Black Shirt: Sir Oswald Mosley and British Fascism* (Penguin Books, London, 2007), p. 566.

44. Post-war MI5 minute sheet; unfortunately, the file which the minute refers to appears to have been destroyed; TNA; KV 2 1 2144 386216.
45. MI5 note, dated 20 June 1952; TNA; ibid.

Chapter 12. Rebuilding Her Life

1. FTA, FT, TS, 'The Political Experience', p. 28.
2. FTA, Letter L78, 9 July 1947.
3. Ibid.
4. Ibid.
5. TNA KV 2 1 2143 386216, Report dated 21 May 1946.
6. FTA Letter L80, 3 August 1947.
7. FTA. A 'Surrey "Lightweight" Diary'.
8. Ibid.
9. Ibid.
10. FTA, letter 6 March 1949 from Sandy to FT.
11. FTA, Diary for 1948.
12. FTA Diary for 1948, entries and doggerel at the back of the diary.
13. Ibid.
14. A note by Taylour in the back of the diary saying that Tufty lived at '29 Ashburn Place, S.W.7 where he didn't live! (but did! Or rather "slept")'.
15. FTA, Note by Proctor entitled 'Activities in World War No. 1'.
16. Ibid.
17. FTA letter L92, from 1948, undated.
18. Ibid.
19. FTA, letters L105 & L107.
20. FTA, letter 107, Sandy Proctor to FT, 6 March 1949.
21. FTA, letters, 4, 24 and 30 August 1947.
22. FTA , Postcard, Joyce Pope to FT, dated 14 December 1947.
23. FTA, letter from Mary to FT, dated 19 September 1948.
24. FTA, ibid.
25. FTA, Envelope of letter postmarked 14 May 1948, Dublin.
26. FTA, Letter from FT to M.E. Carre, 14th May 1948.
27. Ibid.
28. Letter, L92 from 1948, undated.
29. FTA, Diary for 1948.
30. FTA, letter L92, from 1948, undated.
31. FTA, Diary for 1948.
32. Ibid.
33. FTA, letter dated 24 November 1948 to Roger Barlow, President of International Motors, Los Angeles, USA.
34. Barbe Baker's autobiography, available on request from: Richard St Barbe Baker – The Man of the Trees.
35. FTA, Diary 1948.
36. FTA, letter L95, dated 28 July 1948.
37. FTA, Diary 1948.
38. FTA, Diary 1948, entry for 28 August.
39. FTA, letter L98, dated 12 June 1948.
40. Ibid.
41. FTA, letter L100, dated 8 August 1948.
42. FTA, FT, TS 'The Political Experience in Detail', p. 29.
43. Richard Armstrong, 'Fay on Four Wheels', p. 18, unpublished manuscript, 2013.
44. FTA, letter L102, dated 24 November 1948.

45. FTA, letters L105, L107, dated 24 February and 6 March 1949.
46. FTA, letter L108, dated 4 March 1949.
47. FTA, FT, TS, 'I Laughed at Security', Part III, p. 2. In this draft, Taylour uses the pseudonym 'Paul' for Lionel Wills.
48. FTA, letter L109, dated 8 March 1949.

Chapter 13. To the United States – Hollywood

1. FTA, Letter L203, dated 29 April 1949.
2. Ibid.
3. Ibid.
4. Ibid.
5. Photograph of the Jaguar XK 120 and further details can be found: https://en.wikipedia.org/wiki/Jaguar_XK120, Accessed, 6 June 2022.
6. FTA, Ephemera. E5.
7. FTA, FT, TS: 'I Laughed at Security', Part III p. 2/12.
8. Ibid, p1/13.
9. Richard Armstrong, unpublished MS, 'Fay on Four Wheels' (2013), p. 21.
10. FTA, FT, TS: 'I Laughed at Security', Part III., p1/13.
11. Ibid, p. 1/14.
12. FTA, FT, TS, 'The Political Experience in Detail', Pt II, p. 30.
13. FTA, FT, TS: 'I Laughed at Security', Part III, p. 2/14.
14. FTA, Press cutting from Los Angeles *Daily News* 9 December 1949, attached to the synopsis of 'One Love Lasted' or 'One Thing Lasted'.
15. Armstrong, 'Fay on Four Wheels' (2013), p. 21.
16. FTA, FT, TS: 'I Laughed at Security', Part III, p. 1/15.
17. Ibid. p. 2/15.
18. Ibid.
19. Ibid, pp. 2/15–3/15.
20. FTA, FT, TS, 'One Thing Lasted' or 'One Love Lasted'.
21. FTA, FT, TS, 'I Laughed at Security', Part III, p. 3/16.
22. Ibid.
23. Ibid, p. 4/16.
24. Ibid. p. 5/16.
25. FTA, FT, TS, 'The Political Experience', p. 31.
26. FTA, FT, TS: 'I Laughed at Security', Part III, p. 1/17.
27. Ibid.
28. Ibid.
29. FTA, E6, 1951–1952 contracts for West Coast tour.
30. FTA, FT, TS: 'I Laughed at Security', Part III, p. 2/17.

Chapter 14. Racing from Coast to Coast

1. FTA, FT, TS, 'I Laughed at Security', Part III, p. 1/18.
2. Ibid., p1/19.
3. FTA, Letter, L1, dated 29 June 1951, from Northwest Sports Inc. to Taylour.
4. Ibid.
5. Ibid.
6. FTA. FT, TS: 'I Laughed at Security', Part III, p. 1/19.
7. Ibid., p. 2/19.
8. 'A History of the Iconic Bullet Bra – The Endless Night', https://theendlessnight.com/a-history-of-the-iconic-bullet-bra, accessed 15 June 2022.
9. FTA, FT, TS: 'I Laughed at Security', pp. 4/20–5/20.
10. Ibid., p. 5/20.

11. Ibid.
12. 'A History of the Iconic Bullet Bra – The Endless Night'.
13. FTA, FT, TS: 'I Laughed at Security', Part III, p. 5/20.
14. Ibid., p. 1/21.
15. Ibid., p. 2/21.
16. Ibid., p. 5/21.
17. Ibid., p. 8/21.
18. Ibid.
19. Ibid., p. 2/22.
20. *Reading Eagle*, 21 September 1952.
21. FTA, FT, TS: 'I Laughed at Security', Part III, p. 4/22.
22. Ibid.
23. Ibid., pp. 4/22–5/22.
24. Ibid., p. 6/22.
25. Ibid., p. 1/23.
26. Ibid., p. 6/23.
27. Ibid., p. 7/23.
28. Ibid., p. 8/23.
29. FTA, Letter L2. Letter from Lee Phillips to FT, dated 3 December 1951.
30. FTA, Letter L3. Letter from Laura Wilck to FT, dated 15 October 1951.
31. Lee Israel, *Kilgallen* (Delacorte Press, New York, 1979).
32. FT to Dick Bellamy in a letter dated 8 March 1974. In possession of the author.
33. FT to Dick Bellamy in a letter dated 18 March 1974. In possession of the author.
34. FT to Dick Bellamy, in a letter dated 8 March 1974. In possession of the author.
35. FTA, FT, TS: 'I Laughed at Security', PartIII, p. 1/24.
36. Ibid.
37. Ibid., p. 2/24.
38. Ibid., pp. 2/24–3/24.
39. Ibid., p. 5/24.
40. Ibid., p. 1/25.
41. Ibid., p. 4/25.
42. Ibid., p. 3/26.
43. Ibid., p. 4/26.
44. Ibid.
45. Ibid., pp. 5/26–6/26.
46. Ibid., p. 7/26.

Chapter 15. Banned from the USA

1. FTA, FT, TS: 'I Laughed at Security', PartIII, p. 8/26.
2. Ibid., p. 9/26.
3. Ibid., Part IVA, p. 6/27.
4. FTA, Letter L172, dated 26 May 1952, from FT to W.R.Thompson, Davey & Thompson, Bedford Row, London WC1.
5. Ibid.
6. 500cc Race website, http://500race.org/people/alvin-spike-rhiando/, accessed, 10 June 2022.
7. FTA, FT, TS: 'I Laughed at Security', Part IVA, p. 15/27.
8. FTA, FT, TS, 'The Political Experience', p. 33.
9. Ibid.
10. Ibid.
11. Ibid.
12. MI5 note (277a) provided to the US Embassy in London, 20 June 1952; TNS, KV 2 1 21444 386216.

13. FTA, FT, TS, 'The Political Experience', p. 33.
14. Richard Thurlow, *Fascism in Britain, From Oswald Mosley's Blackshirts to the National Front* (I.B. Tauris, London, 1998), p. 218.
15. FTA, FT, TS, 'The Political Experience', p. 33.
16. Ibid.
17. Ibid.
18. Ibid.
19. Oswald Mosley, *Mosley: Policy and Debate. From The European* (Euphorian Books, London, 1954), p. 21.
20. FT in a letter to R.R. 'Dick' Bellamy, dated 4 March 1974. In possession of the author.
21. Ibid.
22. FTA, FT, TS: 'I Laughed at Security', Part IVA, p. 4/29.
23. Ibid., p. 6/29.
24. Ibid., pp. 7–8/29.
25. Ibid., p. 18/29.
26. Ibid., p. 21/29.
27. Ibid., p. 26/29.
28. Ibid., p. 33/29.
29. https://www.shelsleywalsh.com/, accessed 11 July 2022.
30. Ibid., p. 40/29. Although Taylour provided no account of her racing a Bugatti in 1952, Richard Armstrong in his 'Fay on Four Wheels' research has shown that she did, in fact, race a Bugatti on 28 June, when she won the Ladies' Handicap at Snetterton.

Chapter 16. 'Tearing from Place to Place' – the 1952–53 Season

1. http://500race.org/marques/effyh/ accessed 12 July 2022.
2. FTA, FT, TS, 'I Laughed at Security', Part IVA, p. 41/29.
3. Ibid.
4. Ibid., p. 42/29.
5. https://500race.org/people/rod-nuckey/, accessed 12 July 2022.
6. FTA, FT, TS, 'I Laughed at Security', Part IVA, pp. 47–48/29.
7. http://500race.org/people/pim-richardson/, accessed 12 July 2022.
8. FTA, FT, TS, 'I Laughed at Security', Part IVA, p. 52/29.
9. Ibid., p. 53/29.
10. Frank Arthur – Australian Speedway Hall of Fame, accessed, 25 July 2022.
11. FTA, FT, TS, 'I Laughed at Security', Part IVB, p. 12/30.
12. Ibid., p. 1/30.
13. Ibid., p. 5/30.
14. *Daily Telegraph* (Sydney), Wednesday 8 October 1952.
15. *Sydney Morning Herald*, Thursday 9 October 1952.
16. *Sydney Morning Herald*, Thursday 16 October 1952.
17. The History Buff: 'Satan' Lived in Campbelltown (campbelltown-library.blogspot.com), accessed 29 July 2022.
18. *Argus*, Thursday, 23 October 1952.
19. *Australian Women's Weekly*, Wednesday 12 November 1952.
20. FTA, FT, TS, 'I Laughed at Security', p. 7/30.
21. Ibid.
22. Sheila Patrick, 'Racing driver dresses to suit her car', *The Australian Women's Weekly*, 12 November 1952.
23. A search of the National Library of Australia's digital newspaper and magazine data base, TROVE, using the term 'Fay Taylour' and 'newspapers' produced the result of 416 items. Additions are constantly being made to TROVE, so it is likely that there were more than 416.
24. FTA, FT, TS, 'I Laughed at Security', Part IVB, p. 8/30.

25. Ibid., p. 10/30.
26. Ibid.
27. Ibid., p. 11/30.
28. Ibid., p. 12/30.
29. *Sunday Herald* (Sydney), Sunday, 16 November 1952.
30. *Advertiser* (Adelaide), Monday, 17 November 1952.
31. FTA, FT, TS, 'I Laughed at Security', Part IVB, p. 14/30.
32. Ibid.
33. Ibid.
34. Ibid., p. 17/30.
35. Ibid., p. 18/20.
36. Ibid., p. 20/30.
37. Ibid., p. 23/30.
38. *Courier-Mail* (Brisbane), Friday, 28 November 1952.
39. FTA, FT, TS, 'I Laughed at Security', Part IVB, p. 26/30.
40. Ibid, p. 27/30.
41. Ibid.
42. Results in *Truth* (Brisbane), Sunday, 30 November 1952.
43. FTA, FT, TS, 'I Laughed at Security', Part IVB, p. 27/30.
44. *Truth* (Brisbane), Sunday, 30 November 1952.
45. FTA, FT, TS, 'I Laughed at Security', Part IVB, p. 28/30.
46. *Sun* (Sydney), Thursday, 4 December 1952.
47. *Sydney Morning Herald*, Thursday, 4 December 1952.
48. *Sun* (Sydney), Thursday 4 December 1952.
49. *Daily Telegraph* (Sydney), Friday, 5 December 1952.
50. FTA, FT, TS, 'I Laughed at Security', Part IVB, p. 29/30.
51. Ibid., pp. 39–30/30.
52. Ibid., p. 30/30.
53. Ibid., p. 31/30.
54. Ibid., p. 32/30.
55. Ibid., p. 32/30.
56. *Sydney Morning Herald*, Saturday 6 December 1952; and *Daily Telegraph* (Sydney), Saturday 6 December 1952.
57. Ibid.
58. *Sunday Herald* (Sydney), Sunday 7 December 1952.
59. FTA, FT, TS, 'I Laughed at Security', Part IVB, p. 33/30.
60. Ibid., p. 34/30.
61. *Advertiser* (Adelaide), Friday, 12 December 1952.
62. In an interview with the *Australian Women's Weekly*, quoted on Harry Neale – Australian Speedway Hall of Fame, accessed 31 July 2022.
63. *Advertiser* (Adelaide), Saturday, 20 December 1952.
64. *Argus* (Melbourne), Monday, 22 December 1952.
65. FTA, FT, TS, 'I Laughed at Security', Part IVB, pp. 34–35/30.
66. Ibid., p. 33–36/30.
67. Ibid., p. 39/30.
68. Ibid.
69. *Truth* (Brisbane), Sunday, 11 January 1953.
70. In other accounts of her earlier time with 'Charles' in 1929 (see Chapter 4), FT called him 'Cuthbert'.
71. FTA, FT, TS, 'I Laughed at Security', Part IVC, p. 47/30.
72. Ibid., p. 60/30.
73. Ibid., p. 62/30.

74. Ibid.
75. Ibid., p. 63/30.
76. Ibid.
77. Harry Neale – Australian Speedway Hall of Fame.
78. FTA, FT, TS, 'I Laughed at Security', Part IVC, p. 70/30.
79. Ibid., p. 71/30.
80. Norman Jacobs, *Crystal Palace Speedway: A History of the Glaziers* (Fonthill, Stroud, 2012), p. 19.
81. FTA, FT, TS, 'I Laughed at Security', Part IVC, p. 72/30.
82. *The West Australian*, 24 January 1953.
83. 1951 CLAREMONT – speedwayandroadracehistory, accessed 5 August 2022.
84. *The West Australian*, 24 January 1953.
85. *The West Australian*, 30 January 1953.
86. FTA, FT, TS, 'I Laughed at Security', Part IVC, p. 75/30.
87. Ibid., p. 76/30.
88. *The West Australian*, 31 January 1953.
89. Ibid.
90. FTA, FT, TS, 'I Laughed at Security', Part IVC, p. 78/30.
91. *The West Australian*, 31 January 1953.
92. *The West Australian*, 7 February 1953.
93. *Daily News* (Perth), 4 March 1953.
94. *Daily News* (Perth), 10 March 1953.

Chapter 17. Intractable Problems

1. FTA, FT, TS, 'The Political Experience in Detail', p. 34.
2. Ibid., p. 35.
3. Ibid.
4. Ibid., pp. 35–36.
5. The details of this will and its implications for FT are in letters in the FTA, letters L174, 8 March 1950, L175, 13 March 1950, L176, 11 October 1950, L178, 15 February 1956 and L198, 31 August 1956.
6. FTA, Letter L225, dated 5 Jun 1953.
7. *The Irish Times*, 22 May 1953.
8. Ibid., 28 August 1953; 4 September 1953.
9. Richard Armstrong, TS, 'Fay on Four Wheels' (2013), p. 29.
10. Ibid., p. 29.
11. *Sydney Morning Herald*, 11 November 1953.
12. FTA, FT, TS: 'The Political Experience in Detail', p. 36.
13. *Argus* (Melbourne), 22 January 1954.
14. *Daily News* (Perth), 8 December 1953.
15. *West Australian* (Perth), 11 December 1953.
16. Ibid., 12 December 1953.
17. Ibid.
18. Ibid.
19. *Argus* (Melbourne), 13 January 1954.
20. *West Australian* (Perth), 15 December 1953, p. 24.
21. *Advertiser* (Adelaide), 1 January 1954.
22. Ibid., 9 January 1954.
23. *Argus* (Melbourne), 13 January 1954.
24. BAXTER PARK SPEEDWAY (VIC) – speedwayandroadracehistory, accessed 9 August 2022.
25. *Argus* (Melbourne), 22 January 1954.
26. Ibid.
27. *Daily Telegraph* (Sydney), 4 February 1954.

28. There are two interviews with Enid Nunn available on the National Library of Australia TROVE website, [Interviews with Enid Nunn, speed boat driver] [sound recording] / [interviewed by Ros Bowden]. – Trove (nla.gov.au).
29. *Daily Advertiser* (NSW), 8 February 1954.
30. *Sunday Mail* (Brisbane), 14 February 1954.
31. Ibid.
32. *Truth* (Brisbane), 11 January 1953.
33. *Daily Telegraph* (Sydney), 20 February 1954.
34. *Sun* (Sydney), 5 March 1954.
35. Advertisements in the *Sun*, *Daily Telegraph* and the *Sunday Morning Herald*, March 1954.
36. *Sporting Globe* (Melbourne), 17 April 1954.
37. Photographs of two different posters/flyers advertising Fay Taylour's appearances at Wembley, Johannesburg, in the FTA.
38. *Wembley Car Stadium Racing Souvenir Programme* (Johannesburg), Saturday, 14 August 1954.
39. Ibid.
40. FTA, photograph of FT in racing overalls taken in Johannesburg 1954.

Chapter 18. Return to the USA

1. FTA, FT, TS, 'The Political Experience in Detail', p. 39.
2. FTA, FT, TS, 'I Laughed at Security', Part V, p. 1.
3. Ibid., p. 2.
4. Ibid., p. 4.
5. Ibid., p. 5.
6. Ibid.
7. FTA, FT, TS, 'The Political Experience in Detail', p. 38.
8. Ibid., p. 39.
9. FTA, FT, TS, 'I laughed at Security', Part V, p. 8.
10. FTA, Letter, L208, dated 17 July 1956, from FT to John Barclay.
11. FTA, FT, TS, 'I laughed at Security', Part V, p. 8.
12. Ibid., p. 9.
13. Ibid., p. 10.
14. Ibid., p. 12.
15. Ibid., pp. 14–15.
16. Ibid., p. 15.
17. Ibid., p. 35.
18. Ibid., p. 16.
19. Ibid., p. 20.
20. Ibid.
21. Ibid., p. 21.
22. Ibid., p. 22.
23. Ibid., p. 23.
24. Ibid., p. 29.
25. Ibid., p. 30.
26. Ibid.
27. Ibid.
28. *The Shreveport Journal*, 23 October 1956. In the FTA as E.17.
29. FTA, FT, TS, 'I Laughed at Security', Part V, p. 44.
30. Ibid., p. 48.
31. Ibid.
32. Ibid., p52 and p. 56.
33. FTA, FT, TS, 'The Political Experience in Detail', p. 41.

Chapter 19. Life After Racing

1. FTA, FT, TS, 'The Political Experience in Detail', p. 41.
2. FTA, FT, TS: 'I Laughed at Security', Part VI, p. 4.
3. Ibid., p. 5.
4. FTA, photograph album entitled 'Interlude in Texas', and 'Illustrating Part VI of Life Story' On Retiring From Racing'.
5. Ibid.
6. Ibid.
7. FTA, FT, TS: 'I Laughed at Security', Part VI, p. 7.
8. Ibid., Part VII, pp. 58–59.
9. FTA, Letter L226, dated 21 August 1957.
10. FTA, TS: 'I Laughed at Security', Part VI, p. 5.
11. Ibid., p. 6.
12. Ibid., p. 8.
13. Ibid.
14. Ibid., p. 9.
15. Ibid., p. 14.
16. Ibid.
17. FTA. photograph album, 'Texas Interlude 2; Tornado strikes Dallas. The drive West'.
18. FTA, FT, TS: 'I Laughed at Security', Part VI, p. 18.
19. Richard Armstrong, unpublished TS, 'Fay On Four Wheels', 2013.
20. FTA, FT, TS: 'I Laughed at Security', Part VI, p. 19.
21. Ibid., p. 20.
22. Ibid., p. 21.
23. Ibid.
24. FTA, FT, TS, 'I Laughed at Security', Part VII, p. 3.
25. FTA, Letter L160, Taylour to Mr Caradine, bank manager, The National Bank Ltd, 274 Oxford Street, dated 4 December 1958.
26. FTA, TS, 'I Laughed at Security', Part VII, p. 5.
27. Ibid.
28. Ibid., p. 8.
29. FTA, Letter L160, dated 4 December 1958.
30. Ibid., p. 22.
31. Ibid., p. 23.
32. Ibid., p. 25.
33. Ibid., p. 65.
34. Ibid., p. 71.
35. Ibid.
36. Ibid., p. 143.
37. Ibid., pp. 148–149.
38. FTA, FT, TS, 'I Laughed at Security', Part VIII, p. 6.
39. FTA, FT, poem, 'Castro! Why Not?', dated June 1961.
40. Anke Eve Goldmann, The Vintagent, accessed 27 August 2022.
41. FTA, Letter L56, dated 2 September 1961.
42. Ibid.
43. FTA, FT, TS, 'I Laughed at Security', Part VIII, p. 2a.
44. Ibid., p. 2b.
45. Ibid., p. 6.
46. Ibid., p. 5.
47. Ibid., p. 10.
48. Ibid., p. 19.
49. Ibid., p. 13.

50. FTA, Letter L256.
51. FTA, E15, clipping from *Motorcycle* magazine, dated 29 January 1975.
52. FTA, Letter L264, dated 23 December 1966.
53. Ibid.
54. FTA, Letters, L25, dated 18 July 1969, and L46, dated 25 July 1969.
55. FTA, Letter L44, dated 10 August 1969.
56. FTA, Letter, L53, dated 10 August 1969.
57. FTA, Letter 17 August 1969.
58. FTA, Letter L52, dated 2 August 1970.
59. FTA, Letter L69, dated 28 April 1974.
60. Richard Armstrong makes the point that this was on 'the short (1.17 miles) and seldom-used Mountain Circuit – not [...] the longer and faster banked Outer Circuit' at Brooklands. Armstrong, 'Fay on Four Wheels'.
61. Theresa Jenkins-Teague in conversation with the author, 17 April 2013.

Bibliography

Archives

There are two main archives that were used in the writing of this biography – the Fay Taylour Archive (FTA), and Home Office, Security and Police files held at The National Archives (TNA), Kew.

The **Fay Taylour Archive** is in private hands. It is a substantial collection of letters, photographs, ephemera, newspaper cuttings, and Fay Taylour's own autobiographical writings. I am very much indebted to Mairi Ann Cullen for her patient and painstaking work with the FTA, turning what was a jumbled collection into a catalogued and usable source for the book.

The National Archives' files on Fay Taylour are grouped into two volumes. The UK security services watched and reported on Fay Taylour from 1939 until 1976. However, many of the relevant files have, over the years, been destroyed. Nonetheless, a substantial amount of material remains. The National Archive reference numbers can be found in the endnotes.

Newspapers and Magazines

Action
The Advertiser (Adelaide)
Argus (Melbourne)
Australian Women's Weekly
The Cairns Post (Queensland)
Courier-Mail (Brisbane)
Daily Advertiser (NSW)
The Daily News (Perth)

Daily Telegraph (Sydney)
Evening Post
Hoskins Weekly
The Irish Times
The Motor Cycle
New Zealand Truth
News (Adelaide)
The Register News-Pictorial

Sporting Globe (Melbourne)
Sun (Sydney)
Sunday Herald (Sydney)
Sunday Mail (Brisbane)
Sydney Morning Herald
The West Australian

Internet Sources

18b Detainees List (oswaldmosley.com)
1951 CLAREMONT – speedwayandroadracehistory
http://500race.org/marques/effyh/
https://500race.org/people/rod-nuckey/
http://500race.org/people/pim-richardson/
Alvin "Spike" Rhiando – 500race.org
Anke Eve Goldmann | The Vintagent
BAXTER PARK SPEEDWAY (VIC) – speedwayandroadracehistory
Bonhams: The Marjorie Cottle Collection
The College of Anaesthesiologists of Ireland (anaesthesia.ie)
http://www.diamondsmcc.org.uk/profilesoffroad.html
https://en.wikipedia.org/wiki/Jaguar_XK120
Final results Rallye Automobile de Monte-Carlo 1934 (ewrc-results.com)
Frank Arthur – Australian Speedway Hall of Fame
Harry Neale – Australian Speedway Hall of Fame
The History Buff: 'Satan' Lived in Campbelltown (campbelltown-library.blogspot.com)
[Interviews with Enid Nunn, speed boat driver] [sound recording] / [interviewed by Ros Bowden] – Trove (nla.gov.au)
http://www.midgetcarpanorama.proboards.com/thread/16/famous-names-fay-taylour

221

MIDGETS ARRIVE 1934 | CRYSTAL PALACE MOTORSPORT (proboards.com)
http://www.motorcycle-uk.com/vsm/jessie.html
Richard St Barbe Baker – The Man Of The Trees
https://www.shelsleywalsh.com/
SIG SCHLAM (speedwaypast.com)
http://speedqueens.blogsport.co.uk/2011/109/paddie-eirane-naismith.html
https://theendlessnight.com/a-history-of-the-iconic-bullet-bra
Universal Aunts – Established 1921
Wills Lionel (speedwaymuseumonline.co.uk)

Secondary sources

Andrew, Christopher, *The Defence of the Realm; the Authorized History of MI5* (Allen Lane, London, 2009).

Anon., *Persecuted Women in Britain To-Day* (18B Publicity Council, London, no date, probably 1944).

Armstrong, Richard, 'Fay On Four Wheels' (unpublished TS, 2013).

Bamford, Robert & Stallworthy, Dave, *Speedway: The Pre-War Years* (Tempus, Stroud, 2003).

Barnes, James, & Barnes, Patience, 'Oswald Mosley as Entrepreneur', *History Today*, March 1990.

Beddoe, Deidre, *Back to Home and Duty: Women Between the Wars 1918–1939* (Pandora, London, 1989).

Belton, Brian, *Fay Taylour Queen of Speedway* (Panther Publishing, High Wycombe, 2006).

Bouzanquet, Jean-François, *Fast Ladies: Female Racing Drivers, 1888–1970* (Veloce, Dorchester, 2009).

Bridgett, Derek, *Midget Car Racing: Belle Vue Speedway 1934–39* (Fonthill, Stroud, 2013).

Broom, John, *Opposition to the Second World War: Conscience, Resistance & Service in Britain 1933–45* (Pen & Sword, Barnsley).

Ceadel, Martin, 'The First Communist "Peace Society"; the British Anti-War Movement, 1932–1935', *Twentieth Century British History*, Vol. 1 (1), 1990.

Clew, Jeff, *Vintage Motorcycles* (Shire Publications, Princes Risborough,1995).

Clough, Bryan, *State Secrets; the Kent-Wolkoff Affair* (Hideaway Publications, Hove, 2005).

Cronin, Mike, *The Blueshirts and Irish Politics* (Four Courts Press, Dublin, 1997).

Cullen, Stephen M., *In Search of the Real Dad's Army: The Home Guard and the Defence of the United Kingdom, 1940–1944* (Pen & Sword, Barnsley, 2011).

Cullen, Stephen M., *Long Road to Berlin: Socialism, Stalinism and Nazism; Dorothy Eckersley's journey to German wartime radio* (Allotment Hut, Warwick, 2021).

Cullen, Stephen M., 'The British Union of Fascists, the international dimension', *The Historian*, Vol. 80, 2003.

Cullen, Stephen M., 'The Development of the Ideas and Policy of the British Union of Fascists, 1932–40', *Journal of Contemporary History*, Vol. 22 (1), 1987.

Cullen, Stephen M., 'The Fasces and the Saltire: The Failure of the British Union of Fascists in Scotland, 1932–1940', *The Scottish Historical Review*, Vol. 87 (2), 2008.

Cullen, Stephen M., 'Strange Journey; the life of Dorothy Eckersley', *The Historian*, No. 119, 2013.

Davenport-Hines, Richard, *Enemies Within: Communists, the Cambridge Spies and the Making of Modern Britain* (William Collins, London, 2018).

Doherty, M.A., *Nazi Wireless Propaganda; Lord Haw Haw and British Public Opinion in the Second World War* (Edinburgh University Press, Edinburgh, 2000).

Dorril, Stephen, *Black Shirt: Sir Oswald Mosley and British Fascism* (Penguin Books, London, 2007).

Douglas, R.M., *Architects of the Resurrection; Ailtirí na hAiséirghe and the fascist 'new order' in Ireland* (Manchester University Press, Manchester, 2009).

Douglas, R.M., 'The Pro-Axis Underground in Ireland', *The Historical Journal*, Vol. 49 (4), 2006.

Hemming, Henry, *M: Maxwell Knight, MI5's Greatest Spymaster* (Preface Publishing, London, 2017).

Herlihy, Jim, *The Royal Irish Constabulary* (Four Courts Press, Dublin, 1997).

Hoffman, Matthew B., & Srebrnik, Henry F., *A Vanished Ideology: Essays on the Jewish Communist Movement in the English-Speaking World in the Twentieth Century* (State University of New York Press, Albany, 2016).

Huggins, Mike & Williams, Jack, *Sport and the English* (Routledge, London, 2006).

Israel, Lee, *Kilgallen* (Delacorte Press, New York, 1979).

Jacobs, Norman, *Crystal Palace Speedway: A History of the Glaziers* (Fonthill, Stroud, 2012).

Leach, Daniel, *Fugitive Ireland; European Minority Nationalists and Irish Political Asylum, 1937–2008* (Four Courts Press, Dublin, 2009).

Lewis, Jeremy, *Shades of Greene: One Generation of an English Family* (Vintage Books, London, 2011).

Linehan, Thomas P., *East London for Mosley: The British Union of Fascists in east London and south-west Kent, 1933–1940* (Frank Cass, London, 1996).

Macklin, Graham, *Very Deeply Dyed in Black: Sir Oswald Mosley and the Resurrection of British Fascism after 1945* (I.B. Tauris, London, 2007).

Manning, Maurice, *The Blueshirts* (Gill & Macmillan, Dublin, 1970).

Masters, Anthony, *The Man Who Was M; the life of Maxwell Knight* (Basil Blackwell, Oxford, 1984).

Mason, David, *Freddie Dixon; the man with the heart of a lion* (Haynes Publishing, Yeovil, 2008).

McGarry, Fearghal, *Eoin O'Duffy; A Self-Made Hero* (Oxford University Press, Oxford, 2007).

McKibbin, Ross, *Classes and Cultures: England 1918–1951* (Oxford University Press, Oxford, 1998).

Miller, Joan, *One Girl's War* (Brandon, Dingle, County Kerry, 1986).

Mosley, Oswald, *Mosley: Policy and Debate. From The European* (Euphorian Books, London, 1954).

Nicholson, Virginia, *Singled Out* (Viking, London, 2007).

Schapiro, Leonard, *The Communist Party of the Soviet Union* (Eye & Spottiswoode, London, 1960).

Simpson, A.W. Brian, *In the Highest Degree Odious: Detention without trial in wartime Britain* (Clarendon Press, Oxford, 1992).

Tate, Tim, *Hitler's British Traitors: The Secret History of Spies, Saboteurs and Fifth Columnists* (Icon Books, London, 2019).

Thurlow, Richard, *Fascism in Britain: From Oswald Mosley's Blackshirts to the National Front* (I.B. Tauris, London, 1998).

Thurlow, Richard, *Fascism in Modern Britain* (Sutton Publishing, Stroud, 2000).

Thurlow, Richard, 'The evolution of the mythical British Fifth Column, 1939–46', *Twentieth Century British History*, Vol. 10 (4), 1999.

Tidy, Roger, *Hitler's Radio War* (Robert Hale, London, 2011).

West, A.J., *Truth Betrayed* (Duckworth, London, 1987).

Williams, Jack, '"A Wild Orgy of Speed": responses to speedway in Britain before the Second World War', *Sport in History*, Vol. 19 (1), 1999.

Williams, Jean, 'Wisdom, Elsie Mary [Bill] (1904–1972)', *Oxford Dictionary of National Biography* (Oxford University Press, Oxford, 2013).

Index